Periodization and Sovereignty

THE MIDDLE AGES SERIES

Ruth Mazo Karras, Series Editor
Edward Peters, Founding Editor

A complete list of books in the series is available from the publisher.

Periodization and Sovereignty

How Ideas of Feudalism
and Secularization
Govern the Politics of Time

Kathleen Davis

PENN

University of Pennsylvania Press

Philadelphia

Published by
University of Pennsylvania Press
Philadelphia, Pennsylvania 19104–4112

Printed in the United States of America on acid-free paper
10 9 8 7 6 5 4 3 2 1

Library of Congress Cataloging-in-Publication Data

Davis, Kathleen.
   Periodization and sovereignty : how ideas of feudalism and secularization govern the politics of time / Kathleen Davis.
      p.   cm. — (The Middle Ages series)
   Includes bibliographical references and index.
   ISBN-13: 978-0-8122-4083-2 (hardcover : alk. paper)
   1. History—Periodization.   2. History—Political aspects.   3. Time—Political aspects.   4. Civilization, Medieval.   5. Civilization, Modern.
6. Sovereignty.   7. Feudalism.   8. Secularization.   9. History—Philosophy.
10. Historiography—Philosophy.   I. Title.
   D16.9.D295   2008
   901—dc22   2007052496

For my family

This moment of suspense, this épokhè, this founding or revolutionary moment of law is, in law, an instance of non-law. But it is also the whole history of law.

Derrida, "Force of Law"

Contents

Introduction

In the early eighth century, the Northumbrian monk and scholar now known as the Venerable Bede offered his own etymology for the Latin word *tempus*, "time." As usual for him, he considers it in the plural: "Times take their name from 'measure'" (*tempora igitur a "temperamento" nomen accipiunt*).[1] Taken in its various senses, the word "measure" nearly captures the force of *temperamentum*, which derives from the verb *tempero*, "to be moderate, to divide, to regulate." The verb *accipio* ("to take without effort, receive, get, accept") hovers between the active and the passive, and thereby displays the logic of the etymological relation: *tempora* are so called because they *do* moderate, divide, and regulate.[2] Scholars have tended to attribute this emphasis on temporal regulation to the daily monastic routine of tolling bells and calls to prayer, and in so doing have cordoned it off from its far more ambitious, and effective, historical and political designs. Well attuned to the stakes of time as a regulating principle, Bede later became the first author to use *anno domini* (A.D.) dating in a historical narrative, thereby attaching history, in the form of Christian politics, to the sacred at the point of a division in time.[3] This periodization, which is not entirely attributable to Bede of course, continues today to regulate calendars and political life.

In recent decades there has been much attention to the "politics of time," and it has not come untethered from the problematic relation of history with the sacred. Indeed, studies of the politics of time have taken this relation as their conceptual limit, almost always expressed in the form of a divide between a religious Middle Ages and a secular modernity. The arguments center upon historical consciousness and follow along these lines: medieval people subordinated all concepts of time to the movement of salvation history and the inevitability of the Last Judgment, and therefore had no sense of *real*, meaningful historical change; under such circumstances history is already determined, and a "medieval" politics of time is therefore an oxymoron.[4] These arguments often derive explanatory power from economic models of periodization by aligning a transition from ecclesiastical to secular society with a transition from a medieval, rural, agrarian economy to a modern, urban, commercial economy, most typically expressed as the transition from feudalism to capitalism.[5] So commonplace are these ideas that—even though the Middle Ages is well understood to be a constructed category—they have taken on the self-evidentiary status of common sense.

A principal goal of this book is to ask why, in the face of all challenges to teleological and stage-oriented histories, do the monoliths medieval/religious/feudal and modern/secular/ capitalist (or "developed") survive, and what purposes do they serve? What does the regulating principle of medieval/modern periodization hold in place, and what does it help to obscure? What political assumptions go unchallenged when subjugation and lawlessness are labeled "feudal" and aligned with the Middle Ages? What cultural paradigms flourish when a Christian politics of time such as Bede's is declared apolitical, or pre-political? A sincere engagement with these issues requires that the division medieval/modern be put into question together with categories such as "feudal" and "secular," with which it was mutually constituted, and which it holds in place.

Ironically, the boldest, most celebrated critiques of rigid historical paradigms usually reinforce rather than disrupt this periodization. In his justly famous critique of anthropology in *Time and the Other*, for example, Johannes Fabian sets out this claim, with which few would now disagree: "If it is true that Time belongs to the political economy of relations between individuals, classes, and nations, then the construction of anthropology's object through temporal concepts and devices is a political act; there is a 'Politics of Time.'"[6] Fabian finds it necessary, however, to stipulate that the study of such politics must begin by recognizing a "qualitative step from medieval to modern time conceptions," which resulted from the "achieved secularization of Time."[7] Although he is aware that there are other ways to consider this history, he describes what he calls the "sacred vs. secular" divide in sharp terms: "Enlightenment thought marks a break with an essentially medieval, Christian (or Judeo-Christian) vision of Time. That break was from a conception of time/space in terms of a history of salvation to one that ultimately resulted in the secularization of Time as natural history."[8] Thus, even though he insists that "Time belongs to the political economy of relations," Fabian posits a foundational, qualitative break in the nature of time that is apparently outside politics. Rather than considering the narrative of "secularized time" *as* political, as part of a process that, like anthropology, "at once constitutes and demotes its objects,"[9] Fabian considers it simply "achieved." Like Bede, he thereby grounds a political order by attaching it to a relation with the sacred, at the point of a division in time. The fact that this attachment to a relation with the sacred takes the form of a claim to detachment does not alter this fundamental similarity.

By definition, a division in time purportedly outside politics and based on a relation with the sacred both defines and regulates politics. One obvious symptom of the regulative function of such division is the recent substitution of C.E. ("common era") for the nomenclature A.D.—a change that does little to diminish the effect of a globalized Christian calendar, and in fact privileges its order under a rubric that appears both secular and universal. As such, it miniaturizes the processes studied by Tomoko Masuzawa in *The Invention of World Religions: Or, How European Universalism Was Preserved in the Language of Pluralism.* Masuzawa's work clarifies what is at stake in a claim for the Enlightenment's "achieved secularization of Time." As Europe produced its own narrative of secularization, she shows, it simultaneously mapped regions elsewhere in the world according to newly consolidated conceptions of "religion" and religious heritage. With this pattern in mind, I want to call attention to the striking correspondence between Fabian's temporal mapping of European politics according to a "sacred vs. secular" divide, and the geopolitical mapping studied by Masuzawa. In her terms: "One of the most consequential effects of this discourse [of world religions] is that it spiritualizes what are material practices and turns them into expressions of something timeless and suprahistorical, which is to say, it depoliticizes them."[10] This depoliticization must be studied, I suggest, in tandem with its temporal correlate: the constitution of a "religious," pre-political "Middle Ages." The sleight of hand that facilitates the privileged universalism under which *only* "European" politics can identify as "secular," and only "secular" politics can be legitimate, is medieval/modern periodization. By periodization I mean not simply the drawing of an arbitrary line through time, but a complex process of conceptualizing categories, which are posited as homogeneous and retroactively validated by the designation of a period divide.

The grounding of political order upon periodization is the main concern of this book. The sacred/secular divide presupposed by Fabian has long been a commonplace of European history; yet in world politics today and in recent theoretical debate the categories it presupposes generate violence and contention. Likewise, the period concept of the "feudal" Middle Ages adjudicates conceptions of economic as well as political development, and ever more frequently acts as a foil for "democracy."[11]

The problem, which has been obvious for decades, is that units such as sacred-medieval-feudal and secular-modern-capitalist (or democratic) exercise exclusionary force, and require alignment with historically particular cultural, economic, and institutional forms for entrance into an ostensibly global political modernity. Taking up related concerns, medievalists have demonstrated how divisions such as medieval/modern or

Middle Ages/Renaissance impose homogeneities that not only mask the existence of "modern" characteristics in the Middle Ages and "medieval" characteristics in modernity, but also distort the histories of fields such as medicine and philosophy and occlude minority histories such as those of women and the racially or religiously oppressed.[12] Subaltern studies scholar Dipesh Chakrabarty, a longtime opponent of the conceptual divisions constituted by such periodization, characterizes the problem through questions that highlight the overlapping concerns of both medievalists and postcolonial critics: "Can the designation of something or some group as *non-* or *premodern* ever be anything but a gesture of the powerful?" How do we characterize those "whose life practices constantly challenge our 'modern' distinctions between the secular and the sacred, between the feudal and the capitalist, between the nonrational and the rational?"[13]

These questions address political struggles and disparities today—particularly those pertaining to religious violence—but I argue in this book that they cannot be separated from the processes that have constituted the idea of the Middle Ages and its categories. No attempt to grapple with these political dilemmas can afford to ignore the function of medieval/modern periodization as a regulating principle and thereby remain open to the dissimulation of readings such as Fabian's, which postulate historical breaks as fully "achieved" and outside politics. Instead of perceiving that the narrative of "secularized time" simultaneously produced an "other" time and an "Other" of anthropology, Fabian's argument, like many similar and important critiques of "modern" sciences, reinscribes one of colonialism's most cherished stories. The conceptual boundaries constituted by this intellectual history "temper" current theoretical efforts to deal with some of the most intractable political challenges, and indeed bear some responsibility for that intractability. My concern in this book is not to revise definitions of the "medieval" or the "modern," but to address the occlusions and reifications instantiated by the periodizing operation itself, and to show why this matters today. At least two histories of periodization are implicated here: one that generates and protects cultural and political categories by grounding them upon a division between medieval and modern; and one that grounded Christian political order by attaching it, by way of the *anno domini* and the biblical supersession of the New Testament over the Old Testament (which is also to say Christian history over Jewish history), to a division in sacred time. The latter of these is encrypted and redoubled within the former.[14]

This book aims to engage the topic of periodization at the level of its global import. Certainly this topic is a vast one, but I do not want to back away from its vastness too quickly, for it is precisely through the slippage from local history to universal category, from singular event to narrative fulcrum, that the effects of periodization are dissimulated and thus entrenched. The belief in a break between a medieval and a modern (or an early modern) period ever more intensively assumes world-historical implications for categories such as the sovereign state and secular politics—that is, categories with both ideological and territorial stakes—and for exactly this reason the "Middle Ages," like "modernity" before it, has been vaulted from a European category to a global category of time. This globalized Middle Ages operates in two conflicting ways. On the one hand, literary and political history—whether of Europe, Asia, India, or Africa—is increasingly organized along a conventional medieval/ (early) modern divide. According to this scenario, the world moves in unison, in tempo with a once European story written at the height of, and in tandem with, colonialism, nationalism, imperialism, and orientalism.[15] On the other hand, the "Middle Ages" is a mobile category, applicable at any time to any society that has not "yet" achieved modernity or, worse, has become retrograde. In this mode, it provides a template for what Fabian has aptly termed the "denial of coevalness."[16]

Insofar as it has been adopted as a historiographical tactic, even if as a gesture of inclusion, this globalized Middle Ages must be considered in the context of what Lisa Lowe and David Lloyd have perceived as the tendency, under the pressure of contemporary neocolonial capitalism, "to assume a homogenization of global culture that radically reduces possibilities for the creation of alternatives."[17] By providing a singular point of departure, a global "medieval" past anchors this homogenization of cultural forms.[18] More specifically, this singularized point of departure validates the global application of narrowly conceived definitions of political forms—such as modern democracy, feudal (or "rogue") states, and "secular" government—the limits of which have been formulated through the periodization of the medieval and the modern. It is important to emphasize that this periodization also requires a singularized Middle Ages: as soon as we begin to pluralize the "medieval" in any meaningful way, we begin to undermine the condition of possibility of the periodizing operation. The topic of multiple temporalities cannot be usefully broached, I suggest, until the process and the effects of periodization have been taken into account. Periodization as I address it, then, does not refer to a mere back-description that divides history into segments, but to a fundamental political technique—a way to moderate, divide, and regulate—always rendering its services *now*.[19] In an important sense, we cannot periodize the past.

For this reason, the pertinent question regarding periodization is not "When was the Middle Ages?" but "Where is the Now?"—a question raised by Chakrabarty as a challenge to scholarship that presupposes a "certain figure of the now" in its approach to current political dilemmas.[20] He argues that the insufficiently examined historicity of fundamental concepts—such as religion, secularism, democracy, and even politics—renders the logic of many events across the world unrecognizable to dominant strains of critical theory, which adopts an unspoken limit as to how "the now" can be thought.

The history of these fundamental concepts is also the history of medieval/modern periodization, consideration of which is essential to any rethinking of critical theory and its limits. Despite the obvious status of the "Middle Ages" as a constructed category, and despite some recognition of its vexed position in the histories of colonialism and competing nationalisms, the relationship between the historical conceptualization of its defining attributes and the formation of some our most basic historical and political assumptions has not been studied. This book undertakes such study by focusing on two ideas with long and complex histories: feudalism and secularization. These ideas, both notorious in their resistance to definition, anchor "the Middle Ages" as a period concept and supply the narrative bases of the "modern" sovereign state and secular politics. The problem of their definition cannot be extricated from the continuing performance of the periodizing operations that constitute them.

Feudalism and Secularization

My arguments regarding these two complex ideas pertain to a single thesis: *the history of periodization is juridical, and it advances through struggles over the definition and location of sovereignty.* I began this book with the intention of researching feudalism and secularization as concepts, hoping to learn how and why they became such powerful temporal categories. It was a surprise to find that the idea of a "feudal" past for Europe emerged in legal battles over sovereignty, and that the sixteenth-century legists who narrativized the fief not only embraced "feudal law" as the conceptual basis of sovereignty and a social contract, but also competed over its origin story. When this history turned my attention to current theoretical work on sovereignty, it was likewise a surprise to find secularization already there, at the heart of current critical debates over sovereignty and its relationship to law and politics. Before I had the chance to approach it separately, then, secularization appeared in relation to feudalism through sovereignty, and it quickly became evident that the relation of secularization and sovereignty is also key to historical debates over periodization—particularly with respect to the idea of "modernity" as an independent, self-constituting period. Coming full circle, theories of modernity rely upon the legitimacy of secularization to shore up the period divide.

FEUDALISM

So entrenched is the idea of "feudalism" that the few scholars who have attended to early feudal historiography have celebrated its "discovery" of Europe's legal past, thus leaving its details understudied and its claims unexamined.[21] Chapters one and two undertake this study and this examination, with attention to the performance of this historiography in struggles, from the sixteenth through the eighteenth century, over the definition and the possession of sovereignty. As an "-ism," feudalism of course suggests a fully reified object, a status that accords with the belief that it is (or *ought* to be) a phenomenon of the past. We should not be surprised, however, to find that "feudal*ism*" emerged with the decapitating stroke: first nominalized as *féodalité* on the eve of the French Revolution, it was brought to adjudicate between nobility, parliament, and crown, particularly in matters of property, and ultimately to embody the superstitious and fettered past being dragged to the guillotine.[22] In this sense, "feudalism" is one of our most graphic examples of Walter Benjamin's insight that "modernity" simultaneously produced and destroyed the images of tradition to which it opposed itself.[23]

My concern in the chapters on feudal historiography is not primarily with the appropriateness of "feudalism" as a descriptive category for the Middle Ages, an issue with a long, controversial history that has lately been revisited, with productive results, by Susan Reynolds. I agree with Reynolds that the idea of a feudal Middle Ages and the wide range of assumptions that this idea brings with it have led to reductive, generalized, and misleading historical and social analysis.[24] There simply never was a "feudal Middle Ages." My main concern here, however, is with the relationship between the historiographical *becoming-feudal* of the centuries now considered "medieval" and the formation of political concepts long considered central to modern politics. Well before it materialized as an -*ism*, the sixteenth- and seventeenth-century writing of a "feudal" past for Europe mediated the theorization of sovereignty and subjection at crucial moments of empire, slavery, and colonialism.[25]

Chapter 1 traces the early narrative of a feudal European past, which took shape through a search by sixteenth-century jurists for Europe's legal origins, the stakes of which, according to their own arguments, were the nature of sovereignty and the history of *imperium*. For these scholars, feudal law was a way of negotiating the sovereign paradox, as it has been most forcefully described by Carl Schmitt: the sovereign is both inside and outside the law.[26] Through a study of the most important of their legal commentaries, I show that the juridical condensation of a feudal past for Europe both grounded arguments regarding the "free" political subject and a social contract and facilitated the transference of the problem of slavery from the contemporary slave trade to a brutal past. Early feudal historiography fully relies on medieval law and commentary, yet it also constitutes the narrative and conceptual basis of modern politics. The cut of periodization not only obscures this history, but also redistributes its terms—the subjected and the sovereign, the enslaved and the free—across the medieval/modern divide. This chapter therefore advances our understanding of the medievalism at the heart of the theoretical enterprise of modernity, a topic recently explored in other ways by medievalists such as Bruce Holsinger, Carolyn Dinshaw, John Ganim, Allen Frantzen, D. Vance Smith, and Andrew Cole.[27] Tracing "the archaeology of medievalism" in modern critical thought provides, as Holsinger puts it, "a powerful mechanism for questioning traditional schemes of periodization and temporality in the Western tradition."[28]

It is not quite accurate, however, to speak of "medievalism" with reference to the sixteenth- and seventeenth-century historiography of feudal law, and this problem indicates the complexity of the temporalities inherent in periodization. To my knowledge, the scholars who narrativized the fief, and who are now credited with "discovering" feudalism, never used the terms "medieval" or "Middle Ages," and would perhaps have found them perplexing. This is not just a matter of terminology. Although they wrote in a humanist milieu influenced by the linguistic and historical ideals of Petrarch and Lorenzo Valla, and therefore considered the language of earlier legal commentary "barbaric" and its methodology "confused," these scholars nonetheless identified themselves with these laws and commentaries, which they took as the basis of their own legal arguments. For them, the *ius feudali* they studied was customary law of their *own time.* It is difficult to find in their writings any general terms for the past; they refer to specific laws and specific predecessors, and occasionally to the "ancient past" when discussing what we would today call the "early Middle Ages" or even "late antiquity." It was only *after* sixteenth-century legists (particularly in France and Germany) theorized sovereignty, subjection, and a social contract on the basis of the feudal relation of lord and vassal, that legal historians such as Jean Bodin advanced arguments for absolutism by retaining this theory of the social contract, but rejecting the "feudal" as property-based and as aligned with slavery. In other words, at the very moment the colonial slave trade began to soar, feudal law and slavery were grouped together and identified as characteristic of Europe's past and of a non-European present.

Early feudal historiography, then, operated in conflicting modes, one that depended upon and identified with the materiality of a "feudal" past, and one that repudiated material detail as it strove to conceptualize a universal "spirit of the law." This complex pattern of identification and rejection is what made it possible for the category of the "Middle Ages" to emerge as it did in the eighteenth and nineteenth centuries. Despite the humanist literati following Petrarch (for whom, we should remember, the "dark age" was his own time), the "Middle Ages" as we know it today is not a Renaissance idea. It is a much later reification of categories that emerged as a means of legitimizing sovereignty and conquest.[29] By the time thinkers such as Montesquieu, William Blackstone, Adam Smith, and Karl Marx engaged it, for instance, the politically fraught concept of a feudal past had been at work for centuries, and these late analyses owe enormous debts to—and have in turn regenerated—the constitutive work of early feudal historiography. Important as the later, more explicitly "medievalist" discourse is to national, colonial, and imperial politics, it tells us almost nothing about how this periodization occurred, why it is so powerful, or why it is so difficult to establish beginning and end points for "the Middle Ages."[30]

Chapter 2 begins by crossing the channel to seventeenth-century England, where legal scholars who were well read in continental feudal historiography recognized its importance to constitutional debates over sovereignty, conquest, and absolutism, and thus soon began to "discover" that England's past had been "feudal." The first part of this chapter follows the burgeoning of England's feudal narrative, which developed as, and in, colonial discourse. Indeed, the acclaimed foundation of English feudal historiography, Henry Spelman's *Feuds and Tenures*, was written in response to a court decision by which the crown seized colonial property in Ireland, and in which the court had rejected Spelman's interpretation of feudal history and based its ruling upon that of his contemporary, John Selden. For Spelman and Selden, as for the court system and parliament, feudal law became an invaluable—although always ambivalent and therefore dangerous—discourse on sovereignty and subjection, as well as a potentially lucrative theory of property. Whereas the continental debates over the origin of feudal law had centered on the end of the Roman Empire, English debates pivoted on the Norman Conquest (which for Spelman was "colonial" and subjugating), but they continued to mediate struggles over the location of sovereignty: the *merum imperium*, "sheer power," or the "power of the sword."

This chapter section ends with a consideration of recent historiography such as that of J. G. A. Pocock, which, despite its learned and often subtle discussion, erases the performance of the *writing* of a feudal past by suggesting that scholars such as Spelman "rediscovered" feudalism, which had long been "forgotten" in England. Arguments such as this demonstrate how periodization ultimately becomes reified and one-dimensional. While, as Michel de Certeau has shown, historiography "forgets" infinite possibilities for selecting and arranging detail as it carves out an apprehensible concept, Pocock's formulation takes the resulting concept and locates it in the past, as the forgotten object toward which historiography must strive. With such confirmation of "modern" historiography's trajectory, periodization becomes self-evident, and time runs smooth.

Turning to the eighteenth century, the second part of this chapter follows feudal law and its colonial affinities to India. The historiography of English feudal law, including its metamorphosis into feudal*ism*, has always been treated as a domestic discourse. However, a wide-angle approach to William Blackstone's *Commentaries on the Law* shows that, explicitly following Spelman's interconnection of feudal law and colonial conquest (i.e., the Norman Conquest but also England's conquest of Ireland), Blackstone read the history of feudal law through the lens of contemporary colonialism, particularly the battles between the crown and the East India Company regarding the relation of sovereignty, conquest, and commerce. Wanting a *European* past for England—which, according to his admired predecessors, meant a *feudal* past—yet not wanting a past of conquered subjugation to the French, he famously proposed that in England feudal law was a "fiction." The Normans did impose feudal law, but its terms were *de jure*, not *de facto*: the conquest was a bargain. With this Blackstone triangulates an English feudal past, the current policy of the East India Company in Bengal, and the controversial relation of conquest and commerce. The history of feudal*ism*, then, is not to be found in "the Middle Ages," but in a complex and shifting series of such triangulations in the eighteenth and nineteenth centuries.

The potential of this triangulation was not lost on colonial administrators, and a decade later East India Company officials such as Philip Francis leaned heavily on Blackstone's feudal history—including his "feudal fictions"—in writing a revenue plan for the Permanent Settlement of Bengal. The final section of this chapter reads Francis's plan alongside Ranajit Guha's analysis of it in his *Rule of Property for Bengal*, and attempts thereby to pry open and to display the difference between an inchoate "feudal" that was not yet an *-ism* for either Blackstone or Francis (for whom it was still being conceptualized at the intersections of colonial and commercial traffic) and the "feudal*ism*" that Guha, as a Marxist scholar and the founder of the subaltern studies collective, accepted as the "medieval" past and to a degree as a means of understanding eighteenth-century Bengal (which he describes as "quasi-feudal"). Although Guha was among the earliest to challenge the insertion of colonized countries into narratives of transition (medieval to modern, feudal to capitalist, pre-political to political), he nonetheless accedes to the narrative of medieval/modern periodization for Europe, thus missing the degree to which the very colonial history he studies contributed to that formulation. Well before Marx got hold of it, the space of transition out of a "feudal" past was theorized in relation to the challenges of colonial administration. If we straighten out this timeline, the simultaneous creation and destruction of a paired medieval/colonial is made to disappear.

SECULARIZATION

In contrast to "feudalism," the closely related problem of "secularization" suggests a process, at minimum the transference or transformation of something from a "nonsecular" to a "secular" status, whether that something is a plot of land, a priest, a government, or an attitude. As an ecclesiastical term since early Christianity, it has referred to the movement from monastic life to that of secular clergy, and as a legal term in European history after the Reformation it refers to the expropriation of ecclesiastical rights and property. In this sense it shares a history with "feudalism," particularly during the French Revolution's seizure of both Church property and "feudal rights," and its process thus moves directionally with the conceptualization of feudal*ism*, but away from the structures characterized as feudal.

In a less concise and far more controversial sense, secularization has been understood to narrate the modernization of Europe as it gradually overcame a hierarchized and metaphysically shackled past through a series of political struggles, religious wars, and philosophical upheavals. This is the familiar Enlightenment, "triumphalist" narrative of secularization—for which the privatization of religion, along with the freeing of the European imagination from the stranglehold of Providence, came to mark the conditions of possibility for the emergence of the political qualities designated "modern," particularly the nation-state and its self-conscious citizen.[31] It is this narrative that Johannes Fabian invokes, or takes for granted, in the section of *Time and the Other* that I discuss above. Fabian published his influential book in 1983, just before political events began to expose the historicity of this narrative's qualitative story and to force a reevaluation of "religion" and the "secular." Talal Asad describes this change of focus in his 2003 *Formations of the Secular: Christianity, Islam, Modernity.*

The contemporary salience of religious movements around the globe, and the torrent of commentary on them by scholars and journalists, have made it plain that religion is by no means disappearing in the modern world. The "resurgence of religion" has been welcomed by many as a means of supplying what they see as a needed moral dimension to secular politics and environmental concerns. It has been regarded by others with alarm as a symptom of growing irrationality and intolerance in everyday life. The question of secularism has emerged as an object of academic argument and of practical dispute. If anything is agreed upon, it is that a straightforward narrative of progress from the religious to the secular is no longer acceptable.[32]

With the escalation of bloody political struggles over "secular" or "religious" government around the world, scholarship on these categories continues to expand with little consensus, and I make no attempt here to engage the full compass of this debate.[33] My interest is in the role of medieval/modern periodization in the constitution of the fundamental categories in question, and in ways that taking this periodization into account can make a difference in understanding the contours and implications of the debate.

The historiographical and political processes that yielded the narrative of secularization have been much more studied than those of feudalism, yet—despite the obvious role of periodization in the "triumphalist" narrative of secularization—these studies tend to reaffirm rather than critique the medieval/modern divide. I take Talal Asad's work as an example for the moment, since the relation between the "secular," the "religious," and the "modern" in his *Formations of the Secular* demarcates several issues that engage me throughout this book. Asad offers his complex anthropological study "as a counter to the triumphalist history of the secular," asserting that the "religious" and the "secular" are not essentially fixed categories.[34] To the contrary, their definitions and their relation are, at least in part, a function of the juridical. Arguing against the misleading, dichotomized "common assumption that the essence of secularism is the protection of civil freedoms from the tyranny of religious discourse," he suggests instead that institutional powers, in taking *aim* at a "secular modernity," carve out a sense of "religion" and an opposing sense of the "secular" that is "defined and policed by the law."[35] His analyses of juridical processes also demonstrate, as this thesis would suggest, the constant breakdown of West/non-West and modern/premodern binaries.[36] They thereby unravel some of the most elemental, constitutive aspects of the "modern" subject.

Like most works that grapple with the volatile politics of these ideas, however, Asad's analysis is pinned to the category of the "modern," even when he would question it. He posits on the one hand that modernity is a *project*, "people *aim* at 'modernity,'" and he wants to ask "why it has become hegemonic *as a political goal,* what practical consequences follow from that hegemony, and what social conditions maintain it."[37] On the other hand, according to Asad's terms throughout his book, the "secular" is fully circumscribed by the hegemonic project of modernity; it is "a modern doctrine of the world in the world":

> We should look, therefore, at *the politics* of national progress—including the politics of secularism—that flow from the multifaceted concept of modernity exemplified by "the West" . . . But should we not also inquire about the politics of the contrary view? What politics are promoted by the notion that the world is *not* divided into modern and nonmodern, into West and non-West? What practical options are opened up or closed by the notion that the world has *no* significant binary features, that it is, on the contrary, divided into overlapping, fragmented cultures, hybrid selves, continuously dissolving and emerging social states? As part of such an understanding I believe we must try to unpack the various assumptions on which secularism—a modern doctrine of the world in the world—is based. For it is precisely the process by which these conceptual binaries are established or subverted that tells us how people live the secular—how they vindicate the essential freedom and responsibility of the sovereign self in opposition to the constraints of that self by religious discourses.[38]

These are salient questions, and they expose the dilemma wrought by the relation of periodization and sovereignty. Asad is certainly right when he insists that taking a stance on the modern/nonmodern binary is a political move, and this is one of my suppositions throughout this book.

But the way in which the "modern" operates doubly in Asad's passage indicates that, even when questioned, its sovereignty survives complication, a position that does not take into consideration that the "triumphalist history of the secular"—which is also to say the history of medieval/modern periodization—is a principle means by which the idea of the "modern" emerged. If we collapse this relation and thus ignore the means by which periodization binds the "modern" and the "secular," we have already closed off, to use Asad's own terms, the "process by which these conceptual binaries are established." Thus the "secular"—that is, the *world* itself according to this "modern doctrine"—would be already and *only* a "modern" project, in both the temporal and the cultural sense. Asad well recognizes that it is sovereignty, in the form of the liberal humanist "essential freedom and responsibility of the sovereign self" (which he critiques) that is at stake, but frequently in his analysis this also, however inadvertently, becomes a "world" sovereignty already decided. These are some of the issues inhabiting the problem of "secularization" that I take up in Chapters 3 and 4. These chapters, unlike the two chapters on feudalism, focus more on the theoretical premises underlying narratives of secularization than on the historical unfolding of these narratives.

In contrast to the "triumphalist" narrative of secularization, a qualitatively different view of the relation between periodization and secularization is available in the work of Carl Schmitt, Walter Benjamin, and some of their contemporaries. Chapter 3 considers the importance of Schmitt's and Benjamin's work on sovereignty to the context of recent arguments regarding time, "religion," and the "secular." Schmitt's *Political Theology* (1922) has become central to discussions of sovereignty for its insight into the "sovereign paradox." The legal order of a state, Schmitt argues, can never be fully self-enclosed; there is always the possibility that a "state of exception," which he theorizes by analogy to the miracle in theology, might exceed the expectations of all juridical norms. In order to protect its autonomy a state therefore requires a sovereign, whose position it is to *decide* that a state of exception has occurred, and to suspend the existing legal order for the preservation of the state. Schmitt makes it clear that he is dealing with a limit concept. Paradoxically, if a state is to be sovereign in the sense of being "autonomous" (*auto*, "self"; *nomos*, "law"), it must at its core be *antinomic*: it requires a sovereign who is both inside and outside the law, and whose decision, like creation *ex nihilo*, simultaneously defines and breaches the limit of that law. The foundation of this sovereignty, then, is not locatable. One goal of this chapter is to show how medieval/modern periodization frequently serves as a substitute for this absent foundation of sovereignty, and thereby installs certain characteristics of the "modern" in the place of the sovereign. In this sense, periodization functions as sovereign *decision*.

Recent attention to Schmitt has focused on his argument regarding the structure of sovereignty that I outline above, often at the expense of his historical argument. But this structure, epitomized by the famous statement, "Sovereign is he who decides on the exception," is pinned to the equally important historical claim: "All significant concepts of the modern theory of the state are secularized theological concepts."[39] Here, "secularized" does not refer to the narrative of Europe's extrication from theological constraints; it refers rather to the transference of theological forms to the politics of an ostensibly "secular" state, in which theology thus becomes immanent. The crucial aspect of modern sovereignty in this sense is its *essential* indebtedness to preceding theological-political forms. Schmitt works out this indebtedness more explicitly is his less studied *Roman Catholicism and Political Form*. Just as sovereignty is irreducible to pure rationality, so too "modern" politics depends upon theological-political precedent for political *representation*:

that is, for a means of incarnating the "ethos of belief" upon which politics depends.[40]

Understood in this way, secularization disrupts any narrative of clean-cut periodization, and blocks the substitution of medieval/modern periodization for the absent foundation of sovereignty. The second part of this chapter engages the critical reception of this "secularization theory," which was considerably extended by thinkers such as Karl Löwith, and was attacked explicitly as a threat to periodization—most specifically for its suggestion that "modernity," or *Neuzeit*, is not a fully independent, self-constituting period.[41] The postwar backlash against this view of secularization came at the moment when European political hegemony was waning, decolonization was underway, and "world order" was in question, and this reactionary, vehement insistence upon the purity of medieval/modern periodization, cast mainly in religious/secular terms, must be considered in this broader context. This argument for periodization found powerful expression in the work of Reinhart Koselleck, one of the most influential theorists of temporality and "modernity," who shifted the emphasis from secularization to that of historical conceptions of time. In Koselleck's hands, the theory of an eschatologically bound Middle Ages "trapped within a temporal structure that can be understood as static movement," and entirely lacking any meaningful sense of temporality or historicity, reaches an extreme.[42] For him, as I show in an extended reading of an essay from his *Futures Past*, time remained untemporalized until the events of modern politics, particularly the French Revolution, cracked open this temporal stasis and inaugurated a meaningful sense of futurity. This narrative, other versions of which I will examine below, bases the periodization of historical time upon the apprehension of historical time itself, taking as its ground an evacuated "Middle Ages."[43]

Viewed from within the self-defining "modern European" political discourse in which Koselleck is situated, this narrative could make sense. But it cannot be separated from the interrelated discourses of anthropology and Orientalism that it extends, and in effect shores up, as northern Europe's (particularly Germany's) place in "world order" shifted. Anthropology and Orientalism of course generated timeless, suprahistorical, depoliticized tribal and Eastern others in the context of colonialism and imperialism. And, for "self-consciously modern Europeans," as Masuzawa puts it, these discourses "promoted and bolstered the presumption that this thing called 'religion' still held sway over all those who were unlike them: non-Europeans, Europeans of the premodern past, and among their own contemporary neighbors, the uncivilized and uneducated bucolic populace as well as the superstitious urban poor."[44] This is the context in which we should consider mid-twentieth-century efforts to buttress a divide between modern historical consciousness and a theologically entrapped Middle Ages incapable of history, and to disavow the intellectual basis of its own thinking about history, temporality, and periodization.

Theories of periodization and temporality in "the Middle Ages" were more numerous, complex, and embattled than medieval/modern periodization, partly because hegemony was less consolidated, but also, of course, because "the Middle Ages" is not a temporal or geographical unity. Chapter 4 centers on one example, that of Bede, with whom I began this introduction, and juxtaposes two of his texts with an unlikely companion piece: Amitav Ghosh's postcolonial text *In an Antique Land.* The contemplations of temporal division in these texts touch upon, for different reasons and in disparate ways, the possibilities inherent in resisting or *suspending* periodization. Because it moves around the edges of such potential, this chapter, unlike the previous chapters, is more meditation than argument.

I choose Bede in part because he was an extremely influential historian and theorist of temporality, and in part because his political and historical situation differed significantly from that of Augustine, whose important work on time in *The Confessions* and *The City of God* often overshadows other "medieval" conceptions of time. Augustine had little need to theorize a place and time for Christian kingship and political history, but in eighth-century Britain the very existence of the Church was precarious, and in Bede's estimation it required active kings as much, sometimes more, than monks and monasteries. For this reason it is no accident that Bede became the first author to use *anno domini* dating in a political and institutional history, and thus to link—in a way that Augustine does not—the incarnation with political time. Bede elaborated what we could call a secular theology of time, whereby the necessary, ongoing calculation of time becomes a regulating practice, a way of living that in turn generates the history of the world. Perhaps more important, Bede's claims regarding conceptions of history and temporality, like the claims of those who disagreed with him, must be understood as political arguments. As such, they demonstrate the absurdity of the idea of a *single* "medieval" conception of history and temporality; they testify, rather, to a *plural* "Middle Ages," which—in this as in many other categories—undermines the very condition of possibility of medieval/modern periodization.

Amitav Ghosh's *In an Antique Land,* a book familiar to many medievalists for its extensive work on the Cairo Geniza, both critiques and falls prey to periodization. The two main strands of Ghosh's book—the Indian narrator's anthropological quest among rural Egyptian villagers, and his reconstructed story of a twelfth-century Jewish trader and his

Indian slave—are linked by a narrative of historical methodologies: the colonial process of making and effacing a void at the center of history, and the counterprocess of squeezing an alternate history out of the colonial archive. Ghosh attempts to stitch the occluded, "medieval" intercultural affiliations that he finds in the twelfth century to the tenuous connections and interfaith practices of his twentieth-century characters as a way, he seems to suggest, of opening alternate historical trajectories. Medievalism becomes the method for countering a colonial politics of knowledge precisely because this politics instantiates the medieval/modern divide as a form of territorialization. All too often this medievalism slips into romantic tropes, and its engagement with periodization sometimes reinstates symptoms of identity politics. Despite its narrative failings, however, *In an Antique Land* accentuates the strictures and the limits of periodization, and tries to think about how time and politics might be disaggregated. By juxtaposing this text with Bede's, I hope to survey potential contours of such disaggregation.

Historiography

The relationship of literary and historical periodization has its basis in politics, and medievalists have begun to analyze this relation in political terms. A recent book that directly engages the conjunction between political jurisdiction and literary periodization is James Simpson's *Reform and Cultural Revolution*, which aptly describes the stakes involved. Here is his first paragraph: "Despite its size, this book has a very simple, central, and consistent theme: that the institutional simplifications and centralizations of the sixteenth century provoked correlative simplifications and narrowings in literature. If literary history and criticism is, as I believe it should be, ancillary to the complex history of freedoms, then this is a narrative of diminishing liberties."[45] As these two sentences suggest, Simpson understands periodization as politically driven and as having political implications relevant today. His argument that "only new concentrations of political power enable such powerful redrawings of the periodic map" identifies, I believe, the generative mechanism of the periods that have been ingrained by several centuries of intellectual history, and accurately assesses sixteenth-century politics (rather than fourteenth- or fifteenth-century humanism) as critical to medieval/early modern periodization in its predominant form.[46]

In its insistence upon the importance of sixteenth-century centralization, Simpson's approach coincides with Michel de Certeau's description of the relation of *place*, politics, and historiography, and a comparison of these two very different authors can be instructive. Certeau argues that: "In the sixteenth and seventeenth centuries, by being established spatially and by being distinguished by virtue of an autonomous will, political power also occasions restriction of thought." The result, Certeau suggests, is a discourse that, on the one hand, "'legitimizes' the force that power exerts," providing it with a familial, political, or moral genealogy, and on the other hand, "sketches a science of the practices of power."[47] Simpson's book, in part, traces such practices of power, and, more implicitly than explicitly, their legitimizing role as Henry VIII, for instance, repudiates an "old" ecclesiastical and juridical order, which he simultaneously repossesses and defines.

Because Certeau and Simpson approach historiography from quite disparate positions, and yet for conflicting reasons both reaffirm the periodizing cut they analyze, a brief examination of their differing assumptions and conclusions can help to expose the logic of periodization as well as its inherent slippage. Certeau considers the historiographical method he describes not to have been possible before the sixteenth century, and his argument aligns sovereignty with the conceptualization of historical time: "Since the sixteenth century—or, to take up clearly marked signs, since Machiavelli and Guichardin—historiography has ceased to be the representation of a providential time, that is, of a history decided by an inaccessible Subject who can be deciphered only in the signs that he gives of his wishes. Historiography takes the position of the subject of action—of the prince, whose objective is to 'make history.'"[48] This argument recapitulates the fundamental premise of the longstanding, triumphalist narrative of secularization. Wrested from God and claimed for the "world," time only becomes truly historical through a political-theological tear that inaugurates a new "age"—a tear that thereby defines the relation of world and time, and that paradoxically occupies a transcendent position by virtue of banishing transcendence. In this way, periodization becomes its own logic, a self-identity that, through rupture rather than through presence, supplies the necessary platform for a claim to sovereignty. This is the disappearing trick that has made the hegemony of the "modern" so difficult to assail. In this evacuation of "history" from the Middle Ages, it is also the temporal version of colonialism's "people without a history."

Even though Certeau recognizes the periodizing "*decision* to become different" as one of encryption and forgetting, one that "promotes a selection between what can be *understood* and what must be *forgotten* in order to obtain the representation of a present intelligibility," he nonetheless bases his own analysis upon an essential break in the conception of history itself, thus reaffirming the self-substantiating logic of periodization.[49] Crucially, the slippage in Certeau's argument occurs *within* the founding cut of *decision* (Lat. *decidere*, "to cut off"), which for Certeau on the one hand marks the movement of *decision* from Providential to human control, and on the other hand marks the originary historical *"decision to become different,"* within "modern" history. The fact that Certeau critiques the hegemonic operations of "Western modernity" does not undo this affirmation of its claims—or in his own terms, its *forgetting*.

Certeau is heavily influenced, of course, by the work of Michel Foucault, to whom the relationship between periodization and sovereignty was of fundamental importance. Foucault's persistent efforts to disrupt the narrative of a universal sovereign subject generated some of the most effective critique—but also some of the most frustrating repetition—of dominant historiography, a pattern endemic to the paradoxical structure of periodization itself. Foucault's historical analysis often reinstates versions of spatio-temporality established through struggles over history and the possession of sovereignty, mediated by contests over national boundaries and expanding colonial opportunity.[50] It is no coincidence, therefore, that scholars find Foucault both to repeat stereotypes of periodization and to elide the racial formations of colonialism.[51] Foucault's complex engagement with periodization is a voluminous topic that has recently been taken up by medievalists, and I do not attempt to engage it here.[52]

Although he does not engage the theoretical questions that occupy Certeau, Simpson moves directly in on the assumptions supporting such a model of historical time, and precisely reverses their terms. In his redescription, "medieval" cultural practice exhibits a sensitivity and openness to historicity, and, "above all, an affirmation of the possibility of human initiative, whether in politics or theology." By contrast, the sixteenth-century "cultural revolution" repudiates historicity as it insists upon a static, original purity, and stresses "central intelligence and initiative" under the mantle of "a newly conceived transcendence of power."[53] At the very least, the erudition with which Simpson documents this reversal animates Bruno Latour's famous aphorism that "it is the sorting out that makes the times, not the times that make the sorting."[54] There is perhaps some strategic irony in Simpson's clean reversal and his assertion that "there *was* such a thing as the Middle Ages and a 'Renaissance,'" a position that allows for a decisive, massive overturning of historical assumptions—on their own terms.[55] Such declarations jostle throughout the book with demonstrations of how the periodizing *coup* failed, was incomplete, or was so dispersed and inconsistent as not to constitute a division at all.

Periodization has not yielded absolute or unassailable configurations of time and power. Declarations of jurisdiction over time, space, and history in the sixteenth century did not utterly succeeded as *performative* acts, any more than did those of following centuries.[56] Certainly they were epochal *in their own terms* of pronouncing a revolutionary moment in law, which enacted institutional and, less directly, cultural change. To the degree that such change was constituted and executed *as* a break with a past simultaneously defined, this act of periodization instantiates certain limits. But, as David Wallace remarks with reference to the Reformation, "the transformative effects" of such shifts "can never be as comprehensive as their agents, and their agents' chroniclers, would have us believe."[57] The extent to which we grant an existential status to such periodization by *fiat* depends not only upon our willingness to read *with* dominant historiography and its organization of categories, and to comply with the selection and description of texts and events according to the strictures of "modern" intellectual history, but also to cooperate in the slippage between institutionalized limits and historical essence.[58] In other words, it requires us retrospectively to collapse the difference between history and a theory of history, and thus to reify the basis of what is always a *particular* sovereign claim upon "the now."

The most potent critique of this historicism, particularly its mapping of homogenized historical time as a mechanism of epistemological exclusion, has come in recent decades from the arena of postcolonial studies. For this reason, a rich conversation has been developing between medieval and postcolonial studies, and one aim of this book is to bring the history of the relation between medieval/modern periodization and techniques of colonialism (even as they continue today) into sharper focus.[59] As medievalists have recently argued, the genealogies of "the Middle Ages" and of colonialism are intimately entwined. The construction of a "medieval" period characterized by irrational superstition was fully involved with the identification of colonial subjects as irrational and superstitious, and this process bore concrete effects upon colonized peoples through the systems of rule that it generated and legitimized. The idea of a superstitious Middle Ages, in other words, did not preexist the "superstitious" colonial subject upon which it became mapped; rather, they emerged together, each simultaneously making possible and verifying the other. Likewise, the analysis of land systems in colonies went hand in hand with the development of the concept of a "feudal" Middle Ages, and this analysis played out in administrative decisions regarding the organization and control of land for the purpose of extracting wealth, even as it concretized a feudal medieval past. There was no such "superstitious, feudal Middle Ages" *before* colonialism, and doubtless there never would have been such without colonialism; vice versa, colonizers could not have mapped and administered foreign lands and bodies as they did without the simultaneous process of imagining such a "Middle Ages." This argument does not receive its own chapter here, but I hope the reader finds it interwoven, both explicitly and implicitly, throughout these pages.

Part I
Feudalism

Chapter One
Sovereign Subjects, Feudal Law, and the Writing of History

> *But I think partly it was they [the PLO] were coming out of some kind of a feudal background, which made them incapable of understanding the way a democratic society works.*
>
> *Noam Chomsky*

The comment by Noam Chomsky above is not as off-handed as it may seem. Wittingly or not, it participates in a long legal history, which conceptualized a "feudal" past as a means of grounding claims to sovereignty, and then rejected this newly consolidated past as a means of distancing Europe from its others. The feudal-democratic binary that Chomsky takes for granted rests upon the effacement of this political history, and the geopolitical narrative of development implicit in his comment is the most commonplace symptom of this effacement.

This chapter investigates the historiographical *becoming-feudal* of the centuries now considered "medieval," a process initiated by sixteenth-century juridical struggles over sovereignty and slavery. My primary concern is not with the appropriateness of "feudalism" as a descriptive category for the Middle Ages, an issue with a long, controversial history lately revisited by scholars such as Susan Reynolds. My focus, rather, is upon the history of the process that turned the "fief" into a narrative category, a history that begins to tell us why the "feudal"—despite its inaccuracies, contradictions, and anachronisms—persists today as a temporal marker and a lever of power.

The narrative of a feudal European past took shape through a search by sixteenth-century jurists for Europe's legal origins, the stakes of which, according to their own arguments, were the nature of sovereignty and the history of *imperium* (in its related senses of executive power and supreme territorial rule).[1] Ironically, the work of these jurists, who were among the most influential legal theorists of their time, does not fit traditional categories of periodization, even though they generated what would become one of periodization's most influential categories. Perhaps this is why they are relatively understudied, and most of their writings remain in rare books unedited since the sixteenth century. The jurists who narrativized the fief did not use terms such as "medieval" or its cognates, nor did they reject the feudal law they studied. Although they wrote in a humanist milieu influenced by the linguistic and historical ideals of Petrarch and Lorenzo Valla, and therefore considered the language of earlier legal commentary "barbaric" and its methodology "confused," they nonetheless identified themselves *with* these laws and commentaries, which they took as the basis of their own legal arguments: indeed, they vied over a feudal origin story as the basis of sovereign legitimacy.[2] It was only after these professional jurists theorized sovereignty, subjection, and a social contract on the basis of the feudal relation of lord and vassal that legal historians such as Jean Bodin advanced arguments for absolutism by retaining this theory of the social contract, but rejecting the "feudal" as property-based and as aligned with slavery. At the very moment the colonial slave trade began to soar, in other words, feudal law and slavery were grouped together and identified as characteristic of Europe's past and a non-European present. To this history we owe the later, persistent association of the Middle Ages with subjugation, as well as the role of the Middle Ages as the enabling figure of exclusion in much philosophical and political thought.

By the close of the sixteenth century, the narrative of a "feudal" European past was securely entrenched, and the constitutive performance of its early historiography disappeared. As a symptom of this effacement we are left with feudalism's central but always conflicted role in mediating theories of power and temporality, signaled most obviously, perhaps, by the enduringly contested status of "feudalism" itself.[3] More telling, however, is the centrality of feudalism to conceptualizing a *shift* in power relations—for example, the cry to abolish *la féodalité* on the eve of the French Revolution, feudalism's linchpin role in the Marxist paradigm, and accusations of feudalism against "rogue" nations today.[4] Crucial to these processes is feudalism's productive relation with historicism (handled most interestingly by Hegel, to whom I return below), which on the one hand underwrote linearity by bonding "feudalism" and "the Middle Ages," and on the other hand loosed feudalism to roam across time and space, but always as a *temporal* marker, a tick on the clock of development.[5] As the following pages show, early feudal historiography operated in conflicting modes, one that depended upon and identified with the materiality of a "feudal" past, and one that repudiated material detail as it strove to conceptualize a universal "spirit of the law." The conceptualization of a feudal past, in other words, negotiated the tension between positivism and idealism, as well as the tension between freedom and slavery at the heart of "modern" politics.

This chapter focuses mainly on the crucial early decades of feudal historiography's long, conflicted story, and primarily on three of its most dominant characters, all of whom were professional legists: Ulrich Zasius (1461–1535), Germany's leading legal scholar and practicing magistrate; Charles Du Moulin (1500–1566), "the prince of legists," staunch French royalist under Henry II and vociferous antipapist; and François Hotman (1524–1590), a fiery Huguenot and Gallic nationalist.[6] These "feudists" (as they were called) developed a feudal narrative within the larger project of revising and interpreting law, and they worked from differing, sometimes conflicting political positions in the struggles between the Habsburgs and France, and in France's civil wars. The confessional as well as national loyalties of these men drove their scholarship, and their story therefore intersects the nexus of periodization, secularization, and sovereignty that I address below in Chapters 3 and 4. My focus here, however, is not upon the details of their political and religious entanglements, but upon the arguments and the implications of their feudal historiography. These legists and their contemporaries narrativized the fief and conceptualized the feudal relation as a *universal* category of sovereignty, a status that prepared for its extension to a theory of slavery and its contrast to citizenship in the work of Jean Bodin, with which I conclude.

The early historiography of feudal law is a tangle of contradictions for three reasons, which I set out briefly here and explain at length in the course of this chapter. First, this historiography was the medium for competing origin stories: French legists interested in forwarding France's claims to legal independence from the Empire usually argued for a Frankish origin of feudal law, while Italian and German legists interested in defending the authority of Roman civil law and the interests of the Empire argued for a Roman origin (these have been called "Germanist" and "Romanist" positions, respectively).[7] Second, the main players in this controversy ("feudists," as they called themselves) stood in a conflicted relation with the humanist movement that united them. They embraced, on the one hand, the Petrarchan dictate to purge texts of postclassical barbarisms, but refused, on the other hand, an outright rejection of postclassical legal codes and commentary. Third, commentaries on the feudal relation (of lord and vassal) became the foundation of *competing* theories of sovereignty, particularly in regard to absolutism.

As this argument shifted from the hands of legists to those of political theorists such as Jean Bodin, it became key to theorizing the relation of sovereignty and slavery in domestic and international law. In this new role the historiographical condensation of a "feudal" past enabled a narrative transference of the "problem of slavery" from the contemporary slave trade to a brutal past that was ostensibly being left behind. At the same time, it grounded arguments regarding the "free" political subject and a social contract. The *becoming-feudal* of the Middle Ages, in other words, is the narrative and conceptual basis of "modern" politics.

As a way of approaching feudal historiography, we may begin with the simple but salutary reminder that medieval people—even medieval lawyers—did not think of their time as feudal any more than they thought of it as medieval. There were "fiefs" of course, at certain times and certain places, as well as laws governing fiefs. (A fief was a right to, not ownership of property, which was often a portion of land but could also be, for instance, a right to collect a certain tax.) These laws comprised one aspect of medieval contract and property law, and addressed relations between property holders, mainly aristocrats, such as the rules for inheriting, securing, or alienating fiefs; they did not, however, address the status of nonproperty holders, such as serfs.[8] "Feudal law" did not appear *as* law until the twelfth century, when a small collection of academically rarefied texts (commonly known as the *Libri feudorum*) became important for negotiating power relations, after which royalty, popes, and nobility could draw upon these texts and their commentaries to exert pressure and gain political advantage.[9] The centrality of property to any analysis of social and political history argues, of course, for the extension of such laws to consideration within a socioeconomic system, but such late analysis did not arise until the eighteenth-century legal and economic syntheses of thinkers such as Montesquieu, William Blackstone, and Adam Smith. By then, the politically fraught concept of a feudal past had been at work for centuries, and these late analyses owe enormous debts to—and have in turn regenerated—the constitutive political work of early feudal historiography.[10]

There has been scant attention paid to feudal historiography, and not inconsequentially that which does exist came through a search for the origins of "modern" historical method. In his foundational work on the feudists, Donald Kelley argues that we must look beyond their ideological agendas to their role in shaping this historical method: "What is far more interesting" than their political agendas, he argues, "is the way in which our problem [of feudal origins] illustrates the awakening of historical consciousness."[11] I argue, to the contrary, that it is precisely the myth of this "awakening" and the suppressed *writing* of a feudal past that continues to privilege a linear narrative of civil society, which both brackets slavery and preserves a European universal "spirit of the law."

Temporal Contradictions

To a surprising degree, the story of feudal historiography leans upon the strange history of a particular book. The narrative of a feudal past did not begin, as one might think, from study of a broad array of medieval documents and laws, but from the commentary tradition on the twelfth-century Italian *Libri feudorum*, an eclectic collection of treatises, statutes, and northern Italian legislation regarding fiefs. The *Libri* started as a private, mostly Lombard collection, and accumulated in various recensions throughout the twelfth and thirteenth centuries in the context of the revival and teaching of Roman law.[12] In the early thirteenth century, the influential glossator Hugolinus appended a recension of the *Libri* to the corpus of Roman law, and from that point on it circulated with the standard manuscripts of civil law used throughout Europe for teaching, and to a lesser degree for practice. After the legist Accursius glossed it along with the entire Roman code in his authoritative thirteenth-century *Glossa ordinaria*, the *Libri*'s place in the corpus of Roman civil law was secure, although its nonclassical Latin sometimes prompted commentators to question its authenticity—that is, the veracity of its ancient Roman heritage.[13] The *Libri* thus existed in a fairly stable but sometimes vexed relation with the Roman law from which it drew authority, and when jurists took it up in the sixteenth century, this relation would provide the wedge for debate. Ironically, then, feudal law entered legal historiography's mainstream with an ancient Roman passport, by virtue of a twelfth-century humanism that both enabled and put a fold into the "Renaissance" cleansing and recuperation of a legal past.

The history of the *Libri* and its commentary tradition challenges many standard concepts of a feudal timeline. The onset of the *Libri*'s immense popularity and the initiation of its burgeoning commentary tradition in the thirteenth century is "astonishing," Kenneth Pennington notes, and "presents a historical puzzle for two reasons":

First, by the thirteenth and perhaps as early as the twelfth century, the system of personal and property relationships that historians have denominated feudalism was distinctly on the wane. Medieval society was no longer structured around warrior vassals holding fiefs in return for military and other services. Mercenary armies and professional civil servants were instead the new key piece of a changing economic and administrative world. Second, what feudal custom did remain in use varied from place to place. The Lombard customs in the *Libri feudorum* had no necessary similarity to the customs anywhere else in Europe. Yet not only was the *Libri feudorum* the second most popular private law collection after the *Decretum* of Gratian, but it also continued to be published, consulted, and commented on by academics and practitioners throughout Europe well into the early modern period.[14]

This contradiction within feudalism finds its parallel in the many contra-dictions that scholars now acknowledge as inhabiting the term. Penning-ton offers two explanations for the disparities he identifies. First, "written feudal law was largely an academic creation" perpetuated by the pedagogy and tradition of law schools. This suggestion coincides with Susan Reynolds's argument in her *Fiefs and Vassals* that the aca-demic law of fiefs was a creation "of a culture of academic and profes-sional law and of professional, bureaucratic government that had developed since the twelfth century," upon which she builds her conten-tion that this law, read retroactively, has disproportionately influenced medieval historiography.[15] The history of the *Libri* needs much more study, but at minimum its texts must be understood as politically situated arguments, not as transparent evidence of longstanding "medieval" practice. It is worth noting here as well that the emphasis of these aca-demic laws upon bonds of fidelity, sometimes with explicit reference to sexual liaisons, suggests intriguing intersections with the contemporary development of "courtly love."[16]

Pennington observes, second, that the *Libri* was "a work of generali-ties," and therefore flexible enough to offer lawyers a common vocabu-lary for disparate circumstances. Incredible as it may seem, as Magnus Ryan puts it, "A private collection of Lombard customs [i.e., the *Libri feudorum*] was often used to describe fiefs given in return for homage and fealty in Northern Europe, even though the text itself never men-tions homage."[17] In his study of the *consilia feudalia* accompanying legal cases, Gérard Giordanengo, like Pennington, notes a disparity between the chronological and geographical history of these *consilia* (which began in the thirteenth century but did not expand and attract spe-cialists until the fifteenth and sixteenth centuries, mainly in Italy) and medievalists' expectations: "The least that one can say is that these chro-nological and geographical facts do not all correspond to what we know—or what we think we know?—about feudal institutions and their importance in the medieval period."[18] He argues nonetheless for the importance of these *consilia* with regard to sovereignty in an interna-tional context, a point to which I return shortly.

Reynolds's controversial *Fiefs and Vassals* insists upon the need to revisit and to account for the influence of early feudal historiography. It aims, in part, to prove that the late medieval academic laws of fiefs did not develop out of earlier customary laws, and that this academic tradi-tion (mainly based upon the *Libri feudorum*), along with the sixteenth-century interpretation of it, has led to a generalized, homogeneous, and misleading "construct of feudalism." Her book attends as well to the ret-rospective authorizing strategies of the medieval academic laws of fiefs, which have long been read by scholars as simply the codified reflex of centuries of feudalism. Ultimately, Reynolds marshals great quantities of documentation as evidence that over-arching ideas of "fiefs and vassal-age," as well as the later "feudalism," are "post-medieval constructs" of little use in approaching medieval history.[19] Reynolds is certainly right to insist upon the need to revisit "feudalism" with an eye to the process and the effects of its historiography, but empirical evidence will never settle the arguments. "Feudalism" can *only* be a contested category, in that it developed as a medium for conflicts over sovereignty and *imperium*, which inhabit it and sustain it as a contradictory and politically active term. Attempting to come to grips with the *writing* of a feudal past is one way of questioning what David Lloyd calls "the reasons of state that are embedded in the rationalities of history."[20]

Augean Writing

"Quid sit feudum?" the teacher Hostiensis asks rhetorically in the mid-thirteenth century. He then answers, "Nunquam audivi convenientem diffinitionem," and adds, "satis potest magistraliter describi" (What is a fief? Never have I heard a suitable definition . . . for teaching it can be explained well enough).[21] As this pedagogic moment attests, the "fief" never admitted definition, which availed teachers space for interpreta-tion and lawyers malleability in application. Ironically, this indetermi-nacy later enabled sixteenth-century feudists such as François Hotman (1524–1590) to describe the law attested in the *Libri* as "ambiguam" and "incertam," and to imagine himself a juridical Hercules who braved its Augean stable of "barbarous writing" as he produced his *De Feudis Commentatio Tripartita* (1573).[22] The narrative flow of his feudal histori-ography, in other words, purges as it proceeds, and leaves in its wake a recuperated edifice of the law—an apt figure of the feudists' writing of history as they simultaneously rejected and relied upon centuries of medieval legal commentary.

For legists such as Hotman, the *Libri* occupied a pivotal position in legal discourse. On the one hand, its position in the corpus of Roman civil law offered the value (or sometimes the liability) of a Roman pedi-gree. On the other hand, its "barbarous" language offered an affinity with local, contemporary custom. For sixteenth-century scholars imbued with the ideals of humanism and the sense of innovation that it brought to legal teaching, this doubleness corresponded to the philosophical and political tensions inherent to their discipline. As legal scholars the feudists approached the study and reform of law with an admiration for Roman legal principles, but also with an acute awareness of the histori-cal difference between cultures. They therefore acknowledged an irrep-arable disjunction between Roman antiquity and the present, not simply in terms of an intervening "dark age," but also according to the terms of their conviction that laws were culturally specific and thus not transferable. They agreed, therefore, with Petrarch's sense of being cut off from the light of antiquity, as well as with the criticism, forwarded by the "grammarians" gathered behind Lorenzo Valla, that jurists of the preceding centuries had naively attempted to apply Roman law directly to their own world. The desire of legists such as Hotman to cleanse and recuperate the laws of the *Libri*, then, redoubled the larger, idealist legislative project at hand.

In contrast to humanists such as Valla, however, professional jurists such as Hotman refused to relegate the Roman corpus to antiquarian status, and instead turned to reestablishing its text and to studying its principles within a project of comparative jurisprudence that embraced the laws of the recent "barbarous" past. Thus, while Petrarch, Valla, and their "grammarian" followers wanted to expunge the obviously unclassical *Libri* from the Roman legal corpus, and scorned commentaries such as those of the prominent fourteenth-century legist Bartolus of Sassoferrato, most professional jurists rejected this approach. They insisted instead upon both the centrality of the *Libri* (even if they refused its authority for political reasons) and the value of the earlier commentaries.[23] This was true, for instance, even of Andrea Alciato, the Italian scholar hailed as the leading innovator in legal teaching: "Alciato denounced the ignorance of the glossators (*Accursiani*), but he had little more use for the irrelevant 'folly' (consciously using the term of his friend Erasmus) of grammarians, especially of their 'emperor' Valla; and he celebrated the work of Bartolus and such later professional interpreters as his own teacher Giason, 'without whom . . . we should have no science.'"[24] As they took up legal historiography from various points of indebtedness to state power, then, these legists felt themselves to be separated by a gap in time from the valorized principles of Roman law, and distanced, by virtue of its "barbarism," from the more recent past. It was upon the latter, however, that they fully depended, and with few reservations, reclaimed.[25]

The historiographical *becoming-feudal* of the past we now call "the Middle Ages" does not conform, then, to the standard narrative of periodization, and its contradictions belie the idea that medieval/modern (or medieval/Renaissance) periodization emerged simply through the "consciousness of a new age" that established a relationship between the ancient and the modern at the expense of "the Middle Ages."[26] The pattern of this historiography demonstrates why temporal divisions such as medieval/modern must be put into question *with* the categories that constitute them. Periodization, if it is to have a historical legacy, results from a *double* movement: the first, a contestatory process of identification *with* an epoch, the categories of which it simultaneously constitutes (as we see in the feudists under study); and the second a rejection of that epoch identified in this reduced, condensed form (as we will see in Jean Bodin). I argue in part that the conflicted relation of feudal legal historiography with the past, along with its engagement in attempts to theorize sovereignty, generated the temporal boundaries of what would become "the Middle Ages" as sites of contest that only took concrete form with the mapping of sovereign power.

Barbarian Places

The tensions within this legal study abound in the work of Hotman, who describes feudal law in the preface to his *De Feudis* as "ambiguitatem, repugnantiam, et absurditatem," and as written in "barbarica scriptione." Yet, he had only disdain for the "grammariens purifiez" who would reject past law and commentary as "nec lex sed faex" (not law but excrement), a stance poignantly at odds with the Augean metaphor he applies to his own cleansing efforts, and an explicit reminder of the inescapable relation of *fundament* and *fundamental*.[27] Hotman writes here as one of France's leading jurists, as a Huguenot and a proponent of resistance theory (i.e., justification of political resistance to a regime in power), and as a French patriot who argued for public checks upon royal power. Extreme though his politics sometimes were, Hotman in many senses was a typical feudist: on the one hand, his approach to feudal historiography was politically motivated; on the other hand, it operated within the larger humanist projects of reorganizing and systematizing law, considering laws in terms of their historical specificity, and undertaking comparative study ultimately aimed toward distilling universal principles of justice—the *mens legum* or the "spirit of the law."[28] In his thinking, as Ralph Giesey puts it, "the tension remained between those two coexisting attitudes to law which saw understanding in terms of history and yet demanded the demonstration of absolute values," a tension clearly evident in the preface to *De Feudis*, and one that would be an enabling factor in the political application of the feudists' work.[29] Hotman is the most recent of the feudists under study here, but I begin with a discussion of his texts because they so clearly set out the parameters and the implications of this early feudal discourse.

Hotman wrote *De Feudis* while teaching law at Bourges, after having fled Paris and survived the siege of Sancerre during the second Religious War; its publication in 1573, just months after the Saint Bartholomew's Day massacres (from which he narrowly escaped), coincided with the release of a number of his works after he fled to Geneva. As a French nationalist, Hotman claimed a "Germanic" (i.e., Frankish, rather than

Roman) origin for the feudal law attested in the *Libri*, and he called upon these laws to support his arguments against a strong monarchy. But he also considered the *Libri*, like Roman law, to have been corrupted by centuries of sophistic editing. He undertook its explanation and organization both for teaching and for advancing a program of legal reform aimed toward a national code for France—a code based upon historical analysis and the roots of French public law, but a code that nonetheless aspired to universal principles of equity.[30]

Hotman outlines this legal program most explicitly in his earlier, polemical *Antitribonian* (1567), which (as its title indicates) attacks Tribonian, the sixth-century editor of Emperor Justinian's *Digest*, for his misunderstanding and corruption of the legal code.[31] It also argues, however, that Roman law had no authority in France, both because the Roman code was specific to ancient Roman culture, and because Hotman defends the independence of France (and the territories it claimed) from the Empire and from the pope. By contrast, "feudal law *must* be studied, because it is germane to French institutions of public law, whereas Roman Law has no direct application to them."[32] Hotman nonetheless holds fast to an idealizing project, and concludes *Antitribonian* by insisting that the principles of Justinian's code still offered a priceless guide for a program of legal reform. He thus offers an effective description of the process through which conflicting legal practices served political ends, and yet, cleansed of their literal pertinence, were retained and made to yield a universal Roman spirit.

Both this universalism and the specificity of French custom were bound up with colonialism, as *Antitribonian* quickly attests. In an imaginary scene meant to display the absurdity of applying Roman law to France, Hotman stages the centrality of colonialism to this juridical discourse. *If*—he proposes—a lawyer meticulously trained in Roman law but ignorant of French customary law were to present himself "en un palais ou autre siege de ce Royaume," then it would be as though he had come among the savages of America:

> qui ne sçait qu'il y sera presque aussi nouueau et aussi estrange, comme s'il estoit arriué aux terres neuues entre les sauuages de l'Amerique? Car là il n'orra jergonner que d'heritages cottiers ou surcottiers, des droits seigneuriaux, de iustice directe, censiue, recognoissance, de retraits lignagers ou feodaux . . .[33]
>
> [who does not know that it would be nearly as novel and as strange as if he had arrived in the new world among the savages of America? For only jargon is heard there—cottar and surcottar tenancies, seigneurial rights, immediate jurisdiction, jurisdiction over quitrenters, assizes, first right of redemption based on kinship or lordship . . .]

Almost as strange, new, and implicitly as "savage" as the inhabitants of the New World, the French court stands as distant from classical Rome as does America from sixteenth-century France. Hotman's conjunction of "estrange" and "sauuages" fleshes out the full implications of the "barbarism" attributed by humanists to postclassical law, with its foreignness defining the very limits of civility and civil law. Despite the estrangement in this passage of French customary terms and classical law, "it is clear," as Pocock observes, "that these uncouth vocables, 'barbarous' according to all humanist standards, are being contrasted favourably with the classical clarity of Roman law."[34] Like an early version of the "noble savage," Hotman's French court challenges the outmoded mores of classical civilization with autochthonous strength, defying their universal span in space and time, usurping the claim to empire.

At the time Hotman wrote *Antitribonian*, justifying such usurpation was crucial to French claims both in Europe and in Florida, where as newcomers they needed to devise nonpapally sanctioned justifications for colonial rule. Indeed, Hotman's association with the American "savage" would have been even more specific and complex. During the years that Hotman was writing this treatise, the French were challenging the Spanish for colonial territory, and its publication in 1567 comes just two years after the Spanish massacre of French Huguenots at Matanzas Inlet (now St. Augustine). José Rabasa has shown that Protestant response to this massacre associated the well-known and controversial Spanish atrocities against Indians with their massacre of the French colonists, which after 1572 also became associated with the Saint Bartholomew's Day massacres in Protestant colonial historiography. Both cases, Rabasa rightly notes, "deny Indians the status of subjects and the possibility of becoming part of the European community."[35] Indeed, Hotman's scene depends upon the inassimilable status of the American "savage" in order to imagine the internal limits of a legal history that he nonetheless firmly circumscribes as "European."

Such demonstration of the limits of the law is also, however, precisely what demands its supersession by absolute values, the *mens legum*, or "spirit of the law." Mediated by the American savage, who is nonetheless kept safely distant by "presque," French barbarism can authorize and be assimilated into a new European universal. As David Wallace comments, the "discovery" and colonization of the "New World" has always been a principal historical determinant behind configurations of the Renaissance.[36] Citing and furthering Wallace's point, Walter Mignolo argues that this European "discovery" precipitated a "discontinuity of the classical tradition" ultimately constitutive of Renaissance universals: "The foundation of colonial difference, in the sixteenth century, implied the discontinuity of the classical tradition: Indigenous people of the Americas could not be accommodated within the secular history of the world initiated in Greece."[37] Mignolo finds that this breach forced a reevaluation of universal categories, resulting in a redefinition of humanity coupled with racism. This argument, however, is incomplete. The redefined humanity so crucial to colonial rule and to the logic of empire *also* depended upon a reworked, embattled identification of and with a European "past," which was articulated in minute detail yet superseded by a historiographical idealism that ultimately bonded—in the breach, so to speak—the "Middle Ages" and the colonial subject.

Hotman's triangulated scene thus miniaturizes the disciplinary interests and constraints within which legists engaged the "barbarism" of feudal law, sometimes to cleanse it of troublesome discontinuity, but more often to insist upon its "barbarism" in order to reclaim it. This last position, part of the beginning of the "Gothic" rehabilitation that would have such a long political (not to mention literary and architectural) life in the name of nationalisms and colonialism, participated in an already developing debate in which the *ius feudale* performed as a historical ground for political arguments and territorial claims. Hotman's scene clearly also miniaturizes the process by which a "feudal" (and ultimately, a "medieval") past emerged *with* the colonial subject, each simultaneously making possible and verifying the other.

In order to understand how this feudal past became such an important ground, we need to consider the arguments of several feudists who preceded Hotman, and whose work delineated the stakes of this origin search and its connections to sovereignty.

Barbarian Etymology

The rubric "de origine feudorum" dates from the fourteenth-century legal commentator Isernia, who raised the etymological point that *feudum* and its related terms are not classical. Fourteenth- and fifteenth-century commentators such as Isernia were interested in the legal authenticity of the *Libri* within the Roman corpus, and in the continuity of imperial authority that this authenticity would ensure.[38] In the early sixteenth century, this question of etymology shifted to a question of origins bearing upon the legal ancestry of particular states and their claim to *imperium*, both in the sense of the translation of power from Rome, and in the juridical sense of the ownership of power.[39] The fundamental point dividing the French position from the Italian position, for instance, was "whether the king of France recognises the emperor as superior"—a question framed by the larger claim, invoked and debated with reference to imperial and colonial ambition from the first to the eighteenth centuries, that "the emperor is lord of the whole world" (*dominus totius orbis*).[40] Supporting or refuting this claim required historical evidence and a current theory of sovereignty, both of which were supplied, in part, through the historiography of feudal law. Etymology remained a focus of analysis throughout the sixteenth century, and thus became a cutting edge for history as it laid claim to imperial power and to jurisdiction over territory.

The French philologist Guillaume Budé (1468–1540) addressed the issue of feudal law in his influential *Annotations on the Pandects* (1508), a sprawling collection of notes on the first twenty-four books of the *Digest*.[41] Budé was France's most famous early humanist (considered by contemporaries as the equal of Erasmus), a Gallican nationalist and professional servant of the monarchy (although not a professional jurist), and an aggressive champion of French cultural independence. As a humanist dedicated to the task of recovering the text of Roman law distorted by centuries of "barbarous" editing and commentary, and more dedicated than the professional jurists who followed him to Valla's dictum that doctrine was inseparable from eloquence, Budé adopts a *translatio* approach in order to negotiate the tension between his Gallicism and the supremacy that he yielded to ancient Rome. In other words, he concedes the point of a Roman origin and argues for a transfer of leadership to France, which would emerge from the "barbarous shadows" of the past into cultural superiority and independence.[42]

Budé therefore grants a Roman provenance for the fief, which he defines in a way that accords with his support of absolute monarchy, and that limns the process by which feudal historiography performed as a discourse on sovereignty and subjection. The provincials and allies of the Romans often pledged themselves as clients to Roman noblemen, he argues, and "these clients were then obliged to keep themselves and their fortunes forever subjected to their patron and to keep and to venerate his customs." With an eye toward restoring local feudal custom to a position of classical eloquence, Budé then performs a reverse translation: "nobody, I think, can avoid the conclusion that *nostram feudorum consuetudinem* arose from the relation of client to patron. Wherefore, I usually apply the Latin term 'clients' to those called vassals and 'clientele' to that relation and ceremony called 'homage.'"[43] This linguistic reversal places the French laws of fiefs, like French culture, in a position to emerge from the shadows of the barbarous past and to claim the translation of Roman power. The language of fiefs thus operates for Budé, as it would for continental as well as English jurists over the next century, as a cutting edge in the writing of a political history executed through the principles of philology. For the professional jurists following Budé this edge would far more explicitly align with *imperium*, both in struggles over absolutism within states as well as in international conflict over the claim that the emperor is "lord of the whole world."

Few of Budé's compatriots would follow him in declaring a Roman origin for fiefs.[44] The leading German jurist Ulrich Zasius (1461–1535), however, found Budé's client-patron theory, as well as the principle of classicizing vocabulary, suitable both to his support of Charles V's hegemony, and to the larger project of his full treatise on "feudal customs."[45] Writing after the Roman *ius civile* (including the *Libri feudorum*) was "received" in Germany, Zasius opens his *Usus feudorum epitome* by insisting upon the central importance of *feudales consuetudines*, which, he insists, his students must learn even if its "sordid" and "barbarous" language did offend their fine sensibilities. He promises, nonetheless, to ameliorate this law's offensive diction.[46] Zasius adopts the client-patron theory ("Nos credimus feuda a vetustis Romanorum moribus orta" [We believe that *feuda* arose from the ancient customs of the Romans]),[47] but, far less inclined toward absolutism than Budé, he tells the story differently: the Romans, having conquered the provinces of Gaul, Germany, and so on, left behind a large part of the *militae*, who invited many of the inhabitants, largely peasants, to become "clients," granting them lands and property as "clientele." From this beginning, in the course of time, a variety of feudal customs developed.[48] However variable they may be then, for Zasius feudal customs attest to the continuity of empire linked to a common history for Europe.

Zasius also had different motivations than Budé for classicizing the barbarous language of fiefs (although despite his client-patron theory he usually did not substitute "client" for "vassal")—not only because he linked a Roman origin to contemporary empire and thus to his Hapsburg patrons, but also because he wished to validate the imperial authority of feudal customs, past and present, upon which he would base a contractual theory of sovereignty (which I discuss below). Like Budé, he understood the point of classical rhetoric that dictated the inseparability of doctrine and eloquence. Rejecting the theory that the *Libri* was merely a collection of private law, he insists upon the legal authority of feudal customs in both the lay and ecclesiastical spheres: it was not without reason, he says, that this law was inserted into the *corpus Iuris Civilis*.[49] In contrast to Budé, Zasius rejected the "grammarian" approach of Valla and defended the Accursian gloss and "Bartolist" commentaries, retaining their position in legal history even as he recognized and attempted to purge their barbarous shortfalls.[50] In Zasius's *Usus feudorum*, then, the translatability of the *Libri* and its commentaries into classical diction validates the origin and the continuous participation of feudal customs in imperial history, and their linguistic transposition is ultimately a statement about the foundation of power.

For precisely this reason the famous French jurist Charles Du Moulin (1500–1566) railed against it. In the long treatise *De Fiefs* (1539) that opens his *Commentarii in Parisienses consuetudines,* Du Moulin strenuously refutes the legitimacy of the classicizing tactics of Budé, who "barbara feudorum vocabula latinis commutauit" (converted the barbarous vocabulary of fiefs into Latin), and even more strenuously criticizes Zasius's imitation of this practice.[51] For Du Moulin, it was necessary to reclaim and to embrace barbarian etymology in order to insist upon a *difference* in feudal origin that would open the foundation of this law and allow for a competing narrative of sovereignty based on its terms. As Kelley puts it, "Dumoulin protested that his objections to such classicizing rested on no mere verbal quibble; the point was not a change in terminology but a difference in historical origin."[52] Du Moulin effectively positions the "barbarous" language of fiefs as a shibboleth that reveals ethnic distinctions and enforces a territorial claim to sovereignty. Although he dismisses Zasius's linguistic *translatio* as mere fondness for elegant diction, his response points to the increasing importance of this language in legal debates over the nature of European institutions and monarchy, and signals the role it was beginning to play in nationalist historiography and international law.

Du Moulin's embrace of barbarian etymology allowed for an innovative and consequential move, announced in his first sentence: "Merito priore loco ponitur hic materiae fedalis titulus, quum feuda sint proprium et peculiare inuentum veterum Francorum."[53] Fiefs were an invention of the Franks, and from them spread south, first to Gaul, then to Lombardy (with the Lombards, who had learned feudal practices from the Franks), the two Sicilies, Apulia, and many other regions.[54] He rejects the *Libri* entirely as Lombard, late, and derivative—nothing, in fact, except local Italian law, introduced well after the compilation of the Roman corpus (which in any case, so far as Du Moulin was concerned, had no authority in France).[55] Reversing the movement of *translatio imperii,* Du Moulin exploits the cultural capital that had accrued to feudal historiography through the *Libri*'s incorporation in the Roman code, and appropriates it for the Franks. Combining an already established French rejection of the *Libri*'s authenticity (i.e., its authority in France) with a rejection of its claim to historical priority, he merges feudal historiography—now broken free from the *Libri*—with the swelling tradition of Gallic nationalist historiography. Turning to Parisian custom as authority, he effectively builds up an *ius commune* based on feudal custom that could stand up to the Roman *ius civile*. His "Germanist" thesis would quickly link with the project of Gothic rehabilitation, later advanced, for instance, by his friend Hotman, which would carry the politically charged, chauvinistic banner of "feudalism" for centuries and that would, in the eighteenth and nineteenth centuries, become both a heuristic and a tool for colonial enterprise.[56]

De Fiefs thus simultaneously expands feudal custom as a capacious legal and social category, and secures it as an origin myth for French sovereignty—both in the sense of declaring French supremacy and independence from the empire, and in the sense of defining *imperium* as the prerogative of the king, a double-edged argument already developed for feudal custom, although less explicitly, by Zasius for the imperial side. Combining an insistence that only local custom can provide the basis of legitimate law ("Ergo consueutudines nostrae sunt ius commune")[57] with an argument that the sovereign relation encapsulated in the fief had its basis in the *ius gentium* (the "law of nations"), Du Moulin, like Zasius, formulates a theory of sovereignty based upon the fief that exhibits the tension, to quote Giesey again, "between those two coexisting attitudes to law which saw understanding in terms of history and yet demanded the demonstration of absolute values."[58] The implicit universalism of the fief finds resonance in Hotman's savage scene, and a generation later will provide a basis for Jean Bodin to theorize relations of dominance and subjection on an international scale.

So far, I have focused primarily on the process by which sixteenth-century jurists narrativized feudal law as they developed and justified historical and geographical claims to sovereignty. Even more important to the process of periodization, however, is the role of this narrative in struggles over the definition of sovereignty and subjection, slavery and freedom, to which I now turn.

Feudal Sovereignty and the "Law of Nations"

The contrasting views of Zasius and Du Moulin regarding sovereignty are well known to legal historians, and both are based upon a theory of the fief.[59] Zasius held, as Steven Rowan puts it, "that the Roman prince, far from being freed from the law's bonds, was in fact bound by feudal contracts in the same way as a private person (*Princeps Romanus ligatur contractibus sicut privata persona*)."[60] Just as the reciprocal contract of the fief bound the lord and the vassal equally, the prince (or the emperor when Zasius passes judgment in a specific case) was bound by constitutional agreements, including certain legal decisions by his magistrates.[61] For Du Moulin, in contrast, the feudal contract both illustrated and grounded the executive independence of the prince in matters of state, even though he agreed that the prince must keep private contracts. These sixteenth-century struggles over sovereignty were often phrased, in a continuation of a long medieval tradition with classical roots, in terms of the *merum imperium*—sheer power, or the "power of the sword"—ultimately the right to inflict the death penalty. *Merum*, or "pure" *imperium*, was power held by right of office, exercisable according to the holder's discretion without reliance upon a superior. Delegated *imperium*, by contrast, was subject to the prince's control and was thereby considered a form of subjection. Royalists tended to define the *merum imperium* as indivisible and vested solely in the king, with magistrates holding *imperium* only by delegation; those resisting absolutism argued for its divisibility, and distributed fully vested power between king and magistrates.[62]

In their arguments regarding the *merum imperium* Zasius and Du Moulin are grappling, as are their contemporaries, with the conceptual limit of sovereignty, the paradox that, as Carl Schmitt phrases it, the sovereign "stands outside the normally valid legal system, [yet] he nevertheless belongs to it."[63] Classical and medieval political theory explicitly recognizes this paradox, typically expressed in the imperial formula that the prince is simultaneously lawmaker and unbound by law (*legibus solutus*). The "pure" possession of power encapsulated in the *merum imperium* operates at precisely this point: its holder is, by law, outside the reach of law and, conversely, defines its limits. It thus succinctly captures the basic implications of sovereignty: "the sovereign is the point of indistinction between violence and law, the threshold on which violence passes over into law and law passes over into violence," a logic that we will see play out in the theories of Du Moulin and Bodin, and in the seventeenth-century historians I discuss in the following chapter.[64]

In their struggles over sovereignty, sixteenth-century legal scholars were competing to define the *location* of sovereignty, the "power of the sword" that operated as law, but also superseded law. Feudal historiography, conflicted in its relation to the past and characterized by its insistence upon both local specificity and universal ideals, emerged as a means of negotiating the sovereign paradox as legists sought to restrict or to empower absolutism, and to legitimize nationalist and increasingly expansive imperial agendas. The feudal relation, in turn, became the basis for theorizing the sovereign *subject*.

As he theorizes sovereignty, Zasius extends the logic of the binding feudal contract to his argument regarding the *merum imperium*. Even though the making of law comes under the eminence of the prince and jurisdiction proceeds from him, he can neither annul the rights of his subjects nor the judgments of his magistrates, who do not have the power of lawmaking, but do hold *merum imperium* in certain jurisdictional areas.[65] The contractual relation of the fief thus grounds Zasius's attempts to limit and to disperse power, a project furthered by his argument that the fief originated with and thus had an authentic basis in Roman law. This solution does not, however, take account of the prince's status as *legibus solutus*, and Zasius thus faced the difficulty of appearing to subordinate the prince to civil law. Zasius gets around this problem by placing the contractual obligation not under positive law, but under the *ius gentium,* the "law of nations," which was understood to derive more directly than positive law from universal principles of equity and justice. It could, therefore, operate as a moral force both to safeguard each state's right to self-rule and to negotiate relations between states. On the basis of the fief, in other words, Zasius theorized a social contract that is both specifically locatable and universally valid.

The *ius gentium* was (and still is) a self-conflicted category. Like "human rights" today, it shuttled between the often contradictory demands for respect of individual cultures (both tyranny and slavery, for example, were covered by the *ius gentium*) and for an insistence upon fundamental moral principles (such as human liberty), and it could of course always come to the service of politics.[66] By placing the obligation of a feudal contract in the category of the *ius gentium,* Zasius positions it not only beyond the prerogative of individual rulers, but in a sphere of law fast becoming a medium of comparative jurisprudence in the context of burgeoning colonial enterprise. In Kelley's perhaps euphemistic terms, the *ius gentium* "represented the expanding and extra-European horizons of modern political and social thought."[67] The inevitable conjunction of law and violence (or consent and conquest) within any theory of sovereignty, and the obvious role of colonial conquest in Europe's expanding horizons, must be kept in mind as we consider the tension between local custom and universal values in the writing of "feudal law" as part of the *ius gentium.*

Du Moulin, of course, wished to locate sovereignty in the king, and he therefore arrived at a different conclusion from Zazius regarding the contractual relation of the fief and the *ius gentium.* He is perhaps best known for the categorical statement, made in his chapter on "homage," that the king is fully vested with all *merum imperium,* and that seignorial jurisdictions were usurpations. Here, feudal law is the basis of centralized government:

For it is evident in all this realm and in any part of it whatever that the king is by common law vested with all jurisdiction and *imperium,* since he is the most high monarch of his kingdom. . . . And he is vested with these rights by specific disposition of the *ius gentium* . . . and from this it must be agreed that they are mad who think the king vested only with the final appeal, or, if I may use their words, with the last resort, because, on the contrary he is established in every grade and species of jurisdiction in the whole realm. . . . And so by common law and *ius gentium* all jurisdiction of this realm is the king's since not the least jurisdiction may be exercised unless by him or in his name and authority.[68]

To suggest, as has been done, that Du Moulin's argument here amounts to an "attack on the feudal vision of French society," or a condemnation of "feudal relationships," is anachronistic, and entirely misses the constitutive force of feudal historiography.[69] Du Moulin is developing an argument about sovereignty based upon what he claims to be the essence of the feudal contract, which in turn upholds his royalist theory of the *merum imperium*. As I demonstrate below, this conjunction provides the basis for his theory of the relation between an absolute sovereign and his subject, as well as that between freedom and bondage. In sum, Du Moulin's *De Fiefs* establishes the "Germanic" narrative largely responsible for what will become the predominant trajectory of feudal historiography and the development of feudalism as a historical category. At the same time, it relies upon the idea of the feudal relation to theorize "absolutism" on behalf of the state, a stance that will be popular among legists for nearly a century.[70]

To a degree, Marxist historiography offers an explanation for this centrality of feudal theory to arguments for absolutism. In his discussion of absolutism and periodization, for instance, Perry Anderson emphasizes the importance of the Renaissance revival of Roman law to the emergence of "the Absolutist State in the West." He is careful to recognize the connection between this revival and the study of Roman law beginning in the twelfth century:

> The dual forces which produced the new monarchies of Renaissance Europe found a single juridical condensation. The revival of Roman law, one of the great cultural movements of the age, ambiguously corresponded to the needs of both social classes whose unequal power and rank shaped the structures of the Absolutist State in the West. Renewed knowledge of Roman jurisprudence dated back, in itself, to the High Middle Ages. The dense overgrowth of customary law had never completely suppressed the memory and practice of Roman civil law in the peninsula where its tradition was longest, Italy. . . . Beyond Italy, Roman legal concepts gradually began to spread outwards from the original rediscovery of the twelfth century onwards. By the end of the Middle Ages, no major country in Western Europe was unaffected by this process. But the decisive "reception" of Roman law—its general juridical triumph—occurred in the age of the Renaissance, concurrently with that of Absolutism.[71]

Anderson argues that this "reception" of Roman law (which, in all its complications, is what we have been considering here) had a dual, conflicted provocation: it answered to property interests of the commercial and manufacturing bourgeoisie, and it served the royal governments' drive for increased central power. The latter, abetted by aristocratic revision of law in response to changing social and economic conditions, was not a struggle *against* feudalism, he argues, but was rather "*a redeployed and recharged apparatus of feudal domination*," which restructured but maintained aristocratic rule. Anderson therefore suggests, in a collocation taken from Marx, that the revival of Roman law enhanced "feudal Absolutism."[72]

This formulation usefully complicates the politics of medieval/modern periodization, and makes sense of Du Moulin's theorization of centralized power on the basis of the feudal relation. And, even though it does not take account of the *Libri feudorum* and its commentary tradition within and against the Roman legal tradition, it offers an explanation for its importance, both from the twelfth to the fifteenth centuries when, appended to and glossed with Roman law, it steered the course of professionally administered aristocratic laws of fiefs, and in the sixteenth century when its postulation as an origin myth for European sovereignty demarcated a feudal past that in turn organized the content of history in the service of the state. It does not, however, account for the performance of feudal historiography in achieving the ends of "feudalism"—the process, in other words, by which *the self-effacement of the writing of a feudal past* constitutes both the possibility of its existence as a concept and its culmination in this history. Instead, Anderson undoes periodization based upon feudalism and reinscribes it on the basis of "Absolutism." These intertwined paradigms of periodization, however, both emerge from the doubling back of feudal historiography upon itself in an act of mapping sovereign boundaries onto a universalized chronology. The medieval/modern divide is so stubborn because it describes not a passage, but an *aporia*.

This *aporia* accounts for the disappearance of feudal historiography from the temporalization of subjection, which could never have taken hold simply on the basis of a Petrarchan "dark age" that swallowed the light of antiquity, or on the basis of literary and historical projects that proclaimed a new age.[73] The "dark ages" got its teeth, I suggest, largely because feudal historiography meshed with legal teaching and political practice, and because the theorization of sovereignty and subjection on the basis of feudal law easily accommodated a discourse on slavery and transferred it to the past. Once "feudal" sovereignty gained status as a concept and the conflicted narrative that produced it disappeared, the "Middle Ages" could eventuate as distinct, and subjection could be narrated as belonging to the past and elsewhere. Ultimately, the cut of periodization would efface this history and redistribute its terms—the subjected and the sovereign, the enslaved and the free—across the medieval/modern divide.

Feudal Law and Slavery

Feudal law became particularly amenable to a discourse on slavery because in the hands of royalists like Du Moulin—who generally favored what is now termed *absolutism*—its negotiation of the sovereign paradox (sovereignty is the point of indistinction between violence and law, force and consent) brought it into explicit structural alignment with the logic of slavery. As Orlando Patterson has demonstrated in his now justly famous *Slavery and Social Death*, a master's total power or property in the slave requires the exclusion of the claims and power of others in him, and he in them: social death.[74] I am not suggesting that feudal vassals (that is, vassals in the formal relation of fief-holding)—either before or during the sixteenth century—were slaves in an institutional sense, or in the sense of the conditions we usually associate with that term. Rather, in isolating the king as the sole holder of the *merum imperium*, Du Moulin, whom I take as an example here, likewise isolated the political subject from all ties of political dependency other than those with the king. "Pure" sovereignty and slavery, as Hegel's lord/bondsman (or master/slave) dialectic suggests, are inextricably paired.

In feudal historiography this discussion occurs mainly under the rubric of "homage." Du Moulin presents his claims regarding the *merum imperium* in a discussion of *servitus*, which he defines as the "proper" (as opposed to metaphorical) sense of "homage."[75] *Servitus*, he explains, may be either "personal," by which one is bound in personal service/servitude, or "real" (referring to real property), by which one pays rent for land in return for protection and is free (*liberi*). He argues that the act of homage should apply only to bound personal service, but had in recent practice applied in both situations. It is through this indistinction between bondage and liberty in the act of homage that Du Moulin mounts his argument regarding the *merum imperium*.

In discussing the two metaphorical or "improper" applications of homage—those by reason of jurisdiction and by reason of fief-holding—Du Moulin stipulates that the act of homage, as an oath of obedience and a form of self-subjection, necessarily entails the relation of bound personal service. It may not, therefore, properly apply between a free tenant and his lord, whose relation, he insists (in a move that would separate the economic from the political), is merely a real-estate transaction: a form of free exchange. The metaphorical, or "improper," uses of homage are therefore illicit. Invoking both Frankish and Roman history, as well as the old commentators on the *Libri feudorum*, he argues that this precept is held by nature, nations, and the civil law. This extension is important for the future relationship of this theory to slavery, which had traditionally been the purview of natural law and the law of nations, and it will help Bodin to extend homage, as slavery, to international politics.[76]

Du Moulin ultimately insists that the only legitimate *bound* relationship is that between king and subject. Any lord who requires homage from his fief-holders or from those within his jurisdiction behaves as a tyrant, improperly subjecting those who have a free relation with him, and abusing the power that he holds by virtue of the king, who holds the entire kingdom in *dominium directum* (while magistrates and lords hold only *dominium utile*). One can be *subject* only to the king, and may therefore do homage, in the proper sense of pledging *fidelitas absoluta*, only to the king.[77] Du Moulin thereby eliminates the possibility of political interdependencies between subjects, which had occurred, in his estimation, through improper practice of "homage," and he shifts the relation of liberty and bondage entirely to that between king and subjects. He insists, in other words, upon a form of social death, in the sense that the king's total power requires the exclusion of the claims and power of others upon the subject, as well as the exclusion of the subject's reliance upon others for political viability. A generation later, Jean Bodin will register the proximity of this theory to the logic of slavery by describing vassalage as "une vraye servitude d'esclave."[78]

Du Moulin thus sketches out a theory of legal subjectivity that posits the constitution of the sovereign subject, whose speech (possessed of the *merum imperium*) has the literal power to do what it says precisely because of its totalized relation to the subjected subject, whose speech in the act of homage paradoxically declares itself incapable of such a sovereign speech act. Recognizing the interdependency of this relation, Du Moulin places one limitation upon the king, based on the reciprocal nature of the fief. Like Zasius, he holds that neither lord nor vassal can infringe upon the rights guaranteed by their contract.[79] Therefore, even though the king holds *dominium directum* over all honors and jurisdictions, he cannot alienate them from the kingdom, for in so doing he would effectively annihilate himself as king.[80]

Du Moulin's theory of feudal sovereignty, and Bodin's subsequent rendering of vassalage as "une vraye servitude d'esclave," suggest that there may be a historical, as well as a logical, relation between feudal historiography and Hegel's dialectic of recognition in the *Phenomenology of Spirit*. I want briefly to address this implication, for it signals the complex repercussions of feudal historiography's entanglement with colonialism, and this entanglement's subsequent inflection of history's temporal politics. I am not interested here in answering the often-asked question of where Hegel's lordship/bondsman relation originated—a question, I believe, that has no single answer. I want instead to emphasize that the terms and concepts he used had long histories at the time of his writing, histories deeply embedded not only in philosophy but also in legal interpretation and practice, histories that played themselves out in the vocabulary of his contemporaries as they stormed the Bastille or mutinied against slave-masters in Haiti.[81] The caveat to keep literal scenarios at bay as we read Hegel's abstract, or "allegorical," dialectic of self-consciousness becomes both more and less problematic when we consider the histories already at work in his terms, and their negotiation of sovereignty in the context of slavery both before and during Hegel's writing.

We can approach this problem through a specific translation controversy, one sparked by Alexandre Kojève's much discussed translation of Hegel's *Herrschaft und Knechtschaft* as *maîtrise et esclavage*, which Jean Hyppolite reproduced in his 1939 translation of the *Phenomenology* into French.[82] Peter Osborne comments upon this translation and its consequences:

> This translation replaces the feudal terms of Hegel's analysis (to which the English "serfdom" is appropriate) with a notion of slavery resonant with both the world of ancient Greece and the heritage of European colonialism. This would prove to be a brilliant move in the years during and immediately following the Second World War, as Occupation gave way to Liberation and decolonization, revitalizing Hegel's text in hitherto unforeseen ways—as Sartre's and Fanon's appropriations of the model indicate. However, precisely because of its contemporaneity, this translation has led to serious misunderstandings of both the place of this particular dialectic within Hegel's text and its relationship to Marx's work.[83]

Complicated as this reception history is, it only looks one way. Lordship and bondage (in the sense that these were used in feudal historiography) had been in exchange with mastery and slavery since at least the mid-sixteenth century, particularly in the work of Bodin (which Hegel knew), and specifically in a colonial context. So had serfdom, although neither Hegel nor Bodin conflated serfs and feudal law.[84] If we grant that Hegel's *Herrschaft und Knechtschaft* are "feudal" terms—and Andrew Cole has argued there is reason why we should—then we must also recognize that when Hegel took them up they were already heavy with historicism's negotiation of sovereignty and its temporalization of slavery, just as they were during and after the writing of the *Phenomenology*.[85]

As Susan Buck-Morss has shown, the terms of the *Herrschaft und Knechtschaft* dialectic intersected for Hegel with the daily events of the Haitian slave revolt, which occurred just before he wrote the *Phenomenology* (1805–6), and which he followed closely. She argues that Hegel echoed the political language of the revolt, which itself deliberately echoed French revolutionaries' cries against "esclavage antique" (which resonated with those against "la féodalité"). Condemning the failure of scholars to consider the significance of "real slavery" to Hegel's dialectic of recognition, she argues:

> The problem is that (white) Marxists, of all readers, were the least likely to consider real slavery as significant because within their stagist understanding of history, slavery—no matter how contemporary—was seen as a premodern insti-

tution, banned from the story and relegated to the past. But only if we presume that Hegel is narrating a self-contained European story, wherein "slavery" is an ancient Mediterranean institution left behind long ago, does this reading become remotely plausible—remotely, because even within Europe itself in 1806, indentured servitude and serfdom had still not disappeared, and the laws were still being contested as to whether actual slavery would be tolerated.[86]

Buck-Morss is certainly right that the refusal of this significance registers the repeated disavowal of slavery in the narrative of "modern" Europe's rising political freedoms—a form of forgetting that is fundamental to Europe's civil story.[87] "Real slavery" and its relationship to the past are, however, already encoded in the "feudal" terms of Hegel's dialectic, though they are made invisible there too.

For this reason, the translation of Hegel's *Herrschaft und Knechtschaft* cannot be a matter of *either* "lord/bondsman" *or* "master/slave." Such an either/or choice in this instance, especially if we grant that this dialectic resonates for Hegel with the "feudal," obscures the history already at work in these terms. And as long as the writing of feudal historiography remains occluded, its negotiation of the sovereign paradox on the basis of a superseded past, yielding a universal "spirit of the law," will continue to regulate the pulse of history and continue the same patterns of forgetting. In this regard, Kojève's *maîtrise et esclavage* for *Herrschaft und Knechtschaft* is perhaps most faithful, in that it faces up to the repetitive historical logic of slavery in the feudal narrative's mediation of sovereignty.

Timing Slavery

In his *Les six livres de la République,* Jean Bodin explicitly joins the feudal negotiation of the sovereign paradox to the problem of slavery and the international slave trade. His famous discussion of sovereignty in book 1, chapter 8 relies, like Du Moulin's, upon the feudal relation, which for Bodin illustrates both the unencumbered power of a true sovereign (who does not give his oath to his vassal, despite their mutual agreement) and the absolute obedience owed by the subject to the sovereign prince.[88] This reliance upon feudal commentary in defining the mutual exclusion of oath-taking and true sovereignty will be key to Bodin's analysis of oaths between rulers and their relation to slavery in book 1's little-noticed chapter 9.

Chapter 9 addresses the status of feudatory princes, and opens by dividing space and time according to the initiation of feudal law: the question of feudatories "deserveth a speciall Chapter by it selfe, for that it hath no communitie with the auntient markes of Soueraigntie, which were before the right of Fees, vsed in all Europe and Asia, and yet more in Turkie than in any place of the world."[89] This spatiotemporal claim allows Bodin to make arguments about the political relations of European states from their incipience to his own moment, while the territorial extension of "fees" to all Europe and Asia allows him to corroborate his evidence against universal standards, particularly "the Turkes." The figure of the tyrannical Turk was well established by the time Bodin wrote, and was used by Hotman, for instance, to contrast French freedom to the extreme of Turkish government, in which a ruler controlled men like cattle and beasts.[90] But Bodin, who rarely flinches at the implications of the sovereign paradox, uses the Turkish image here as elsewhere as a limit case for his argument that a strong monarch protects, rather than restricts, his citizens' liberties. Freedom is the point of this chapter, which asks whether tributary and feudatory princes may be sovereign, and immediately raises the issue of slavery with a quotation from Martial: "esse sat est servum, jam nolo vicarius esse: / Qui Rex est, Regem Maxime non habeat" (To be a slave it is enough, I will not serve a slave: / Who is a king, friend Maximus, no other king must have).[91] A feudatory king, in other words, is servile, and his subjects no better than *vicarii*, the slaves of a slave.

Bodin had already dwelt at length upon slavery in chapter 5, and his discussion of slavery and state governance in that chapter leaves no doubt that the contemporary threat of Spain and Portugal, figured in terms of their invasive and destabilizing reintroduction of slavery, informs the conjunction of feudal law and slavery in chapter 9. Taken together, these two chapters offer a paradigm of the process by which the intertwined politics of historiography and colonialism simultaneously demarcate temporal and territorial boundaries.[92]

Slavery in chapter 5 is both past and imminent, both memory and threat. Bodin condemns slavery as immoral and dangerous to the political stability of the state, a practice contrary to nature that had been abandoned and nearly forgotten in Europe, but was now spilling back over its borders with the abuses of the Portuguese and of France's archrivals, the Spanish, as they trafficked in Africa and the Indies. Bodin's narrative suggests that the moral and territorial integrity of European states, particularly France, solidified with the eradication of slavery, first with the manumission of "true slaues" (around the twelfth century) and then increasingly with the enfranchisement of manumitted men, who had continued to live under a "bond of seruitude."[93] He therefore distinguishes the status of "true slaves" from what is usually termed medieval serfdom, but nonetheless considers the latter a form of slavery inimical to the liberty of the commonwealth. Since Bodin theorizes the commonwealth on the model of the household, within which slaves form part of the family, slavery necessarily implies a divided house.[94] He thus associates slave-holding with civil war, both in the Frankish past and in his own time, and the enfranchisement of slaves with "libertie" and with national strength.[95]

Early in this chapter Bodin claims that slavery exists in the whole world, "excepting certaine countries in Europe."[96] He finds, however, that the recent encroachment of slavery within Europe through the actions and example of the Portuguese threatens to erase this territorial distinction by undoing time. Slavery is returning, he writes, "to the imitation of the Portugals, who first called in againe Seruitude, now for many worlds of yeares buried in forgetfulnesse in Europe; and are in short time like enough to disperse the same ouer all Europe, as is now alreadie begun in Italie."[97] The renewal of slavery would unbury the past, and reverse the process of forgetting that is necessary, as Ernst Renan observed long ago, for "the creation of a nation."[98] Unity is only possible if the violence of past difference is forgotten, a point that accords with Bodin's description of slavery as violent division within the household, and its disappearance as the story of France's emergence as a unified state with secure liberties.

Because the unburying of the past comes as an imposition from the outside, it also threatens the violent breakdown of the borders between Europe and its others, exposing even Christians to exportation and captivity: "For now a good while ago Africa and Asia, and the Easterne part of Europe also haue accustomed to nourish and bring vp in euery citie, stocks of slaues, in like manner as if they were beasts, and of them to make a great marchandise and gaine. For within this hundred yere the Tartars (a kind of Scythian people) in great number with fire and sword entring into the borders of Moscouia, Lituania, and Polonia, carried away with them three hundred thousand Christians into captiuitie."[99] Bodin's account of slavery's reentry into Europe describes the violation of a double spatio-temporal border. For Europe and especially France, slavery had been *past*, and its secure enclosure through encryptment and forgetting founded the very possibility of civil unity and territorial as well as moral integrity. For the rest of the world, slavery continued into the *present*, and this political, moral, and temporal difference had marked its boundaries with Europe. Portugal and Spain, as European countries that begin to practice slavery elsewhere and then reintroduce it to Europe, disrupt these borders from both within and without, invading it with its own repressed basis of unification, and instantiating a European self-difference that confuses the delineation of its territory and raises the divisive past from its grave, thus dissolving the very distinctions that define sovereign territory and enable the exercise of true sovereignty.

Chapter 5 does not mention feudal law, which for Bodin concerned relations between property holders—not serfs or slaves as he is considering them historically. The slavery he associates with the feudal relation results from a determined analysis of the logic of sovereignty, which he distills to the conclusion that any prince who holds anything in fealty is not sovereign. Like Du Moulin, he finds that homage always entails a bond of personal service and subjection:

Wherfore we conclude, that there is none but he an absolute soueraigne, which holdeth nothing of another man; considering that the vassall for any fee whatsoeuer it be, be hee Pope or Emperor, oweth personall seruice by reason of the fee which he holdeth. For albeit that this word *Seruice*, in all matter of fees, and customes, is not preiudiciall vnto the naturall libertie of the vassall; yet so it is, that it importeth a certaine right, dutie, honor and reuerence that the vassall oweth vnto the lord of the fee: which is not indeed a servitude reall, but is annexed and inseperable from the person of the vassall, who cannot be therefrom freed, but by quitting his fee.[100]

Possession of the fee therefore constitutes the bond of subjection. In contrast to Du Moulin, Bodin differentiates the vassal from the king's natural subject, who is always bound to his sovereign and cannot be released from his oath, whether or not he holds a fee. Relying, that is, upon definitions of oath, service, and loyalty developed in feudal historiography, Bodin creates a distinction that solidifies the state by separating loyalty from the contingency of fee-holding, and at the same time shifts this contingency to the question of sovereign borders between states. It is then but a short step to demonstrate that a king who holds territory in vassalage to another loses his sovereignty. To emphasize the totality of this loss, Bodin demonstrates (giving special attention to the self-subjection of English kings to the French) the humiliation entailed in homage, with poignant examples of abjection that recall the details of Hegel's struggle for recognition. He ultimately concludes that subjection to another's sovereignty through homage is indistinguishable from the condition of a slave—as the benchmark Turks esteem it, "une vraye servitude d'esclave."[101]

Saving the time-honored French freedom, Bodin's comparative history eventually depicts the world to be, or to have been, a tangle of dependencies. In book 2, he pursues the interweave of feudal law and slavery, suggesting that feudal bonds and homage must no longer underpin the properly governed European state, while elsewhere, rightly or not, they provide the means of territorial subjection, bondage, and tribute.[102] His contention that slavery belongs to Europe's past (historically and by moral right), his detachment of the subject's loyalty from property relations, and his mapping of homage as a condition of territorial enslavement all depend upon—even as they reject—the "feudal" European past consolidated by earlier feudists in their struggles to theorize sovereignty and subjection.

Ultimately, Bodin's schema associates feudal bonds with Europe's past and with slavery in the present, which, according to his narrative of Europe's rising political freedom, must be located elsewhere. Despite Bodin's condemnation of slavery, his argument maps coordinates of dominance and subjection onto space and time in such a way that the slavery at the heart of empire is, as Buck-Morss puts it, "banned from the story and relegated to the past." It accurately enough describes the trajectory of both the feudal image and the application of feudal law over the next several centuries—not of course because Bodin predicted it, but because he worked within a juridical tradition conflicted in its relation to the past and struggling to distill universal principles for warring states that were, simultaneously, consolidating their rule and expanding their horizons through a spatiotemporal logic that would ultimately designate categories it would name "the Middle Ages" and the "Third World."

Chapter Two

Feudal Law and Colonial Property

Defective Titles

> *It is said that all Isles and Continents (which are indeed but greater Isles) are so seated, that there is none, but that, from some shore of it, another may be discovered. Some take this as an Invitation of Nature to the peopling of one soil from another. Others note it, as if the Publique Right of Mutual Commerce were designed by it. Certainly the severed Parts of good Arts and Learning, have that kind of site.*[1]

"Above all, freedom," John Selden's motto, appears top right on the first folio of the *Codex Mendoza*, a large pictorial and textual account of Mexica life and history, commissioned by Charles V and compiled in Mexico City by native scribes and interpreters under supervision of Spanish friars. The codex sailed from Veracruz on the Spanish treasure fleet in 1541, came into the hands of French privateers who attacked the Spanish fleet, and, along with much other treasure, landed in the coffers of Henry II of France. From there it came into the control of the king's cosmographer André Thevet, thence by sale to Rickard Hakluyt, chaplain to the English ambassador to France, then to Samuel Purchas, and finally to the English jurist and historian John Selden.[2] The history of the codex thus neatly fulfills the terms of the colonial, mercantile, and epistemological geography set out in Selden's passage above, which comes from the dedicatory letter to the second edition of his *Titles of Honor*, a massive documentary and argumentative account of European political and social institutions. Selden spent his parliamentary career working against the claims of absolute monarchy and for common law protections for subjects, so the fact that his motto graces the *Codex Mendoza*, now shelved in the Bodleian as Ms. Arch. Selden.A.1, is doubly poignant.

This irony would eventually also haunt the fortunes of *Titles of Honor*, which reached out to foreign shores of "arts and learning" in part to put both England and Selden on the map of European humanist scholarship, but more particularly to compile a detailed history of Europe and England that supported constitutional law against empire and absolutism. Central to this argument as it had been waged on the continent was the discourse on feudal law that I explore in the previous chapter. Selden, who was well read in the feudists and had studied their method of using feudal historiography in constitutional debate, began to phrase English history in feudal terms in his 1610 *Jani Anglorum Facies Altera*, and then more expansively in the first edition of *Titles of Honor* (1614).[3] With a heavy debt to the Huguenot constitutionalist François Hotman, he became the first scholar to import continental feudal historiography and its negotiation of sovereignty into English politics.[4] English jurists began to "discover" that England had been "feudal," and as will become clear, they did so by way of "peopling" another isle.

Close on Selden's heels was his fellow antiquarian Henry Spelman, who took note of the rift between English and continental legal historiography and the fuss it had caused ever since Hotman, in his *De Verbis Feudalibis*, famously criticized Thomas Littleton's *Tenures* (upon which Edward Coke had later based his authoritative *Institutes of the Laws of England*) as "incondìte, absurdè, et inconcinnè scriptum."[5] Indeed, it was the problem of this rift that had encouraged Spelman in his pursuit of feudal law, in terms that correspond to Selden's metaphors of geography and commerce: "I do marvel many times that my Lord Cooke, adorning our Law with so many flowers of Antiquity and foreign Learning; hath not (as I suppose) turned aside into this field [of *foedal law*], from whence so many roots of our Law, have of old been taken and transplanted. . . . They beyond the seas are not only diligent, but very curious in this kind; but we are all for profit and 'lucrando pane,' taking what we find at market, without enquiring whence it came."[6] The current politics of knowledge—which Spelman shrewdly recognized as an issue of profit and commerce, as we will see—required an English legal historiography that was ordered, reasonable, Latinate, and schooled in the European *koine*. Spelman set out to provide this with his *Archaeologus*, a legal glossary on the model of Hotman's *De Verbis Feudalibis*.

The toehold of feudal law in English historiography was slender at first. Selden's careful argument in *Titles of Honor* was couched in a capacious history of world proportions (beginning with the biblical flood), and it traced a lineage for fiefs along the lines of Du Moulin's and Hotman's, integrating England into the story with care for his constitutional concerns.[7] Spelman's Latin *Archaeologus* (1626) remained in manuscript for decades, although Selden used it for his 1631 edition of *Titles of Honor*. Feudal law gained importance as the struggle between king and Parliament became more intensively historical. The arguments pivoted upon the Norman Conquest, and it gradually became evident that a history of feudal law beginning with the Anglo-Saxons would strengthen the argument for an "ancient constitution," while a history of feudal law as introduced by William I, and thus by conquest, would favor the king.

These arguments were of course densely intertwined with many contemporary political and ideological struggles, particularly religious, and thus intersect with my discussion of "secularization" in Chapters 3 and 4. As John Ganim points out, Selden was trained and employed by Sir Robert Cotton, whose manuscript collection largely made Selden's constitutional work possible, but through which Cotton also "sought to establish a relatively independent lineage for a newly established Church of England."[8] This early scholarship also participates in the textual weave of Orientalism, and as the passage from Selden's preface above and his purchase of the *Codex Mendoza* imply, he was an early and ambitious participant in this field.[9] Spelman poured his energies into tracts defending Church property from the state, and, as Allen Frantzen notes, he sponsored the chair in Anglo-Saxon at Cambridge, the first occupant of which was John Wheelock, who simultaneously held the chair in Arabic. Wheelock recognized the connection between Anglo-Saxonism and Orientalism, Frantzen observes, and "plays on the connection in the preface to his edition of Bede [the *Ecclesiastical History*], where he identifies the 'Saxon muses' and the 'Arabic sisters' with his patrons."[10] These intersections with religious strife and with the discourse of Orientalism are but suggestive indicators of the degree to which England's feudal narrative, like its continental predecessors, emerged as a political argument in national and international political contests, particularly those having to do with sovereignty, slavery, and colonialism.

Ultimately, it was not Selden but Spelman who wrote the definitive treatise on English feudal law. His *Feuds and Tenures* (1639) grounded the historiography of English "feudalism" and English property law for centuries. For William Blackstone, who relies heavily upon this treatise in his *Commentaries on the Laws of England*, it was the "cornerstone" of English property law, and for J. G. A. Pocock it identifies Spelman as the "principal architect" of the "feudal revolution in English historiography."[11] Unlike Spelman's more antiquarian *Archaeologus*, *Feuds and Tenures* is heatedly political, not because Spelman deliberately waded into parliamentary struggles, but because the feudal terminology of his earlier *Archaeologus* had been disparaged by a court of law, in a case that involved the seizure of colonial property by Charles I on the pretext of feudal historical precedent. This is a point that cannot be overemphasized: *Feuds and Tenures* emerged *in*, and *as*, colonial discourse. Spelman seems to have understood the implications, and his response to the court's decision in *Feuds and Tenures* makes it perfectly clear that the political force exerted by the *writing* of "feudal law" quite literally inscribed contemporary territorial boundaries and ethnic subjection as it drew lines through historical time.

The historiography of England's "feudal law" in the seventeenth century thus stays true to the sixteenth-century continental heritage that I trace in the previous chapter. In the two parts of this chapter I continue to follow the "becoming" of feudalism, first through the seventeenth-century story of Selden, Spelman, and the contemporary political struggles over sovereignty and conquest, then into the eighteenth century, when "feudal law" traveled to India, and from there negotiated with William Blackstone's *Commentaries on the Law.*

SHIBBOLETH

> *Their very names pretend no Saxon* antiquity, but as the *Ephramites* bewrayed their Tribe by their language, so by their names these fruits discover themselves to be of *Norman* progeny.[12]

The French names that betray themselves in the passage from *Feuds and Tenures* above are terms that Spelman defines as belonging to feudal law, such as "Wardship," "Relief," and "Livery," which were common in English jurisprudence in his day. He invokes the story of the shibboleth in Judges 12:1–15 in order to reveal a double boundary: one between ethnic groups, as these terms betray a Norman, rather than a Saxon, genealogy; the other, a division in time, the conquest of 1066, which for Spelman draws a line through English feudal law and across the European geography of power. The Saxons, Spelman argues, practiced one type of feudal law, that of "feuds" and military service according to "the ancient manner of the Germans." But the Normans introduced the historically later and specifically French practices of feudal aids or "grievances," which they spread through "the multitude of their Colonies."[13] Spelman's allusion to the shibboleth, like the story in Judges 12, thus entails border crossing (linguistic and territorial), ethnic violence, and sovereign conquest. He had well learned from sixteenth-century jurists that feudal etymology has a cutting edge.

The story behind *Feuds and Tenures*, however, involves another conquest, that of Ireland. *Feuds and Tenures* responded directly to a celebrated 1637 court case, *The Case of Tenures upon the Commission of Defective Titles argued by all the judges of Ireland*, involving English reorganization and colonial control of land in Ireland under Charles I.[14] The Commission for Defective Titles was established to review the titles of landholders in Ireland, and under Charles it was reorganized to extract greater revenue from, or to confiscate, land held by the primarily Catholic "old English" in Ireland.[15] Under the administration of Sir Thomas Wentworth, the commission had by 1637 increased the yearly revenue to the crown by more than £3,000.[16] In the "Case of Tenures," the court invoked and rejected Spelman's history of feudal terminology in his *Archaeologus*, in favor of that of Selden's 1631 *Titles of Honor*, in order to void a land patent and find for the crown. Spelman's *Feuds and Tenures* responds to this challenge on its own terms, combining a philological tour de force with an insistence upon the territorial violence and subjection at stake in the history of "feuds."

The court in the "Case of Tenures," in finding for the king, relied upon the narratives of legal origins recently formulated by Selden and Spelman. It rejected Spelman's theory that feudal law was introduced to England with the Norman Conquest and embraced Selden's view, expressed in the 1631 edition of *Titles of Honor*, that feudal law had been continuous since the time of the Anglo-Saxons. In the process of discussing these narratives the court explicitly brushed aside the many legal sources (such as Bracton's *De Legibus et Consuetudinibus Angliae*) that considered English tenures prior to the new narrative of "feudal law" and judged the validity of the land patent in question strictly according to this recent feudal historiography.[17] The court clearly recognized "feudal law" as a discourse on sovereignty and a potentially lucrative theory of property. The Scottish author Thomas Craig had specifically urged this point in recommending the adoption of this law to James I, to whom he dedicated his *Jus Feudale* in 1603: "for, no matter how far the subdivision of the soil of Britain were carried, every acre would be held of Your Majesty in fee (to use our legal expression), and the possession of every holding would carry with it the obligations of a faithful servant."[18] It was in this spirit that the court applied Selden's and Spelman's feudal historiography, not only to void the patent in question in this case, but, as Paul Christianson puts it, "to buttress an extension of royal claims which seriously undermined previously secure land tenures."[19] With this the court achieved a double irony, for Selden's battles against the crown had prompted him to alter the stance of his 1614 *Titles of Honor*, which held for a Norman introduction of feudal law. His resistance to absolutism and his desire to find evidence of an "ancient constitution" from Saxon times prompted him to alter this argument, and in his 1631 edition to suggest feudal continuity.[20] More than he realized, the geographical imaginary of Selden's dedicatory letter, with which I open this chapter, had already defined his subject.

SLAVERY AND THE SHIBBOLETH

Spelman wrote *Feuds and Tenures* in response to the words of the court decision that "Sir Henry Spelman was mistaken, who in his *Glossary verbo Feudum*, refers the Original of *Feuds* in *England*, to the *Norman* Conquest.

It is most manifest, that *Capite* Tenures, Tenures by *Knights service*, Tenures in *Socage, Frankalmoigne, etc.* were frequent in the Times of the *Saxons.*"[21] By retorting to this decision with the narrative of the shibboleth, Spelman glosses the political stakes of feudal historiography's territorial claims, as well as the degree to which the court, in disagreeing with his version of feudal origins in order to find for the king, had all the more accurately interpreted feudal logic. The conclusion of Spelman's response, which I discuss below, presses the implications of this logic by defining Norman "feuds" as servitude "deriv'd even from very bondage," an argument reminiscent of the analyses of sovereignty and slavery by Du Moulin and Bodin studied in the previous chapter. Spelman thus exposes the extent to which the sovereign discourse of "feudal law" had always been about slavery.

By the time of the "Case of Tenures," the implications of the Norman Conquest for English sovereignty had been crucial to the arguments between king and parliament for decades. The parliamentary debate over the 1628 Petition of Right presented to Charles I focused expressly on this concern: if William I had imposed law by right of conquest, then English law was founded on the basis of unrestrained regnal power, and would itself be an argument for absolute monarchy. All care was taken by the Commons, therefore, to insist that William had contracted with the English to confirm their existing law, or that the Magna Carta, by virtue of a regnal contract, had limited the king's power by statute.[22] This was not, of course, an insular debate. It participated in the bitter contests over sovereignty waging throughout Europe, heightened by the religious wars and competition for colonies, which raised the same problem of legality and conquest. Much discussion in parliament, for instance, focused on the *De Legibus* (1612) of the legal theorist and theologian Francisco Suárez, who had countered James I's English oath of allegiance with his *Defence of Catholic and Apostolic Faith*, and whose works, couched largely in terms of natural law, weighed heavily in international legal debates.[23]

At stake was the location of sovereignty, in the boldest Schmittian terms. In disputing whether the Petition of Right ought to include a "saving" of the king's absolute authority, for example, Philip Maynwaring in the House of Lords and Robert Mason in the House of Commons cited the same section from Suárez in order to insist, and to deny, that a king is above the law—and in particular to determine whether the English king could or could not be restricted by statutes such as the Magna Carta that limit the "absolute power of a conqueror."[24] The members of parliament are here grappling, as is Suárez in greater detail, with the conceptual limit of sovereignty, the paradox that the sovereign is both outside and inside the juridical order.[25] Thus Mason concedes:

"A conqueror is bound by no law but has power *dare leges*. His will is a law."[26] Mason's premise succinctly captures the basic political problem as it is rephrased by Giorgio Agamben: "the sovereign is the point of indistinction between violence and law, the threshold on which violence passes over into law and law passes over into violence."[27] Suárez sets this paradox in motion as he considers the various modes by which a king may validly accede to power: since true power is not possessed inherently or by natural law, it must ultimately derive from the consent of the community; yet when royal power arises on the basis of war, "this mode" of accession, like the modes of communal selection and hereditary succession, "includes, in a sense, the consent—whether expressed or [implicitly] due—of the state."[28] This ambivalence would always hover (as it does today) within state affairs at "home" and "abroad."

Not coincidentally, I believe, English legists took up the narrative of "feudal law" and its association with slavery at the very moment that the crown began to issue land patents in America, in tenurial terms that would be integrated into feudal historiography, just as in "The Case of Tenures." Although I cannot pursue it fully here, I want to suggest that there is a relation between England's self-conscious, belated entry into "feudal law" and its self-conceived belatedness in the European race for colonies, as well as its efforts to compensate for this lag in part through its rule in Ireland.[29]

Suárez, of course, wrote in the larger context of the Spanish slave trade and conquest in the Americas, and his argument for the legitimacy of a contract between conqueror and people was tied to a validation of slavery (all men are born free, but one can, by contract, cede one's liberty). Indeed, he exposes the relation of slavery and sovereignty by illustrating sovereign power through the example of slavery: "Once the power has been transferred to the king, he is through that power rendered superior even to the kingdom which bestowed it; since by this bestowal the kingdom has subjected itself and has deprived itself of its former liberty, just as is, in due proportion, clearly true in the case of the slave, which we have mentioned by way of illustration. Moreover, in accordance with the same reasoning, the king cannot be deprived of this power, since he has acquired a true ownership [*dominium*] of it."[30] As discussed in the previous chapter, the feudists upon whom Spelman and Selden drew had throughout the sixteenth century debated the definitions of sovereignty and slavery in exactly these terms, in a discourse developed through the historiography of the "origins" of "feudal law."

The land patent in question in the "Case of Tenures" had already been defined, officially and institutionally, within the matrix of terms that I have been considering here: law and conquest, sovereignty and subjection. In *A Discovery of the True Causes Why Ireland Was Never Entirely*

Subdued, John Davies, James I's attorney-general of Ireland, discusses the English land reform in Ireland and criticizes English kings from Henry II to Henry VIII for failing to finish the job of conquest. He then praises James I for his military thoroughness and for securing Ireland's subjugation through establishment of English law: "For heretofore, the neglect of the law made the English [in Ireland] degenerate and become Irish; and now, on the other side, the execution of the law doth make the Irish grow civil and become English."[31] The vital element of this subjugation was a thorough reform of land ownership through two commissions, one of which, the Commission on Defective Titles, granted the patent under dispute in the "Case of Tenures":

> But now, since His Majesty came to the Crown, two special commissions have been sent out of England for the settling and quieting of all the possessions in Ireland: the one for accepting surrenders of the Irish and degenerate English, and for regranting estates unto them according to the course of the common law; the other for strengthening of defective titles—in the execution of which commissions, there hath ever been had a special care to settle and secure the undertenants, to the end there might be a repose and establishment of every subject's estate, lord and tenant, freeholder and farmer, throughout the kingdom.[32]

Davies is quite clear as to his point: the whole island "hath been brought into His Highness's peaceable possession, and all the inhabitants, in every corner thereof, have been absolutely reduced under his immediate subjection"—precisely the terms by which Craig had recommended feudal law to James I and VI, and Suárez had described sovereign power by "consent."[33] With this pairing of military conquest and establishment of law, rephrased as "peaceable possession" and "immediate subjection," Davies exposes the indistinction between law and violence constitutive of "civil" order ("the Irish grow civil and become English"), the indistinction that would, of course, always haunt the logic of "civilizing" colonial enterprise.

The temporal division of Spelman's feudal shibboleth splits English history and feudal law precisely at the point of this indistinction between law and violence, liberty and slavery. He insists that the court had misinterpreted his earlier text, which distinguished between Saxon feuds and "such *feuds* as the Law of *England* taketh notice of at this day"—that is, the terms for which the court needed a pre-conquest origin in order to find for the king. He concludes with a history that counters the validity of the court's decision and exposes its rationale:

> It was neither my words nor my meaning to say, that he [William I] first brought in either Feuds or Military service in a general sense, but that he brought in the Servitudes and Grievances of Feuds, viz. *Wardship, Marriage* and such like, which

to this day were never known to other Nations that are govern'd by the *Feodal Law.* There is a great difference between *servitia Militaria* and *servitudes Militares*: The one, Heroick, Noble and full of Glory, which might not therefore be permitted in old time to any that was not born of free parents; no, not to a king's son (as appeareth in *Virgil,*) wherein our Saxons also were very cautelous, and accounted a Souldiers shield to be *insigne libertatis*: the other, not ignoble only and servile, but deriv'd even from very bondage. Let not this offend: I will say no more.[34]

With this final linguistic distinction Spelman cuts straight to the logic of the court's reliance upon feudal historiography, and yields the implications of his shibboleth: the difference under discussion is that between *servitia Militaria* and *servitudes Militares*, liberty or bondage. *Foedal law,* pronounced with a German or a French accent, is the shibboleth. Just as the word "shibboleth" betrays violent difference within a single word, so "feudal law" carries within it not a pure distinction between liberty and bondage but their *indistinction* in sovereign discourse, the paradox evident in Suárez's discussion of sovereign power, and soon to be taken up by Hobbes and Locke. Because the historiographical concept of "feudal law" emerged as a means of negotiating the paradox of sovereignty, it—like the "Middle Ages" to which it will soon be firmly attached—has always been both privileged origin and condemned past, the double bind, and the shibboleth that divides.

Time and the Shibboleth

The seventeenth-century English debates regarding the Norman Conquest and feudal law, like the earlier continental struggles, were essentially over the location of the sovereign exception, the *merum imperium*—sheer power, or the "power of the sword"—now marvelously literalized in the figure of William the Conqueror. Like the continental legists, too, the English battled on the field of periodization, the narrative space of the origin or foundation of the law. As Selden and Spelman's attempts to control the narrative of "feudal law" make clear, and as judicial reliance upon this narrative emphasizes, the form of its remembrance was becoming crucial, as it already had on the continent, to the structure by which sovereignty was situated in the present. In the tradition examined here, "feudal law," historicized in a debate over origins and simultaneously mapped onto conquered territory, negotiates the difference in the exercise of the sovereign exception between its presence (spatial and temporal) and its imagined foundation.

To the degree that it has succeeded in its "Augean" task, to borrow Hotman's term, the narrative of "feudal law" has effaced the process of its own emergence and thus become "real." We can trace the structure of this effacement in the work of J. G. A. Pocock as he assesses seven-teenth-century British legal historiography. Pocock criticizes English common law historians, especially Edward Coke, for a blinkered insular mindset—specifically "their ignorance of the *feudum* and feudalism"—that prevented their recognition of the legal inheritance connecting England with the continent. To an astonishing degree, this analysis repli-cates the linguistic emphasis of the feudists themselves. Pocock remarks of Coke, just as Spelman had, "in fact, it could well be maintained that he knew all there was to know about feudal law in England, except the single fact that it was feudal."[35] For Pocock, scholars such as Spelman "rediscovered" feudalism, and therefore the roots of English legal his-tory: "The common law was above all a law regulating the tenure of land, and the rules of tenure it contained in fact presupposed the exis-tence of those military and feudal tenures which had been imported by the Normans; but this fact had been forgotten and could only be redis-covered by comparing English law with those continental laws which were avowedly feudal—since even the meaning of the word had been largely forgotten in England."[36] Pocock's learned study has been enor-mously influential and an invaluable catalyst in its field, and for this rea-son its rhetorical method and historical assumptions are important. I single out his work because in its complexity, and through its obviously legitimate point regarding the introduction of Norman tenures, his analysis illustrates the process by which the performance of "feudal law" in the negotiation of sovereignty is made to disappear.[37]

Neither feudal law nor feudalism functions as a monolith for Pocock, who devotes much cogent discussion to the political motivations behind particular narratives of feudal law in the sixteenth and seventeenth cen-turies. Precisely because he does attend to feudal mythmaking, his tropes of "forgetting" and "rediscovery" split feudal law: one feudal law, representing the Middle Ages, precedes the debates of early modern his-toriographers; the other changes shape with their political arguments. "Feudal law" thus becomes both an early modern object of interpreta-tion and a medieval entity that—like a foreign continent—preexists the effort of interpretation, but ultimately becomes the fulfillment of this historiographical search for truth. We can align this temporal operation with what Certeau describes as the labor that "promotes a selection between what can be *understood* and what must be *forgotten* in order to obtain the representation of a present intelligibility, and thus to enable the writing of history."[38] Pocock's trope of "forgetting" redoubles this historiographical operation by exactly inverting it. While for Certeau historiography "forgets" infinite possibilities for selecting and arrang-ing detail as it carves out an apprehensible concept, Pocock's formula-tion locates the resulting concept in the past, as the forgotten object toward which historiography must strive. This erasure of the *writing* of "feudal law" confirms historiography's trajectory and periodization, and time runs smooth.

With this smoothing out of time, feudal law and colonial practice come to seem distant and unrelated, and the process by which their entwinement negotiates the difference within the sovereign exception becomes invisible. It is in this state that feudal law sets sail for India.

The Edifice of the Law

> *"The National Assembly," declares the famous decree of the 11th August 1789, "totally abolishes the feudal régime." How could one thenceforth deny the reality of a system which had cost so much to destroy?*
>
> —*Marc Bloch*, Feudal Society

On April 14, 1767, William Blackstone made one of his rare parliamentary appearances, having been called upon as a jurist to weigh in on a debate waging between the British crown and the East India Company. At issue was whether the legal right to the territorial revenues and possessions in Bengal, acquired by the company between 1757 and 1765, belonged to the crown or to the company, a question that entailed delicate interpretations of property and sovereignty. The company's revenues, long key to the London money market, had gained increasing prominence as a national concern (military, diplomatic, and economic) after the end of the Seven Years' War in 1763 and after the company's apparent instant wealth with the assumption in 1765 of the Diwani (the right to collect the territorial revenues of Bengal, Bihar, and Orissa). The crown held unquestioned sovereignty over the company's possessions as "English settlements," a point stipulated in the company's charter of 1698. However, the possession of (and thus the right to) extracted revenues was far more difficult to determine, in that it hinged upon an interpretation of whether the lands had been acquired by conquest (hence belonging to the crown) or by mercantile purchase or bargain (hence belonging to the company).[39]

The sticky problems of factual interpretation and legal definitions were made more complicated by the company's sleight of hand, in that it had arranged for the Mughal Emperor to retain de jure sovereignty over the territories, while it held this sovereignty de facto. As Lord Clive later described it to the House of Commons: "the great Mogul (*de jure*, Mogul, *de facto* nobody at all). . . . The Nabob (*de jure* Nabob, *de facto* the East India Company's most obedient humble servant)."[40] Sovereignty was everywhere and nowhere at once, signaling the unresolved, and—within the parameters of the legal system, unresolvable—relation between conquest and commerce. Versions of this question had cropped up throughout the company's history, and turned upon the very questions of property and sovereignty that feudalism was called upon to negotiate.[41]

In 1767 this intractable and politically dangerous issue came not to a decision but to a settlement, and its unresolved questions continued to plague relations between the government and the company for decades. Projects of imperial and mercantile conquest, often indistinguishable from the interests of commerce, threatened the stability of these terms, which were mediated, moreover, by parliamentary debates over the political and economic stakes of the East India Company administration, the abolition of the slave trade, and the despotic potential of the rising national debt (also linked to the imperial enterprise).[42] But the grounds upon which such battles were fought are my interest here, and to glimpse those we can turn to Blackstone's *Commentaries on the Law*, the first two volumes of which had just been published to immediate acclaim in 1765 and 1766.[43] What kind of historical work underlay the juridical ideas of conquest and commerce that Blackstone would bring to consideration of such a question?

LEGAL FICTIONS

For Blackstone, English law was anchored in history, an approach, as David Lieberman points out, in accordance with the eighteenth-century model (recently exemplified by Montesquieu) that situated rational study within historical inquiry, and with Blackstone's belief (deeply set in current political arguments that appealed to the past for authority) that history provided explanatory power for the system of modern law. Natural law, however, underlay and informed Blackstone's historical thinking, forming a relation that is important to my argument here. Never slipping into historical determinism, Blackstone balanced legal history with legal theory, insisting both that civil law had its basis of legitimacy in ancient custom, and, since law is the perfection of reason, that legal determinations contrary to reason were "not law."[44] Yet, as Lieberman puts it, he managed "to avoid any careful distinction between an historical explanation and a moral justification."[45]

Blackstone's strategies for negotiating this fissure emplot the relationship in his laws between conquest and commerce. I suggest that in the *Commentaries*, the natural law (Reason and universal history) and the English law (understood as a particular, continuous history) upon which Blackstone grounds his legal system, interchange at the point of their breach—a breach of territorial conquest inextricable from the historical breach of commerce. In other words, the moral and the historical are jointed precisely at the point of rupture. The terms of their interchange are the feudal and the colonial, which are caught up together in an intricate, mobile spatio-temporal web. Blackstone gives us a good sense, I believe, of the logic and the legacy of the law as it emerged from this eighteenth-century moment, and if we are to think an ethics compatible with difference, rather than fully accede to a justice system founded upon an exclusionary historicism, we need to trace the pattern of the breach linking history and ethics, medieval and colonial, commerce and conquest.

The question of conquest versus commerce on the floor in April 1767 was already, and would continue to be, a broader topic of hot political dispute between those who favored global expeditions for purposes of commerce only and those who defended the right of imperial conquest, a debate directly tied to the history-based struggle between crown and parliament over sovereignty.[46] Blackstone quite logically categorized this as an issue of property and raises the topic of colonial conquest early in his chapter "Of the Rights of Things." Having already defined the right to property as natural, but the right to inheritance as civil (thus historical) (I 1–15), he takes his stand on the issue of imperial conquest while discussing natural law. In the process of telling a universalizing story of social development, vaguely set in early biblical times and focused on the needs of grazing and early agriculture, he comes to "migration, or sending colonies to find out new habitations." After confirming that cultivating uninhabited territory is well within the "law of nature," he suddenly breaks his narrative frame with a direct reference to contemporary colonial debate: "But how far the seising on countries already peopled, and driving out or massacring the innocent and defenceless natives, merely because they differed from their invaders in language, in religion, in customs, in government, or in colour; how far such a conduct was consonant to nature, to reason, or to christianity, deserved well to be considered by those, who have rendered their names immortal by thus civilizing mankind" (II 7). Here, moral violation erupts as disorder in narrative sequence, with the result that contemporary colonial conquest establishes—in the breach and *prior* to the story of European civilization—the basic moral principle of property. In the space of double violation, that of natural law and that of narrative sequence, the moral and the historical meet. Giving no other examples of such violation of natural law, Blackstone returns immediately to the distant past and to his narrative of the developing idea of property, for which the growth of civilization would eventually require civil laws. Colonial violence, then, sits at the foundation of the law, securing the principles of nature, reason, and even Christianity. But with its shift to primordial time—the time, one supposes, of the "natives" in question—colonial conquest stands anterior to the civil laws that would adjudicate, in Blackstone's narrative, both between Europeans and between the feudal past and the commercial present, where, already eliminated, the "natives" do not appear.

The moral breach of conquest silently oversees Blackstone's nationalistic story of the foundation of feudal law in England, taken up several chapters later in the same volume. The basis for understanding the English civil constitution and landed property is for Blackstone "the feodal law, a system so universally received throughout Europe, upwards of twelve centuries ago, that Sir Henry Spelman does not scruple to call it the law of nations in our western world" (II 44; cf. I 36). This feudal heritage nonetheless raised the same problems of sovereignty and conquest as it had for Selden and Spelman in the previous century, since for Blackstone feudal law had been introduced to England by the Norman Conquest, with the dire implications that this important foundation of English law was an act of colonial violence and a breach of the ancient constitution. Furthermore, Blackstone's understanding that under feudal law all lands were held by the king posed problems for his Whig sensibilities.[47]

Wanting a *European* past for England—which, according to his admired predecessors, meant a *feudal* past—yet not wanting a past of conquered subjugation to the French, Blackstone famously proposed that in England feudal law was a "fiction." The Normans *did* impose feudal law, he states, but its terms were de jure, not de facto. The conquest was a bargain: the English adopted the change "by common consent of the nation. . . . In consequence of this change, it became a fundamental maxim and necessary principle (though in reality a mere fiction) of our English tenures, 'that the king is the universal lord and original proprietor of all the lands in his kingdom'" (II 51). And, he reasons, the oppression of the English that followed resulted from the Normans not keeping up their end of the fiction:

Our English ancestors probably meant no more than to put the kingdom in a state of defence by establishing a military system; and to oblige themselves (in respect of their lands) to maintain the king's title and territories, with equal vigour and fealty, *as if* they had received their lands from his bounty upon these express conditions, as pure, proper, beneficiary feudatories. But, whatever their meaning was, the Norman interpreters, skilled in all the niceties of the feudal constitutions, and well understanding the import and extent of the feudal terms, gave a very different construction to this proceeding; and thereupon [behaved] as if the English had in fact, as well as theory, owed every thing they had to the bounty of their sovereign lord. (II 51)

With this remarkable echo of the practices of colonial commercial enterprise, Blackstone resolves the problem of force at the foundation of the law by insisting upon the reality of the "*as if*"—the difference between de jure and de facto, which underwrites narrative coherence for England as sovereign *and* European. More important, the credibility of the *"as if"* separates "law"—here the system of civil law based on agreement rather than violence (thus the possibility of bargain and commerce)—from force, the actions of "seising," and "massacring" that are foundational to, yet necessarily outside or prior to civil law. The breach of the Norman Conquest, then, is not territorial; it is the annihilation of the space of fiction separating a polite commercial people from the force of civilization. For Blackstone, the English will reconstitute that space, negotiating with the Normans and thus bargaining their way back into history.

"Feodal fictions" such as Blackstone's would in turn provide coherence for other kinds of narratives. A decade later, as we will see, the East India Company official Philip Francis would use it to legitimize his land policy for Bengal, and a century after him Marx would lean toward the opinion that in India, "any traditional ownership of all land by the sovereign was, as in feudal Europe, no more than a legal fiction."[48] The point is not whether Francis and Marx were right or wrong about the English or Indian past, but that the eighteenth-century historiography of feudalism, formed in relation to colonial enterprise, redoubles itself in projects that contemplate a European and a colonial future.

Just as colonial conquest in Blackstone's narrative precedes feudal law, the needs of "commerce" in his lifetime had anticipated "feudal fiction." The convention of such fiction, in a slightly different sense, was already at the heart of jurisprudence. "Legal fictions" were (and still are) accepted legal practice, necessary to bridge the difference between outmoded statutes and contemporary commercial needs.[49] In volume three (1768), Blackstone defends this often criticized device, specifically couching his argument in terms of feudal law. He explains that commercial society's need for a "speedy decision of right, to facilitate exchange and alienation" (III 268) (one might think of the hectic trading in East India Company stock) far outstripped the old feudal code, the practices of which had decayed until "at length the whole structure was removed" (III 267). As both the inherited foundation of the law *and* as that superseded by the fast-paced mobility of everyday commercial exchange, the feudal code marked the necessary anachronism of law itself.

In a final effort to defend legal fictions and to justify the law's anachronism, Blackstone reaches for a metaphor that will solidify the place of the feudal code and join it to commercial life. He lays hold, remarkably, on literary fiction—in the new vogue of the gothic that we saw taking shape in a different context centuries before in Hotman's feudal law: "We inherit an old Gothic castle, erected in the days of chivalry, but fitted up for a modern inhabitant. The moated ramparts, the embattled towers, the trophied halls, are magnificent and venerable, but useless, and therefore neglected. The interior apartments, now converted into rooms of convenience, are chearful and commodious, though their approaches are winding and difficult" (III 268). In Blackstone's gothic metaphor, the *castle* is not the fiction. The "winding and difficult" approaches of his castle stand in for the "legal fictions" he is trying to explain—the necessary "minute contrivances" of "fictions and circuities" that hamper entrance to the halls of remedial justice. The castle stands in for a real past, venerable and militant, the authorizing edifice of the law. But one can only enter this past, as Blackstone's fictitious "approaches" tell us, through historical imagination. This near confession of the past's fantastic status deepens with the effect of the castle as literary trope, invoking, for instance, Horace Walpole's recent and sensational *Castle of Otranto* (1765). Monumentality, however, might counter this hint of fabrication: castles are spectacularly visible. For a London audience, Blackstone's image could also have referenced Strawberry Hill, the nearby site of Walpole's famed pseudo-gothic castle, complete with ramparts and battlements, and "fitted up for a modern inhabitant." Walpole's castle—and, eerily, Blackstone's law—stand precursor to the next century's architectural gothic revival, which monumentalized a national past and extended it, as symbol of the law, to colonial space. This project, as Kathleen Biddick has taught us, imbricated the professionalization of the British university with the disciplinary practices of colonial rule, thus materializing the etymological bond between edifice and edification.[50]

Undeniable as Johnson's stones and as nostalgic as Ruskin's, straddling de facto and de jure, gothic castles memorialized a medieval past built to overshadow the gaping fictions of its entryways and the anxieties of its modern inhabitants. "Feodal" and "legal" fictions are, to borrow terms Gayatri Spivak applies to Marx, "theoretical fictions, a methodological presupposition without which the internal coherence of an argument cannot be secured."[51] As such they anatomize the fissures of the arguments, or the edifices—England, modern Europe, and periodization—that they sustain.

"Feodal fiction" did not have to wait for the gothic revival to take solid colonial form. For those like Blackstone writing in the 1760s, feudal law interlaced colonial affairs and anxieties with political debates at home, but a decade later it got its traveling papers. Moving to the colonial scene in the 1770s, we will find Blackstone's "feodal fiction" working its way into the Indian landscape, in the company of emerging theories of political economy.

A RULE OF PROPERTY

During the 1767 parliamentary inquiry into the East India Company's affairs, the company secretary Robert James flatly stated, "We don't want conquest and power; it is commercial interest only we look for."[52] James was undoubtedly playing the company hand in the commerce/conquest debate, but (for the moment at least), many company officials did favor curbing acquisitions in the interest of securing permanency for those they held. As the company chairman Sir George Colebrooke put it to the House of Commons in 1769, "By extension of territory the Roman Empire was dissolved. Let us try to give a permanency to these acquisitions, and by doing so secure the prosperity of Great Britain."[53] Permanency and prosperity became key terms in parliamentary and company discussion of East India, and concern for these, in the wake of company abuses, scandal, and ineptitude, prompted calls for reform. As one result, Lord North's Regulating Act (1773) sent a five-member Supreme Council to Bengal, where they would attempt to design a land policy for East India that would, through establishment of permanent property rights (with an echo of the Commission of Defective Titles in Ireland), guarantee the permanence of British prosperity and dominion.[54]

In his *Rule of Property for Bengal*, Ranajit Guha provides the classic and enduring study of this contentious process, with particular focus on the thought of Philip Francis, primary author of the 1776 revenue plan that, after an embattled history, ultimately became an important basis of the Permanent Settlement of Bengal. Passed in the India Bill of 1784 and instituted through a 1793 proclamation by Lord Cornwallis, the Permanent Settlement guaranteed Indian proprietors that the tax assessments upon their lands were "fixed forever." For Francis and its other proponents, the settlement ensured the right of private property in land, designed in turn to guarantee prosperity through agrarian reform and promotion of trade.[55] Its ruinous legacy has been a matter of debate,[56] but my focus here is on the role of the "feudal" in the logic of the eighteenth- century officials who first designed the plan, and on the role of "feudal*ism*" in Guha's analysis of that logic. "Feudalism" spins a dizzying weave throughout *A Rule of Property*, both because Francis and his peers sometimes contemplated Indian property relations through a feudal optic, and because Guha, from a different vantage, does as well.

For Guha, feudalism and the Middle Ages are categories prior to rather than objects of his inquiry, although he is sensitive to Francis's reception and redeployment of feudal historiography. This remains the case in subaltern studies scholarship, even though, as Bruce Holsinger has shown, the collective has often engaged the work of medievalists, particularly in its early years.[57] Of primary importance to this engagement were theses on feudalism and the work of Marxist medievalists such as Rodney Hilton, whose readings of peasant revolts, for example, resonated with and greatly facilitated Guha's goals in *Elementary Aspects of Peasant Insurgency in Colonial India*, which draws on peasant studies from many periods and locations, although medieval examples predominate. Guha's engagement with eighteenth-century historiography in *A Rule of Property* gives us a bead on the continuing performance of that historiography in postcolonial critique, and offers just one of many reasons why medievalists and postcolonists should rethink history together.

Time and the "Quasi-feudal"

> *How was it that the quasi-feudal land settlement of 1793 had originated from the ideas of a man who was a great admirer of the French Revolution?*

This question, Guha tells us, prompted his great study. To find the answer, he traces the philosophical and political mooring of the plan in the emerging ideas of the Enlightenment.[58] Skeptical of the received wisdom that British policy in India proceeded simply as a series of experiments, he details the intricate, mobile weave of company policy-making with political and economic thought, and he argues that the Permanent Settlement mapped the Enlightenment's conceptual struggles over property, economy, and the limits of government onto Indian soil. His book sometimes controverts this argument, however, attesting to the genuine study by British officials of East Indian property relations and their attempts to deal with them, and the European lens that Guha brings to his topic has been the subject of critique. Likewise, he asserts that "No understanding of the eighteenth-century imagination can be complete without an appreciation of these attempts to find for the sprawling Spirit of the Laws a procrustean bed in Bengal." Yet he charts a one-directional influence, from Europe to India, that would shape an order "much as a hard-blowing wind would shape the dunes."[59]

His book evidences a different story, one of multidirectional, intersecting traffic—England to India, India to Scotland, Scotland to France, France back to England, France, Scotland, and England back to India—which shows how the pragmatic, material experiences of the British in India fed into the very conceptual struggles about feudalism and property that would eventually take form in Francis's revenue plan. Guha straightens out these temporal complexities, and the framework of his question above, which identifies "feudal*ism*" with the specter made visible by the French Revolution, explains why. Indeed feudal*ism*, as a concept and as a term, appeared in Europe only decades before the French Revolution—decades of high Orientalist rhetoric and wars of imperial conquest, and the same decades often cited as those that ushered Europe into the era of the modern nation-state.[60] Although Guha is fully aware that "feudalism as an historical concept was still very young when Francis wrote about it," he apparently believes, like Pocock, that it was being "discovered."[61]

The ambivalence within and between Guha's uses of the term "quasi-feudal," which he applies not only to Francis's plan but also to the already existing conditions in India, points to the spatio-temporal work accomplished by "feudalism." The English officers were stymied by the agrarian system of India, of which they knew nothing, and "at every step they came up against quasi-feudal rights and obligations which defied any attempt at interpretation in familiar western terms."[62] Here, "quasi" negotiates the incommensurable difference between Indian and western systems—but "feudal" applies to both—a postulate that leaves "feudal" as the unquestioned base term. Despite Guha's insistence upon Indian difference, the "feudal" slips in to fill the gap. Similarly, in discussing Francis's resistance to the idea of sovereign feudal ownership in India, Guha "roughly" translates Indian terms into the European feudal vocabulary used by Voltaire: "The grant of *jagir* and *wakf*, corresponding roughly to fief and *bénéfice* in the European sense, was explained away by [Francis] by the same kind of argument as Voltaire used: 'the land continues to be deemed a part of the Zemindary; the sovereign only grants the revenue of it.'"[63] Guha's translation thus infuses a generic "modern-European" feudal "reality" not only into Francis's thought process, but into pre-British Indian property relations as well. The possibility of claiming specificity for Indian property relations is cut off by a regularizing translation into the terms of Europe's fabricated past. *This past* (we could imagine Blackstone's castle here) then mediates Guha's reading of the settlement's history.

Of course Guha, writing in the 1950s, could not have anticipated the historical challenges to feudalism over the past two decades, and he was certainly hampered by the fact that the eighteenth-century British historiography of feudalism has always been studied as an issue of domestic politics.[64] Moreover, Guha has been at the forefront of subaltern studies scholars in challenging the transitional narratives of Marxism, which had positioned Indian peasants as "backward" and "pre-political," even as he retained the aspects of Marx's thought that had always been crucial to postcolonial studies.[65] He has thus done much to resist this linear narrative and to expose the implications of universalist narratives of capital, and his work has been important to those who continue the interrogation of "history," including, of course, my own work here.

It is not surprising that a book titled *A Rule of Property for Bengal* would tell a story of feudalism's mutation into the departure point for an economic theory of development. The "feudal law" I have explored so far, although shaped by colonial anxieties and pressures, little resembles the received Marxist concept of feudalism underpinning Guha's thought, even though its basic terminology (such as fief and benefice) and its grid of medieval property relations do provide its groundwork. Guha's investigation into Francis's working climate, however, traces the fold of this politicized historiography of feudal law into the developing theories of political economy that were catalyzed by the dire conditions in contemporary France. The historical, political, and economic influences spinning around Francis as he sat at his desk in Calcutta are tangled beyond separation, but Guha's study outlines in miniature, I believe, their major intersections and transformations in the highly charged 1770s.

Two dissimilar Orientalist projects discussed by Guha illustrate the circulation of British-Indian experiences in the developing ideas of feudalism and political economy: that of Voltaire and that of the physiocrat Henry Pattullo. Voltaire and other *philosophes*, chafing against the French monarchy and eager to bring the example of idealized Oriental governments against it, dismissed the claims of travelers' tales (such as Bernier's) that in India the king was proprietor of the soil, and that the peasants (prior to British intervention) were equivalent to medieval serfs. Dissatisfied with his compatriots' work, Voltaire turned in his *Fragments sur l'Inde* to the writings of disaffected company officials returning from India to England. Notable among these were Alexander Dow's *The History of Hindostan* (3 vols., 1768–70) and William Bolts's *Considerations on Indian Affairs* (1772), both serialized and popular in Britain and France.[66] As Guha notes, "[Voltaire] turned to what was then the most recent literature on the subject in English, the histories and dissertations which had been coming out in a steady flow since the Company's acquisition of Diwani, influencing opinion not only in England but to some extent in France as well. Voltaire mentioned Holwell and Dow [company officials], and actually quoted Scrafton in support of his own view that the custom of hereditary succession proved beyond doubt the existence of private property. . . . Francis in turn quoted Voltaire."[67] The early reports of company officials thus inform Orientalist attacks against the *ancien régime* as well as the concomitant, heightening rhetoric of feudalism.[68] This politically charged Orientalism then finds its way, via Francis, back into the feudal framework informing colonial policy.

The physiocrat Henry Pattullo, who had also read Bolts and Dow, had little interest in the past and never mentions feudalism. He argued for reform of Bengal's agricultural system, understood to have been ruined by British mismanagement and to be comparable to the French countryside. Having never visited India, he based his "Essay upon the Cultivation of the Lands, and Improvements of the Revenues, of Bengal" upon

English reports and his own conjectural conversions of Bengali geography and economy into a European calculus: "We shall therefore, surely come nearest to probability and to truth, if we shall suppose these lands to be lett at a medium, for one rupee the bega, or about six and eight-pence an acre, which is a full, sufficient general rent in any country. Upon which computation the sixty millions of begas, would yield seven millions and a half of our money nett into the [East India] company's treasury."[69] Never anti-aristocratic, indeed they were intimates of the court, the physiocrats nonetheless advocated reforms with subversive potential, and after 1789 they were interpreted as anti-*régime*. Marx will read this ambivalence as facilitating the sublation of feudalism to capitalism.[70] In 1776, Francis read Pattullo, particularly his advocacy of permanent property rights, as a way to catapult Bengal into lucrative commerce.

These contrasting modes of analogizing Bengal and Europe frame Francis's linkage of feudalism with modern political economy. For the details of political tradition and feudalism, however, Francis turned to Blackstone, with whom he shared a fundamental ambivalence toward a feudal past. He relied heavily on Blackstone's idea for the integrity (despite conquest) of an "ancient constitution," which he converted into a legitimizing device for his plan.[71] The trope of the "ancient constitution"—which became as common in writings on East India as it was in British politics—could be invoked to support any number of claims, but Francis used it to ground his argument for the tradition of private, inheritable landed property in Bengal.[72] As Robert Travers notes, "Just as some English whigs had learnt to deny the imposition of new feudal laws by the Norman conquerors, Francis argued that the natural wisdom of the Mughals led them to preserve entire the ancient customs of Bengal, represented in particular by the great landed estates of the ancient *zamindars* of Bengal."[73] Francis could thus forward his argument for permanent property rights as one that was *already* based on the country's ancient constitution, which had been interrupted not by Mughal conquest, but by British mismanagement.

This claim for private property conflicted with Blackstone's definition of feudal tenure as sovereignty in the crown, yet Francis frequently speaks of Indian property relations as feudal, likening the relationship between Mughal prince and zamindars to that of a "liege lord and his vassals,"[74] and depicting zamindars as feudal landlords.[75] He thus writes himself, as had Blackstone, into a position of adopting a feudal framework whose basic tenet had to be denied. The claim for crown sovereignty in India was already in place, of course, and seemed corroborated by the solicited testimony of some local Indian officials.[76] Francis therefore appeals most directly to Blackstone not for a solid definition of feudal law, but for the "feodal fiction" necessary to hold together his self-conflicted narrative. "It is true," he admits, "the forms of the royal Sun-nuds, or grants, to the Zemindars, suppose them to hold of the sovereign *in capite*, but this I consider as a kind of feodal fiction, which the sovereign in fact never pretended to avail himself, as constituting a right to assume or transfer the possession."[77] For Francis, "feodal fiction" is the lever by which a feudal system will be turned, based on private property in land, into a developing commercial economy. As Sudipta Sen writes of company policy more generally at this juncture, "In the Indian prince in a Moorish guise, they also saw a familiar feudal past, the specter of whose decay they had been witnessing in contemporary France. This, often as a sleight of hand, provided valuable justification for wrestling privileges of revenue away from the Rajas and Zamindars by undermining the moral basis of their autonomy."[78] Just as it had in "The Case of Tenures," this feudal historiography—now spectacularly displayed as "feodal fiction"—performed as a colonial discourse on sovereignty and a lucrative theory of property.

Francis, like Blackstone, labored under the compulsion of a universalizing historicism that necessarily subsumed "facts" to "principles," as he wrote to Lord North: "In proportion as I acquired local and particular Knowledge, it has been my constant Rule to compare facts with Principles. . . . Hitherto I see no reason to question the Truth of those general propositions, which struck me at the first View of the deplorable State of this Country, and which, tho' drawn from the sources of European Policy, must hold good at all Times and in all Places, if as I believe, they are founded in Truth and right Reason."[79] According to this reasoning, Francis's plan makes sense. If universal history were to hold together, and if Bengal were to be inserted into an economic policy of development based on European principles, then despite its differences from Europe (which Francis clearly recognized), Bengal had to emerge from a feudal past ("the law of Nations in our Western orb") into economic prosperity. It had, in other words, to be, and not be, medieval *at once*. "Feodal fiction" acts as the hinge for this ambivalent narration. The convoluted temporalities at work here will ultimately create the appearance of a linear development from medieval feudalism to modern capitalism, or, more accurately in this case, India's failure to accomplish this transition.

The ambivalence in Francis's plan redoubles with the effect of mimicry discerned by Homi Bhabha in his discussion of colonial discourse. Clearly, for Francis India cannot enter history *as* Europe. Rather, "as a subject of difference that is almost the same, but not quite," it must persist in a difference that would confirm British dominion.[80] Francis designed his plan of economic growth *not* so Bengal might become a viable commercial society on the level of the British, but so it might be permanently subjected as a source of revenue under British dominion. As he states in the letter introducing his plan to the company Court of Directors: "the plan, which I have now the honour to submit to your consideration, makes the recovery and welfare of the country its first and principal object. This I consider as the medium, through which alone the East-India Company can derive a fixed and permanent advantage from their territorial acquisitions."[81] Francis's insertion of India into a universal narrative thus "parodies" history, and its double vision splits apart his Enlightenment argument for native welfare, independence, and civilized prosperity.

A CALCULUS FOR DURATION

Francis allows a glimpse of the path of encryption by which development is made to seem both temporally linear and geographically uneven. He argues for inheritance laws that would reduce the very large zemindaries (landholdings) to more profitable small estates, the benefits of which were a matter of current debate in France and England.[82] In favoring small estates Francis sides with, among others, David Hume, whom he cites: "Such moderate estates, as require economy and confine the proprietors to live at home, are better calculated for duration."[83] Hume proffers more here than his opinion on agricultural economy. His preference for moderate landholding over concentrated wealth in a few hands distanced from "home" registers his anti-imperialist stance, and frames the political and economic anxieties of a nation caught up in debates over the relation of proprietorship to national economy and politics. His chiasmus stresses both that life at "home" is the root of "economy" (*oikos nomos*: "law of the household"), and that defining a relation to land is also a calculation in time, a bid for surviving in history. In the context of Francis's plan, this emphasis on duration amplifies the ironic echo between permanent land rights in Bengal and the goal of "a fixed and permanent advantage" for England. Nonetheless, it would seem to argue for a direct correspondence between Indian and European agricultural development.

But Francis misquotes Hume, who casts his sentence not as I have cited it above, but in the past tense: "Such moderate estates, as they required economy, and confined the proprietors to live at home, were better calculated for duration; and the order of knights and small barons grew daily more numerous, and began to form a very respectable rank or order in the state."[84] This sentence is from Hume's *History of England*, and refers to the breakup of large Norman estates in thirteenth-century England, which Hume describes as "feudal."[85] A feudal setting, then, allows Hume to locate his view of the contested categories of property and political order, along with his fears about the instability of an eccentric economy, in a past that provides a formula for duration. Francis reverses and redoubles the effect of Hume's temporalizing move. Silently converting Hume's theorization of a transitional moment in medieval property relations from the past tense into the present, he turns a retrospective historical calculus into calculated colonial practice. Hume's sentence becomes axiomatic for Bengal through the double erasure of the medieval past and the "facts" of colonial space.

The point, then, is not simply a misquotation, but the catachrestic force of graphing the retrospective desire for a stable home economy onto a colonial location marked not simply as the past, but as the *space of transition* out of a feudal past that is simultaneously being theorized in relation to the colonial. Francis converts speculation into Truth by converting grammatical change into material practice. In the gesture of effacing the incommensurate difference between a shift from past to present and from history to implementation, the simultaneous creation and destruction of a paired medieval/colonial is made to disappear. While the grammatical erasure of Hume's past tense vanishes an English past and an English landscape, its conversion into the present tense would for Francis become actualized in the form of the Permanent Settlement. Medieval feudalism and private property, highly unstable as categories mediating European struggles for identity, gain stability only where modernity is not, and India becomes fixed as always just escaping a Middle Ages nobody ever had.

Here, perhaps more than in Europe, "feudalism" materializes at the moment of its annihilation, leaving as a trace of its (non)existence the consequences of a ruinous land policy. We could think again here of Benjamin's suggestion that "modernity" simultaneously produces and destroys an image of tradition to which it opposes itself, an image that becomes visible as new beauty just as it vanishes.[86] But in this colonial moment, the simultaneously produced and destroyed image of a feudal past is made visible by the hard valence of the colonial practice that performs the vanishing act. Such a moment warns that a "transition" from "feudalism" to capitalism was, in an important sense, colonial before it was European. Designed both for permanence and development, stasis and change, the settlement inducts India to the space of durable transition between those temporalities, or more accurately, an illogical space of suspension—a suspension not unlike the "waiting room of history," but also not unlike the suspension of the law at the heart of sovereignty.

This sovereign suspense of the law and its inherent relationship to periodization is the topic of the following two chapters, which turn from the narrative of "feudalism" to that of "secularization."

Part II
Secularization

Chapter Three

The Sense of an Epoch
Secularization, Sovereign Futures, and the "Middle Ages"

This chapter proposes to excavate the structural and historical link between medieval/modern periodization and the increasingly contentious, often violent function of "religion" in political life today, and suggests that critical recognition of this link and its relation to sovereignty is crucial to understanding and assessing this function.

By its own account, the burgeoning analysis of religion and secularism in the political arena founders upon its central terms of "religion" and the "secular." The limits of these terms, as I discuss at length in my introduction, took shape through a double process by which Europe simultaneously narrated its own secularization and mapped regions elsewhere in the world according to newly consolidated conceptions of "religion" and religious heritage. Briefly, if somewhat reductively: the liberation of Europe's political, economic, and social life from ecclesiastical authority and religion was defined as the very basis of politics, progress, and historical consciousness; correlatively, Europe's "medieval" past and cultural others, mainly colonized non-Christians, were defined as religious, static, and ahistorical—thus open for narrative and territorial development.[1] Gil Anidjar has put it most bluntly: "secularism is a name Christianity gave itself when it invented religion, when it named its other or others as religions."[2] For this reason, there can be no neutral discussion of "religion" or the "secular," any more than there can be of the "medieval" or the "modern."

While the "triumphalist" Christian narrative of secularization described above is fast losing credibility, critical analysis continues to struggle with its temporal legacy, as the growing popularity of the term "post-secular" attests. This term, suggests Hent de Vries in his introduction to the recent volume *Political Theologies: Public Religions in a Post-Secular World*, should be understood "not as an attempt at historical periodization . . . but merely as an indicator for—well, a problem."[3] This problem, which refracts the history I describe above but which lodges today in myriad, differently experienced situations, is not one that can, or even should be definitively settled. I do not advance an argument for a "post-secular" that seeks to resituate "religion," but do suggest that the problem entrenched in these terms can be better negotiated as the relationship between their political and historical elements is worked out. There has been a great deal of attention to the *geo*political history of this relationship, but almost none to the important role of its temporal component, medieval/modern periodization.

Sovereignty has long been a keyword in discourses on secularization; indeed, it can be said that the claim to separate out the "religious" and the "secular" is above all a bid for sovereignty. In this chapter I study the historical and structural aspects of this relation and its connections to periodization through an analysis of several texts by Carl Schmitt, particularly his *Political Theology* (1922), and to a lesser extent through texts by his contemporary Walter Benjamin. In contrast to the previous two chapters, which reassess the historical unfolding of a periodizing narrative, this chapter concentrates upon the theoretical underpinnings of the relation of periodization as a theory of history to political sovereignty.

As I discuss more fully below, Schmitt phrases his analysis of sovereignty in terms of *secularization*, which for him refers not to the narrative of Europe's extrication from theological constraints, but to the transference of theological forms to the politics of an ostensibly "secular" state, in which theology thus becomes immanent. The crucial aspect of modern sovereignty in this sense is its essential indebtedness to preceding theological-political forms, a point that was elaborated and extended to a theory of history by Karl Löwith in the 1940s. The second part of this chapter studies the fierce reaction to this theory precisely because it disrupted a clean-cut medieval/modern, sacred vs. secular divide. This reaction—which insists upon a "secular," political, and historically conscious modernity, in contrast to a "religious" Middle Ages devoid of meaningful political or historical consciousness—delineates the stakes of medieval/modern periodization. Ultimately, its insistence upon "secular modernity" as a self-constituting sovereign period exposes the degree to which claims to sovereignty found themselves upon periodization.

Periodization and Decision

"No political system can survive even a generation with only naked techniques of holding power. To the political belongs the idea, because there is no politics without authority and no authority without an ethos of belief."[4] In these sentences from his *Roman Catholicism and Political Form*, Schmitt critiques the presuppositions of the "rational" techno-

cratic state. In the wake of Max Weber's famous articulation of a "disenchanted" world, and in the context of the nascent Weimar Republic's
interwar struggles, Schmitt found the rational/irrational dichotomy to
be a subterfuge by which liberal democratic pluralism proffered itself as
a neutral political form. As Christoph Menke observes, the ground of
Schmitt's concept of sovereignty "consists in the critique of a political
order which considers itself neutral, in the sense that it considers itself
to be relieved of the confrontation with, and implementation with
respect to, its other."[5] This critique, which to an extent is shared by Benjamin, holds promise for political theorists today, despite Schmitt's ultimate support of dictatorship.

Schmitt has become famous for invoking his theory of the exception
(*Ausnahmezustand*, sometimes called a "state of emergency") in 1932, a
decade after he wrote *Political Theology*, to argue for implementing the
emergency powers section of the Weimar Constitution, Article 48,
which, although it was originally intended to neutralize him, ultimately
helped clear the way for Hitler's rise to power.[6] But when in the 1920s
both Schmitt and Benjamin contemplated sovereignty in the context of
the nascent, struggling Weimar Republic, each with distaste for bourgeois liberalism and parliamentary compromise, the implications of this
argument were not fully apparent. Schmitt read Benjamin's "Critique
of Violence" with admiration, and Benjamin read *Political Theology* as an
adept diagnosis of the temporal and "theological" structure of sovereignty and the importance of this structure to the contemporary crisis
of political legitimacy.[7] Their arguments differ, but Schmitt and Benjamin both labored unsparingly upon the theological aspects of this structure. Perhaps not surprisingly then, attention to their work has
intensified in direct proportion to the escalation of "religion" in political rhetoric since the 1980s, sometimes to recognize the danger but also
to explore the potential of the relation between political and religious
forms. The theories and legacies of Schmitt and Benjamin have been a
crucial starting point, for example, to Julia Reinhard Lupton's important examination of the "positive ethical potential" of rethinking universalism through the historical relation of citizenship and religious
fellowship.[8]

Schmitt's theory has resonated with political advocates on both the
left and right. It continues, as Étienne Balibar notes, to "haunt the
defenses as well as the critiques of national state sovereignty," and
Schmitt's connections with the Frankfurt School and with Leo Strauss
remain topics of intense debate.[9] Most important has been Schmitt's theory of the exception and his insight into the "sovereign paradox." The
legal order of a state, Schmitt argues, can never be fully self-enclosed;
there is always the possibility that a "state of exception," which he theo-

rizes by analogy to the miracle in theology, might exceed the expectations of all juridical norms. The exception "can *at best* be characterized as a case of extreme peril, a danger to the existence of the state, or the like," but by definition it cannot actually be predefined or "made to conform to a preformed law."[10] Constitutional development tended toward honing legal order into a pure mechanistic system for which all circumstances are calculable, thus eliminating, in Schmitt's eyes, the state's capacity to recognize the exception, to confront that which is incalculable according to its laws.

In order to protect its autonomy, Schmitt argues, a state therefore requires a sovereign, whose position it is to decide that a state of exception has occurred, and to suspend the existing legal order for the preservation of the state. Schmitt makes it clear that he is dealing with a limit concept. Paradoxically, if a state is to be sovereign in the sense of being "autonomous" (*auto*, "self"; *nomos*, "law"), it must at its core be *antinomic*: it requires a sovereign who is both inside and outside the law, and whose decision, like creation ex nihilo, simultaneously defines and breaches the limit of that law. Rigorously true to the concept of sovereignty as underived power, the decision is "independent of argumentative substantiation. . . . Looked at normatively, the decision emanates from nothingness."[11] The foundation of this sovereignty, then, is not locatable. One goal of this chapter is to show how medieval/modern periodization frequently serves as a substitute for this absent foundation of sovereignty, and thereby installs certain characteristics of the "modern" in the place of the sovereign. In this sense, periodization functions as sovereign *decision*.

Schmitt's historical argument helps to clarify this function of periodization. Recent attention to *Political Theology* has focused primarily on the structure of sovereignty that I outline above, often at the expense of his historical argument. But this structure, epitomized by the famous statement, "Sovereign is he who decides on the exception," is pinned to the equally important historical claim: "All significant concepts of the modern theory of the state are secularized theological concepts."[12] By this, as I note above, he means not the extrication of European state forms from theological constraints, but the transference of theological concepts to those forms. Understood in this way, secularization disrupts any narrative of clean-cut periodization, and blocks the substitution of medieval/modern periodization for the absent foundation of sovereignty. Schmitt's point is that current attempts to interpret the mechanisms of the modern constitutional state as scientific are doomed because their premises are false. At its core and in its minutest detail, jurisprudence is theological:

Whoever takes the trouble of examining the public law literature of positive jurisprudence for its basic concepts and arguments will see that the state intervenes everywhere. At times it does so as a *deus ex machina*, to decide according to positive statute a controversy that the independent act of juristic perception failed to bring to a generally plausible solution; at other times it does so as the graceful and merciful lord who proves by pardons and amnesties his supremacy over his own laws. There always exists the same inexplicable identity: lawgiver, executive power, police, pardoner, welfare institution. Thus to an observer who takes the trouble to look at the total picture of contemporary jurisprudence, there appears a huge cloak-and-dagger drama, in which the state acts in many disguises but always as the same invisible person. The "omnipotence" of the modern lawgiver, of which one reads in every textbook of law, is not only linguistically derived from theology.[13]

Schmitt wishes the state to recognize and act upon its theological form, rather than repress this inherent sovereign structure. He would therefore have disagreed with the purpose, but not with the historical analysis, in statements such as Anidjar's that "secularism is a name Christianity gave itself when it invented religion, when it named its other or others as religions." It is a matter of "disguise," of "cloak-and-dagger" drama, by which the (Christian European) state hides the prerogative of its sovereign decision (or the "power of the sword," *merum imperium*) under a cloak of science and ostensibly universal, pure reason.

Moreover, Schmitt insists upon the full interrelation of the structural and the historical in this sovereign form:

All significant concepts of the modern theory of the state are secularized theological concepts not only because of their historical development—in which they were transferred from theology to the theory of the state, whereby, for example, the omnipotent God became the omnipotent lawgiver—but also because of their systematic structure, the recognition of which is necessary for a sociological consideration of these concepts. The exception in jurisprudence is analogous to the miracle in theology. Only by being aware of this analogy can we appreciate the manner in which the philosophical ideas of the state developed in the last centuries.[14]

I suggest that this intersection of the structural and the historical in "secularization" provides a way of understanding the workings of medieval/modern periodization and the limits it poses to any rethinking of sovereignty, for it is periodization that provides the means for disavowing the continuity of theological forms. "Secularization," in the sense of a break with the sacred, is generally understood to have occurred in the course of the sixteenth to the eighteenth centuries. This break can be designated as achieved only if the time of the "sacred" has a clear historical referent, which cannot be supplied by the centuries considered transitional. A reified "Middle Ages," made to serve as exemplar and proof of the "religious" or the pre-secular state, is therefore inevitably ushered in to act as a foil for the modern, secular, rational state. Medieval/modern periodization has so successfully sustained the "cloak-and-dagger" drama of "secularization" that it is often called upon to solve theoretical dilemmas. In this role, as I will show later in this chapter through a reading of Antonio Negri's work, it often undermines theoretical attempts to resist the hegemonic idea of the modern nation-state.

We find a sense of secularization with affinities to Schmitt's in the work of Walter Benjamin, who had also dealt with the "divine" suspension of all existing law in his "Critique of Violence," but who differently conceives the relation between sovereign decision and theological form.[15] Benjamin's *The Origin of German Tragic Drama*, which acknowledges its heavy debt to Schmitt's *Political Theology*, also addresses the alignment of sovereignty and history with respect to epochality. The "true object" of the German *Trauerspiel*, Benjamin explains, is "historical life as represented by its epoch," and "the sovereign, the principal exponent of history, almost serves as its incarnation."[16] In this, Benjamin suggests, drama coincides with politics: "The Sovereign represents history. He holds the course of history in his hand like a scepter. This view is by no means peculiar to the dramatists. It is based on certain constitutional notions."[17]

Rather than validating this sovereign representation, however, Benjamin calls it into question by linking it to the problems of literary representation and interpretation, thereby intersecting several aspects of Schmitt's invocation of "drama" and political representation:

Confronted with a literature which sought, in a sense, to reduce both its contemporaries and posterity to silence through the extravagance of its technique, the unfailing richness of its creations, and the vehemence of its claims to value, one should emphasize the necessity of that sovereign attitude which the representation of the idea of a form demands. Even then the danger of allowing oneself to plunge from the heights of knowledge into the profoundest depths of the baroque state of mind, is not a negligible one. That characteristic feeling of dizziness which is induced by the spectacle of the spiritual contradictions of this epoch is a recurrent feature in the improvised attempts to capture its meaning.[18]

By emphasizing the "*necessity* of that sovereign attitude which the representation of the idea of a form demands" (my emphasis), Benjamin returns us to the paradox of the sovereign decision, which must be made—and can only be made—in the face of its own undecidability: technically, representation is impossible. Whereas Schmitt negotiates this paradox by predisposing sovereign decision to the interests of the state, Benjamin, as Samuel Weber argues, concentrates upon the disarticulation of sovereignty. On the one hand, Benjamin recognizes that the necessity of sovereign decision "demands completion of the image of the sovereign, as tyrant." On the other hand, the sovereign "who is responsible for making the decision to proclaim the state of emergency, reveals, at the first opportunity, that he is almost incapable of making a decision."[19] Rather than representing the solidity of an epoch, the sovereign instead represents its impossibility in the form of his own madness: "there is this one thing to be said in favour of the Caesar as he loses himself in the ecstasy of power: he falls victim to the disproportion between the unlimited hierarchial dignity, with which he is divinely invested and the humble estate of his humanity."[20] Benjamin's depiction of this mad Caesar perhaps gives reply to the image of a rational, secular modern state and the world order over which it would lay claim.

"Secularization Theory"

Some of the postwar challenges to this logic of world order embraced and expanded the sense of "secularization" proffered by thinkers such as Schmitt and Benjamin. In so doing, they focused upon the relation between bids for political sovereignty and the periodization of history. Most influential was the "secularization theory" popularized by Karl Löwith's *Meaning in History*, which argued, far more generally than Schmitt and with critical sensibility toward his theory of sovereignty, that modern historical concepts such as Progress are secularized versions of Christian ideas, particularly eschatology: for Comte as for Hegel, history had its end at its beginning, and for Marx the proletariat were a chosen people with a redemptive mission.[21] An expatriate German with Jewish lineage writing in the aftermath of the war, Löwith admired the historians he studied—from Marx, Hegel, and Comte to Joachim, Augustine, and Orosius—but he found their belief in a trajectory of fulfillment a critical failure: "The world is still as it was in the time of Alaric; only our means of oppression and destruction (as well as of reconstruction) are considerably improved."[22] For Löwith, there is nothing legitimate about historical "periods"; to the contrary, they are means of legitimizing political ends. Löwith's work is important for its insistence that conceptions of historical time must be understood as political strategy—and in the case of periodized, progressive history, as a means of aggression.

With a keen sense of the political stakes of periodization, Löwith argues that peace requires a revised sense of periodicity, and his claims focus upon the relation between political legitimacy and the quality of historical time. Periodization operates doubly in Löwith's argument. First, and crucially, he insists that the popularly accepted periodization of historical thought (that is, the dismissal of "prescientific" history as nonhistorical) is incorrect. He controverts, in other words, the standard conception of the philosophy of history as "modern," which we have already seen redacted, for instance, in Certeau.[23] Löwith writes:

Arguing that the philosophy of history from Augustine to Bossuet does not present a theory of "real" history in its finitude, wealth, and mobility but only a doctrine of history on the basis of revelation and faith, [modern philosophers] drew
the conclusion that the theological interpretation of history—or fourteen hundred years of Western thought—is a negligible affair. Against this common opinion that proper historical thinking begins only in modern times, with the
eighteenth century, the following outline aims to show that philosophy of history originates with the Hebrew and Christian faith in a fulfillment and that it
ends with the secularization of its eschatological pattern.[24]

With this, Löwith undercuts the foundational claim of "modern" sovereignty by exposing its disavowal of the history upon which it constitutes
itself. Having dismissed the validity of a "modern" break in the conception of history, Löwith turns, secondly, to the destructive capacity of
"secularized" eschatology, which he sees as having its theoretical basis
in the Christian concept of a break with and the supersession of the old
law, later materialized through political institutionalization. In this
sense, the "secularization," as well as the periodization, of time and politics occurs first with Christianity's "incarnation" of spiritual principles,
and breaks from the classical pattern of recurrence (which, following
Nietzsche, he favors). Löwith's sense of "secularization," then, like
Schmitt's, is not a story of Europe's gradual extrication from religion,
but rather the sublimation of theology in the "world": *Heilgeschehen*
merged with *Weltgeschichte*—a pattern that, unlike Schmitt, he found
disastrous.[25]

Criticism of Löwith based upon whether or not his "secularization"
theory is correct entirely misses his point that periodized, telic history is
the conceptual basis and the legitimizing tool of world-scale aggression.
It is on this basis that he regrets the New Testament teaching that
Christ's birth "shattered once and for all the whole frame of history," a
temporal break from which a secular and incarnate, rather than a spiritual world destiny was imagined with increasing intensity from the time
of Augustine. In this, despite their differing philosophies, Löwith shares
with Schmitt, as with their contemporary Erich Auerbach, a central concern with the political weight of the incarnation and its representative
power in law and politics.[26] In his treatise *Roman Catholicism and Political
Form* (1923), Schmitt finds in the Roman Catholic Church the authorizing logic of political representation: based upon the historical reality of
the incarnation, "the Church is a concrete personal representation of a
concrete personality," the model of a "juridical person" with the power
to represent the *civitas humana*.[27] It is precisely the loss of such personal
representation and its legitimating authority (with the dissolution of the
monarchy in the nineteenth century) that for Schmitt inaugurates political crisis, and although Löwith wishes for a different outcome he works

from the same premise regarding the secular politics of the incarnation, which is precisely what sacred/secular periodization would both disavow and extend.

Löwith saw the eighteenth century's self-styled rejection of tradition as a second wave of secularization that redoubled the worldly imposition of the Christian paradigm: "The secular messianism of Western nations is in every case associated with the consciousness of a national, social, or racial vocation which has its roots in the religious belief of being called by God to a particular task of universal significance."[28] Whereas for Schmitt the (mainly Protestant) retreat to private religion amounted to "abandoning the world" to a crude materialism, for Löwith the "secularization," especially the politicization, of spiritual ideas makes nonsense of religion: "A Holy Roman Empire is a contradiction in terms."[29] Both, however, address the "theological" at the core of political legitimacy, Schmitt to urge the necessity of a sovereign who would cut across incalculability with a *decision* upon the exception, and Löwith (like Benjamin) to plead for sustaining the "incalculability" of history and politics.[30] Indeed, Löwith insists upon the very contingency and incalculability that Schmitt had theorized with the "exception," and argues against the preemption of incalculable "decision" by the interests of a state and a homogeneous "people," the identification of which Schmitt had aligned with the sovereign decision.[31] Recognizing that periodization operates both as a decision that constitutes a "people" and as the temporal platform for such pre-calculation, Löwith deliberately undermines "modern" claims about the meaning of history (secularization) and the concept of sovereignty resting on that meaning.

A Sovereign Age

Response came in the form of Hans Blumenberg's strident *The Legitimacy of the Modern Age* (1966), which limns the stakes in its title.[32] Up to this point, the discussion of "secularization" had primarily focused upon political legitimacy and sovereignty. By recasting the issue as one of the "modern age" (*Neuzeit*), Blumenberg made explicit that this question of "legitimacy" turns upon historical time itself, and he determined to counter the threat to periodization. A refutation of "secularization theory" at large, Blumenberg's book specifically targeted Löwith and Schmitt, but also criticized any related theories, such as Weber's on Puritanism and capitalism. Writing in the 1960s, Blumenberg is ready to offload what he sees as guilt-ridden concern for the politics of supersession and to reclaim possession of history in the name of a self-substantiating modernity. Keeping Schmitt's language of sovereignty, but shifting the question of legitimacy to periodization, he likens "the secularization theorem" to a parting curse by theology as it declares the new, rightful heir its usurping bastard. The "secularization theorem"

is (in its position in history) something in the nature of a final *theologumenon* [theological dictum] intended to lay on the heirs of theology a guilty conscience about their entrance into the succession. . . . Not only does the secularization thesis explain the modern age; it explains it as the wrong turning for which the thesis itself is able to prescribe the corrective. It would be the exact reverse of the claim that the young Hegel had described as the task of the critique of religion in his time: "Despite earlier attempts, it has been reserved for our times especially to claim as man's property, at least in theory, the treasures that have been squandered on heaven; but what age will have the strength to insist on this right and to take actual possession?"[33]

The *right*, not the fact, of possession is the issue, and for Blumenberg its resolution utterly depends upon the legitimacy of periodization. In order to defend the status of this right as literally a matter of property (and by extension of propriety), he insists that the term "secularization" in the philosophy of history metaphorizes its juridical meaning as the illegitimate seizure of Church property, even though he grants that the philosophical history of the concept does not support this reading. By way of a double negative and an appeal against rhetoric, he argues that this essentially improper, metaphorical "alienation of a historical substance from its origin" cancels out, or delegitimates, any illegitimacy thus attributed to the succession of the modern age.[34] This insistence upon the impropriety of metaphor replays the argument of the sixteenth-century French jurist Charles du Moulin (whom I discuss in Chapter 1), as he cancels out all "improper," metaphorical uses of feudal "servitude" and reclaims them as rightful possessions of an absolutist king. This correspondence is no coincidence, for both cases involve an appeal to a literal truth as they attempt to resolve the logical paradox of absolute sovereignty: Du Moulin for the king; Blumenberg for the "modern age."

By way of a reply to Schmitt, Blumenberg negotiates the problem of a pure self-founding by describing *Neuzeit* as an "emergency self-consolidation"—an epochal "postmedieval self-assertion" in the face of necessity (such as the religious wars). This necessity, which, like Schmitt's *Ausnahmezustand* requires suspension of the norm, gives *Neuzeit* a historical grounding without historical continuity, thus granting it legitimate epochal status. In this way, Blumenberg explains modernity's self-assertion in terms of a sovereign *decision* analogous to Schmitt's definition of sovereignty ("Sovereign is he who decides on the exception"): "The concept of the legitimacy of the modern age is not derived from the accomplishments of reason but rather from the necessity of those accomplishments. Theological voluntarism and human rationalism are historical correlates; thus the legitimacy of the modern age is not shown as a result of its 'newness'—the claim to be a modern age does not as such justify it.''[35] Justification comes instead from the historical necessity that calls it into being. Whereas for Schmitt it is the sovereign who decides upon the state of exception and thus suspends the law, Blumenberg collapses the sovereign and the exception, and consigns *decision* to history, which periodizes itself. And although it is understood by all parties that "world order" is the topic under discussion, the question "whose history?" (a correlate, we could say, of "Who decides?") does not arise. In this way, the paradox of a self-constituting modernity is folded into the cut of periodization itself, and the "modern" can emerge as unproblematically sovereign.

Periodization, History, and the Secular

For a more extensive example of this periodizing logic and its role in recent theories of time and modernity, I turn to work that grapples—under the influence of Schmitt's *Political Theology* and in the context of this debate over periodization—with the issues of secularization, sovereignty, and temporality: that is, to Reinhart Koselleck's semantics of historical time.[36]

Koselleck's collected essays on historical semantics (increasingly since their English translation as *Futures Past*) have become a touchstone both for critics who are invested in theories of temporality and modernity, and for those who want to lean on a respectable theory of periodization in order to skirt or to epitomize the Middle Ages (often the same people, of course). Koselleck's work is undoubtedly of profound methodological importance for studies in temporality, but this importance is all the more reason to consider his reliance upon periodization, and the relationship of this reliance to controversies regarding the history and theory of sovereignty. Koselleck's analyses of European historiography distill decades of debate over secularization and periodization on both sides of the Atlantic, and in large measure sanitize its politics. Directly and indirectly, his essays have made it easy for theorists to bypass the political intricacies of periodization, and to support reductive versions of temporality that frequently undermine the very arguments being made. His *Futures Past* is thus both an example of and a factor in critical theory's difficulty with addressing, and sometimes even recognizing, events that defy preconceived concepts of religion, secularism, democracy, and politics.[37]

For my purposes here, the germane issue is not empirical correctness or error, but the elision between a theory of history and the historical change it purports to examine. In Koselleck's case, I believe—not least because of the critical matrix in which he worked—this slippage exposes the logic of medieval/modern periodization, its historical and conceptual relation to sovereignty, and its implications for the relation of religion and politics with which I began this chapter. I argue in part that by shifting the target of critique from political legitimacy to conceptions of historical time, Koselleck—like many of his contemporaries—not only substitutes a medieval/modern break for the absent foundation of sovereignty, but also supplies this substitution with a narrative form.

Koselleck was deeply influenced by his personal and academic relationship with Schmitt, and the effects of *Political Theology* as well as other works by Schmitt appear throughout *Futures Past* in subtle form.[38] By contrast, Koselleck's earlier *Critique and Crisis* (1959) quite explicitly engages Schmitt's theory and its political fate as it attempts to explain the rise of National Socialism and the cold war in terms of European philosophies of history. Political crisis for Koselleck "presses for a decision," in association with "the philosophies of history that correspond to the crisis and in whose name we seek to anticipate the decision, to influence it, steer it, or, as catastrophically to prevent it."[39] "Critique," therefore, bears the heavy responsibility of decoding European history in order to avoid its repetition. The eighteenth century serves as both example and the "common root" of this history, in that "it failed to note any connection between the critique it practiced and the looming crisis," and thus unwarily hastened toward "an unexpected decision."[40] Koselleck's early work, then, is driven by an attempt to take responsibility for European violence and to cultivate a more politically and historically aware brand of criticism.

In its effort to understand how Europe's utopian hopes went wrong, *Critique and Crisis* is also indebted to the "secularization theory" popularized by Löwith, whose argument and the response to it by Blumenberg were integral to the politics of time inhabiting "secularization" by the time Koselleck wrote *Futures Past.* Likewise integral to this argument was the degree to which periodization had become the linchpin of the controversy. Blumenberg had criticized Koselleck's *Critique and Crisis* for its confirmation of "the process of secularization that transposed eschatology into a progressive history," and while Koselleck does not explicitly acknowledge the "secularization" debate in his essays in *Futures Past,* he takes up its central issue as it was articulated by Blumenberg: the qualitative difference of modernity [*Neuzeit*] from a "Middle Ages" oriented to eschatology.[41]

Koselleck focuses his argument on changing historical conceptions of time, a point that continues today as a core issue—if not *the* core issue—for theories of modernity. It is the generative problem, for instance, of Peter Osborne's *The Politics of Time*, which situates itself in relation to

Heidegger's *Being and Time*, but also relies heavily upon Koselleck and Blumenberg as it analyzes the "purely anticipatory, timeless end" that "temporalizes historical time (historicizes temporality) in the same way that the anticipation of death temporalizes time in general."[42] According to this argument, as the indebtedness to Koselleck suggests, there could be no sense of temporalized historical time in the "Middle Ages." Arguing against Löwith, Osborne states that refuting the secularization theory is crucial to a philosophy of "secular modernity," one that would posit an ontological structure of historical time without relegitimating theology on post-Hegelian grounds:

> In particular, to what extent can [this ontological status] be understood independently of the *theological* connotations with which it is inevitably associated in the context of the Judaic-Christian tradition? After all, is not the idea of a timeless exteriority, productive of history yet in principle outside its grasp, even more unequivocally theological than the immanent end of Hegel's "true theodicy," which we would have it displace?
>
> Unless we can counter this all-too-common charge, we remain vulnerable to the threat of a dialectical reversal which would detect in our quest for the ontological structure of historical time a relegitimation of theology on post-Hegelian grounds.[43]

It would be possible to find in such an argument an idea of the "secular" without the "secularization" described by Löwith, if it were not that it reinscribes the pattern by which medieval/modern periodization is substituted for the absent foundation of sovereignty, thus yielding the "incalculable" in politics as the prerogative of the "modern."

Koselleck stipulates from the outset of *Futures Past* that "historical time, if the concept has a specific meaning, is bound up with social and political actions," each with its own temporal rhythm. Agreeing with Herder that at any one time in the Universe there are innumerably many times, he posits that each epoch evinces its own understanding of the interlinkings among events, and indeed that such historical understanding is precisely what determines an epoch. In contrast to his earlier work, he identifies a change in the comprehension of *temporality* as exactly what constitutes the dissolution of one epoch and the emergence of another, and in order to study this change he takes as his central question: "How, in a given present, are the temporal dimensions of past and future related?"[44] The title *"Futures Past"* (*Vergangene Zukunft*) thus refers in part to a bygone way of experiencing a relationship with the future, particularly that of a "medieval" past sealed off from the future through its own closed and now past sense of the future.[45] Some of Koselleck's essays explore temporalities of "modernity" in rich ways—such as negotiating the gap between experience and expectation, or encountering a once imagined future—but they never come untethered from the foundational exclusion of "medieval" time.

Koselleck's goal of identifying such historical-political conceptions of time in any "given present" engages directly with the definition of epochality that Schmitt had already set out in *Political Theology*: "The metaphysical image that a definite epoch forges of the world has the same structure as what the world immediately understands to be appropriate as a form of its political organization. The determination of such an identity is the sociology of the concept of sovereignty."[46] Schmitt never hesitates to explain this "identity" as one that results from conquest and territorialization of both land and ideas, principally as determined by Europe's mapping of the world.[47] Koselleck's "given present"—at its core a political question of "the now" as discussed in my introduction (that is, "a certain figure of the now" that masks the historicity of its fundamental concepts)—must be understood in these terms. His theory of periodization may be persuasive when viewed from within the self-defining "modern European" political discourse in which he is situated, and indeed it has accrued many advocates. But it cannot be separated from the contemporaneous and interrelated discourses of "world order" such as anthropology and Orientalism, which defined Europe's others in precisely the terms Koselleck applies to the Middle Ages, and which in effect it extends.[48]

World order is a central issue for *Futures Past*. These essays developed out of Koselleck's work on the multivolume dictionary of historical concepts, *Geschichtliche Grundbegriffe*, which he coedited throughout the 1960s and 1970s with Werner Conze and the medieval historian Otto Brunner.[49] Brunner is best known for his *Land and Lordship* (1939), an important text in the movement of the 1930s and 1940s against the dominant state-oriented models of medieval German history. *Land and Lordship* reconceptualized late medieval Austrian constitutional history and advanced a model of a Germanic *Volk* state meant to shatter liberal-bourgeois versions of medieval antecedents to the modern national state, and to shore up the political theory of the Third Reich. In Brunner's own terms, his critique evinced "present-day relatedness" (*Gegenwartsbezogenheit*), in that it secured "the historical foundation of the Third Reich's law and constitution, not those of the 'bourgeois *Rechtsstaat*' and its basis in absolutism."[50] After the war Brunner redirected his theory from German to European civilization—the origin, he believed, of what would inevitably become a global culture rooted in the social structure of premodern Europe (stretching from tribal roots up to 1800)—and he continued to pursue the relatedness of that structure to Western civilization as a world order.[51] Indeed, this is the task of the dictionary of historical concepts, *Geschichtliche Grundbegriffe*, which in Koselleck's terms aimed to examine "the dissolution of the old world and the emergence of the new in terms of the historicoconceptual comprehension of this process."[52] Koselleck's historical semantics, then, grew out of an intense need to revise and to reconcile the account of history with a workable but singular vision of "the now," understood in terms of temporality itself, and legitimated through a narrative of periodization.

Throughout his essays Koselleck focuses on the years 1500 to 1800 ("early modernity" or *frühe Neuzeit*) as "the period in which modernity is formed," and argues that during this time the possibility opened—gradually and sporadically—for history to become "temporalized."[53] All of the essays are variations on this central tenet, explicitly stated and glossed in the opening essay, "Modernity and the Planes of Historicity," which I use as my base text, so to speak, for exploring Koselleck's theory of temporalization and for working through its implications for the relation between periodization and sovereignty. I read, as does Koselleck, within the double frame he provides for his opening scene.

The scene is that of Albrecht Altdorfer's famous *Alexanderschlacht* ("The Battle of Alexander and Darius on the Issus"), a painting commissioned in 1528 by Duke William IV of Bavaria for his newly built summer home. It is epochal in every sense:

> Upon an area of one and a half square meters, Altdorfer reveals to us the cosmic panorama of a decisive battle of world-historical significance, the Battle of Issus, which in 333 B.C. opened the epoch of Hellenism, as we say today. With a mastery previously unknown, Altdorfer was able to depict thousand upon thousand of individual warriors as complete armies; he shows us the clash of armored squadrons of horse and foot soldiers armed with spears; the victorious line of attack of the Macedonians, with Alexander far out at the head; the confusion and disintegration which overtook the Persians; and the expectant bearing of the Greek battle-reserves, which will then complete the victory. (3)

Standing at the opening of Koselleck's transitional early modern period, William IV's "Christian-Humanism" and Altdorfer's unprecedented mastery align with the initiating moment of Hellenism, thus confirming humanism's self-proclaimed association with classical Antiquity, and more importantly, linking this aesthetic moment to military conquest, empire, and the trajectory of world history. Despite the initiatory status he grants it, however, Koselleck views this scene and its ducal setting as irrevocably tied to the past, a point he explains through discussion of anachronism. He first notes the deliberate and artful use of anachronism by Altdorfer, who had researched the battle and inscribed upon each army's banner the number of its combatants, including the number of dead, even though in the painting these future dead remain among the living. But Koselleck posits a second element of anachronism as more apparent "to us" *as* anachronism, by which he means Altdorfer's invocation of contemporary figures and battles, such as the Emperor Maximilian or the defeated Turks at the siege of Vienna, whom Altdorfer's Persians resemble "from their feet to their turbans," to the effect that the painting is both historical in the minutest detail *and* contemporary in its typologically charged political nuance.

To Koselleck, however, this anachronism attests not to a deft handling of historical time, but to an absence for Altdorfer of a temporal dimension: for him, fourth-century Persians look like sixteenth-century Turks not because he does not know the difference, but because the difference does not matter (4–5). The *Alexanderschlacht*, in other words, exemplifies a premodern, *untemporalized* sense of time and a lack of historical consciousness. In contrast to Friedrich Schlegel, who at the end of Koselleck's early modern period admired the *Alexanderschlacht* from a critical-historical distance "as the greatest feat of the age of chivalry," Altdorfer's historical overlays evince an eschatological vision of history, evidence that the sixteenth century (and by degrees also the seventeenth and eighteenth centuries) remained locked in a static, constant temporality that proleptically saturates the future as always a repetition of the same: "*Sub specie aeternitatis* nothing novel can emerge" (16). In such a system, there can be no *event* as such: anticipation and arrival are together sucked into the black hole of sacred history, which is not temporalized because its time is essentially undifferentiated. Koselleck thus emphatically reasserts the periodization of the philosophy of history that Löwith had critiqued.

Despite Koselleck's intense focus on a Christian theology, his version of premodern untemporalized history never acknowledges the earlier periodization instantiated by the incarnation—that is, the temporal logic whereby Christianity subsumed and superseded Jewish history—as it had been explicated, for instance, by Löwith. Koselleck's analysis thereby confirms that even when it is most introspective, the "purported 'secularization' of modernity," as Kathleen Biddick argues, "has never overtaken this core Christian conception of supersession."[54] Koselleck once has occasion to reference this history as he argues for the subsumption of Altdorfer's historical consciousness by an impending End: "Altdorfer, who had assisted in the expulsion of the Jews from Regensburg . . . knew the signs" (6). The choice of Altdorfer's politically charged *Alexanderschlacht* thus encrypts the problem of supersession and the temporal rupture of the incarnation, even as it bonds the painting's vision of the future to a medieval, fully closed, and untemporalized past.

Koselleck's method of reading the *Alexanderschlacht* also allows him to absorb medieval and early modern state politics into the "plane of historicity" he theorizes. Prior to modernity, he argues: "This always-already guaranteed futurity of the past effected the closure and bounding of the sphere of action available to the state. . . . The state remains trapped within a temporal structure that can be understood as static movement" (17). Because Koselleck's analysis of periodization is tied to the issue of religion, the Reformation opens both his early modern period and the possibility of politics. It initiates the possibility of breaking from "medieval" stasis for two related reasons that are now familiar from many accounts of a period break: first, as a movement of religious renewal it "carried with it all the signs of the End of the World," yet the End did not happen, but was increasingly deferred, weakening the grip of the Church over the future. Second, the bloodbaths of religious war prompted the Religious Peace of Augsburg (1555), which set aside the requirement of religious unity and thus "concealed within itself a new principle, that of 'politics,'" a principle further advanced by the Peace of Westphalia (6–8). Politics thus begins to break the cyclic grip of prophecy, for which it substituted rational foresight and planning.

In his own postwar analysis of transitions in world order, Schmitt had already discussed the historicity of stasis and action, prophecy and politics, and, like Löwith, he refutes medieval/modern periodization upon the basis of conceptions of history. Insisting upon the powerful sense of history inherent to Christian politics since the time of Paul, Schmitt invokes the concept of *katechon*, the "restrainer" (or "lawless one," *anomos*), named by Paul in the Second Letter to the Thessalonians, which had long been interpreted as the Roman Empire's function of staving off the coming of the Antichrist.[55] I address this idea and the limits of Schmitt's argument at length in Chapter 4, but the salient point here is that Schmitt refuses the eschatological, atemporal paralysis that Koselleck attributes to the Middle Ages. He argues instead that the concept of *katechon* signaled a time full with a "secular" meaningfulness of history:

I do not believe that any historical concept other than *katechon* would have been possible for the original Christian faith. The belief that a restrainer holds back the end of the world provides the only bridge between the notion of an eschatological paralysis of all human events and a tremendous historical monolith like that of the Christian empire of the Germanic kings. . . . This took the form of a lucid Christian faith in potent historical power. Anyone unable to distinguish between the maxims of Haimo of Halberstadt or Adso and the obscure oracles of Pseudo-Methodius or the Tiburtinian sibyls would be able to comprehend the empire of the Christian Middle Ages only in terms of distorting generalizations and parallels, but not in terms of its concrete historical authenticity.[56]

As if in ironic response to Schmitt's warning that the inability to distinguish between medieval prophetic and historicist genres would result in "distorting generalizations," Koselleck insists upon a binarized and linear sorting that moves from stasis to action, prophecy to politics, religious to secular.

For Koselleck this linear transition does not culminate with the Enlightenment (which only shimmered at the edge of the period), since "the reoccupation of a prophesied future by a predicted future had not yet fundamentally ruptured the plane of Christian expectations. This is what harnesses the republic of rulers to the Middle Ages, even if it no longer conceives of itself as Christian" (16). It is the French Revolution, unsurprisingly, that inverts the horizon of expectations, as the coup d'état that closed the old era and opened the temporalization of historical time.

Medievalists have long since tired of such attributions of stasis, closure, and homogeneity, so distortive that they nearly defy response. But response on an empirical basis would in any case be beside the point, for the problem that engages Koselleck as well as his predecessors and successors on this topic is not at all empirical, despite frequent recourse to empirical evidence. It is a philosophical struggle concerning the radical newness—or the possibility of the radical newness—of *Neuzeit*, and its arguments, as well as its relevance for us today, turn on the structure of sovereignty and its relation to theology.

This relation and its dissociation from empiricism coalesce in Koselleck's conclusion, which returns us to the *Alexanderschlacht*, now hanging in Napoleon's bathroom. Through a chiasmic exemplar that sets a "premodern" Napolean on the later side of the 1800 marker, and a "modern" Diderot on the earlier, it teaches us that the temporalizing cut of modernity can easily absorb forerunners and backsliders into its logic, as any master category will. Diderot, well prior to the Revolution but from a "point of departure [that] is modern," had augured the advent of Napoleon, not with a commonplace premonition of the Revolution, but more presciently, with a prediction of its aftermath and the authorial void into which Napoleon would step. Beyond that, Diderot could only say, "What will succeed this revolution? No one knows. *Quelle sera la suite de cette revolution? On l'ignore.*" Steeped though his reasoning was in "classical literature on civil war, ancient theories of despotism and historical cycles, and the critique of enlightened absolutism," Diderot's thought of an undetermined future made his viewpoint "modern." Napoleon, on the other hand, envisioning himself as a parallel to the great Alexander, pondered the *Alexanderschlacht* in his private chambers, drawn, sometimes at least, to "premodern" thoughts: "The power of tradition was so strong that the long-lost, salvational-historical task of the Holy Roman Empire shimmered through the supposedly new beginning of the 1789 Revolution" (19–20).

So we end where we began, with a ruler pondering his own figuration in the scene of the *Alexanderschlacht*'s cosmic, typological sweep. Nothing, yet everything, has changed. How has this happened? Koselleck has explained the emergence of modern politics by narrating the elimination of religion and religious expectations from the realm of political decision (11). In this he accords with Schmitt's historical account that together deism and the idea of the constitutional state had "banished the miracle from the world," by which he refers not to "private religion," but to religion's authorization of political legitimacy. Until the nineteenth century, Schmitt argued, the conception of God and the conception of the sovereign were aligned (rightly in his opinion) vis à vis transcendence of the world and of the state.[57] But unlike Schmitt, Koselleck has all along been narrating a double break: a historical break with a religious mode of ruling the state, and a qualitative break within the conceptualization of temporality itself. In his account, the elimination of religion and religious expectations yields not only politics, but meaningful historical time, and at the critical juncture they fuse. His example is Robespierre, who looks into an accelerating, open future and sees "a task of men leading to an epoch of freedom and happiness" (7). Politics and meaningful time unite in this "human" task.

Koselleck's argument, however, is far from utopian. Like Löwith, he sees conceptions of historical time as tied to political calculation, and considers the "modern" orientation toward an open future as susceptible to utopian goals that become prescriptive and thus rob this future of its actuality. But his periodization and linearity can only figure such recuperation as backsliding, or—to put it in terms of the "theology" he would disavow—apostasy. In his analysis of sovereignty, Schmitt had stayed focused on the problem of the *exception*, and his tenacious insistence that the exception must be thought by analogy to the theological because by definition it requires a sovereign decision unfounded in norms, and his insistence that this analogy underlies a materialist, not a spiritualist, philosophy of history, offer strong grounds for questioning versions of political sovereignty founded upon the qualitative exclusion of a "past" and claims to occupy the space of "secular" world order. By contrast, Koselleck's definition of politics as the evacuation of theology from political decision would seem to leave the basis of decision unexplored. But this is not the case. His merger of political decision with the temporalization of time indicates that its explanatory basis is "modernity" itself. In just this way, modernity becomes a sovereign period, and its periodization the basis of sovereignty.

Periodization and Resistance

In order to outline the process by which medieval/modern periodization thwarts attempts to grasp the promise of the "exception" and incalculability, or to think new political forms and alternate temporalities, I turn briefly here to Antonio Negri's engagement with the structural and historical elements of Schmitt's theory. Negri grapples with Schmitt as he attempts to theorize the possibility of a radically democratic "constituent power" that is never closed down by, or recuperated as, "constituted power." He wishes, in other words, to develop an understanding of a power that suspends law without turning into yet another foundation for law. For Negri, the "paradigm of constituent power is that of a force that bursts apart, breaks, interrupts, unhinges any preexisting equilibrium and any possible continuity." Schmitt's thinking on the exception thus comes "very close to a material definition of constituent power."[58] Schmitt's "miracle" of the exception approximates the force of constituent power in that it is incommensurate with constitutional norms and judicial limits, which Negri wishes to resist. As Negri observes, however, Schmitt's advocacy of "decision" for the sake of protecting the state would preemptively cancel the potential of constituent power from the start:

The "decision" that Carl Schmitt sees as marking the very possibility of law, the identification and conflict of friend and enemy, and that he sees as running through the whole system, shaping it and overdetermining it—this act of war represents the maximum of factuality, cast as absolute immanence in the juridical system. This immanence is so profound that at first sight the distinction between constituent and constituted power fades, so that constituent power appears according to its nature as originary power or counterpower, as historically determined strength, as a set of needs, desires, and singular determinations. In fact, however, the existential matrix through which constituent power is defined is stripped away from the beginning, brought back to the abstract determinations of violence, of pure event as voluntary occurrence of power.[59]

Thus, Negri argues, Schmitt's version of the sovereign "decision" recuperates constituent power into state power and sovereign violence, even before such constituent power has a chance to emerge.

Schmitt's theory of sovereignty certainly does lodge in the necessity of protecting the state. As he puts it in *Political Theology*: "The existence of the state is undoubted proof of its superiority over the validity of the legal norm. The decision frees itself from all normative ties and becomes in the true sense absolute. The state suspends the law in the exception on the basis of its right of self-preservation, as one would say."[60] To the degree that Schmitt predisposes the sovereign decision to the interests of the state we could say that it is not a "decision" at all in his own terms, and this is the most potent critique of Schmitt. Such a decision, rather than coming, as he suggests, "*ex nihilo*"—out of sheer incalculability that requires a decision like a leap of faith—would instead be a calculation, already interested in preserving someone's norm.[61]

In order to resist such recuperation by the state, and to think constituent power as an un-recuperable, unprecedented revolution, Negri attempts to theorize a pure *event*, a breakthrough that has its basis only in itself. There can of course be no event without some aspect of repetition and thus recognizability, and Negri therefore argues for a negative relation, not with existing institutional power, but in time. He turns, in other words, to periodization, in the form of a religious/secular break (which he will also define as a medieval/modern break), in order to ground constituent power: "Constituent power has always a singular relationship to time. Indeed, constituent power is on the one hand an absolute will determining its own temporality. In other words, it represents an essential moment in the secularization of power and politics. Power becomes an immanent dimension of history, an actual temporal horizon. The break with the theological tradition is complete."[62] Negri discusses this founding break as though it is unproblematic—*as though* its conception were a blank space rather than a politically saturated act, and *as though* the differentiation of the "religious" from "the secular" were not a fundamental means of "defining and policing" (to use Talal Asad's terms) state control of an ethical sphere.[63]

It soon becomes evident, moreover, that this temporal break is also for Negri the opening of "history," in the sense of the capacity to apprehend meaningful historical change. Negri cites Koselleck's argument that such a sense of history only began to become possible in the "Renaissance," in order to posit an origin for constituent power based upon a medieval/Renaissance break: "This notion [of revolution] takes us back to the historical origins of the concept of constituent power. The term was probably introduced for the first time during the American Revolution, but it belongs to the development of Renaissance political thought from the fifteenth to the eighteenth centuries as an ontological notion of the formative capacity of historical movement . . . the foundation of the new science that constitutes history."[64] Far from being unencumbered, then, and despite his insistence that "it has excluded any reference to the concept of sovereignty," Negri's constituent power takes its grounding in the foundations of the very sovereign formations he wishes to resist, particularly the "modern secular state." Just as Schmitt's "exception" is from the beginning predisposed to a calculated *decision* for the state, "constituent power" as Negri defines it here is recouped from the start by the sovereign *decision* of periodization, already enrolled in the service of the state. Like Certeau's analysis of the periodizing "*decision* to become different," Negri's argument reaffirms the self-substantiating logic of periodization, which in turn binds the "modern" and the "secular"—or, to return to Certeau's terms, the process by which their establishment (and thus also their exclusions) is *forgotten.*[65]

A different approach to hegemonic state power is available in the thinking of Dipesh Chakrabarty, who sometimes looks to the "Middle Ages" while contemplating the political dilemmas posed by the European narrative of a religious/secular break. I engage this work briefly here for what we learn from its sincere engagement with the dilemmas wrought by the periodizing schemes of medieval/modern, religious/secular.

Chakrabarty addresses the "European story of 'the disenchantment of the world'" (that is, the qualitative narrative of secularization) as constitutive of the institutional assumptions operating in "political modernity" today, which render the agency of "gods and spirits" unrecognizable, foreclosed. He begins with the problem that positivistic ("secular") history has "close ties to law and other instruments of government" (it is the modus operandi of law courts, for instance), and therefore grants, on the one hand, the necessity of working within this political system in order to protect minority rights.[66] But he argues, on the other hand, that the version of historical time underpinning this model is inadequate for thinking political modernity in colonial and postcolonial India.[67] Aware, then, that Europe's secularization narrative legitimizes the colonizing logic of historicism, which posits a "human sovereignty" that reapplies the categories of colonization, Chakrabarty proposes an alternate, coexisting model based upon, following Derrida, *"the non-contemporaneity with itself of the living present."*[68] Insisting that the experience of historicity is necessarily "heterogeneous," irreducible to a single strand that would align the modern/secular against premodern/religious, he argues for the "breach that the stories of godly or ghostly intervention make in history's system of representation." He therefore explores the possibility of writing (without historicizing) a subaltern past that ascribes "real agency" to the divine or supernatural in the affairs of the world, and that can stand as our *contemporary,* "illuminating a life possibility for the present." To imagine this possibility he turns to the Middle Ages, the history of which could not be written, he argues, if it were not in some sense contemporaneous with the historian—despite its strong association with "the supernatural and the magical."[69]

Two important points emerge from Chakrabarty's analysis. First, the Middle Ages operates doubly within it. It signifies the occlusion within European politics of its "own" history of reliance upon a transcendent principle, and given its wealth of accessible documentation, the European Middle Ages offers epistemological access to a "time of the gods." This cross-temporal connection is aporetic rather than direct—a "time knot" as Chakrabarty puts it—to the past of a likewise occluded colonial culture. Second, as a counterargument to the imposition of sovereignty based upon the narrative of secularization, this association with a "time of the gods" (which Chakrabarty refuses to discuss as that of "religion") has the effect of exposing the degree and continuing effect of colonialism's coproduction of the "Middle Ages" and subaltern pasts. Chakrabarty has incurred strong criticism for this argument, both because it appears to align contemporary non-European societies with Europe's "medieval" past, and because it seems to abet the rising power of an aggressive and intolerant "religious" (particularly Hindu) political right wing in India. To this he replies that conceiving the choices as " 'Reason and truth' on the side of democracy and humanism," or " 'faith'—a 'tissue of superstitions, prejudices and errors' "—simply repeats the Enlightenment's terms.[70]

This argument arises against a deeper background of nationalist historiography inextricable from medieval/modern periodization. As Gyan Prakash explains, early Indian nationalist historiography accepted the British "periodization of Indian history into the Hindu, Muslim and British periods, later addressed as the ancient, medieval and modern eras." Chauvinistic Hindu nationalism violently replays this periodization, writing India as "essentially Sanskritic and Hindu—glorious in ancient times, then subject to Muslim tyranny and degeneration in the Middle Ages, which made it an easy target for British conquest."[71] Chakrabarty's challenge to "secular" historicism thus places him between the blades of several Enlightenment Middle Ages, and his oppositional model both replicates and counters the "modern" terms of debate and the dilemma posed by the categories of "religion" and the "secular"—on their own terms. His argument thus elucidates the relation between periodization and the binarized struggle today between a call for secularism that would ostensibly protect minority rights, and the incentive to turn to religion as a site of resistance to Enlightenment ideals and to the "secularized" norms of the majority.

Chakrabarty's analysis also exposes the stakes of periodization as he attempts to think a different, radically disruptive, conception of "time." By exploring the possibility of writing subaltern pasts that ascribe "real agency" to the supernatural in the affairs of the world, he challenges, in effect, the state's prerogative over the *exception*. His turn to "gods and spirits" could be read as less a careless abetting of violent "religious" groups than a diagnosis as to why struggles over sovereignty are waged in terms of "religion" today. His argument for a breach in history's system of representation attempts to reopen the claims of "secular universals," or as he phrases it, "keep them always open to their own finitude." This, he suggests, quoting Benjamin, could allow for "working the universalist and global archives of capital in such a way as to 'blast . . . out of the homogeneous course of history,' times that produce cracks in the structure of that homogeneity."[72]

The Sense of an Epoch

The potential for imagining such an opening is configured quite differently by Benjamin than by Schmitt. Despite the later antipathy between them, Schmitt's and Benjamin's early investigations of theology and law were complementary—they tracked the same philosophical problems, crucial to their moment, though sometimes with differing vocabularies. In their mutual concern with the total suspension of the law, both considered what today we would call the "performative," the ability of language to do what it says. For Schmitt, the suspension of the *exception* opens the space of the sovereign decision, which "becomes instantly independent of argumentative substantiation and receives an autonomous value."[73] This decision is constitutive, that is, fully performative, even though it may be false; indeed such falsity proves the purity of the decision in its invulnerability to challenge. Schmitt understands the structure of the decision perfectly well: its occasion is utterly singular, an "independently determining moment," and it cannot respond to the multiple interests of the population that it will effect; for precisely this reason it requires a single individual, the sovereign. It depends, like any speech, upon former institutions and could thus miscarry, although Schmitt's sovereign acts under Hobbes's principle, "*auctoritas, non veritas facit legem*," and thus maximizes the chance of success. The theological analogy enters here on two counts: the *exception*, like a miracle, exceeds all norms, and the *decision*, like an act of God, but also a means to an end, performs law. As my discussion of Koselleck's theory suggests, and as I have attempted to illustrate throughout these chapters, periodization can, and historically does, operate in just this way, as a simultaneous abeyance and instantiation of law—as the means to a political end. Its history, as Koselleck rightly notices, is the history of the law, and thus leaves a trail of constitutive violence—which is not to say, of course, that this violence can succeed absolutely.

In Benjamin's terms such decision is not "divine" but "legal" violence, and justice will not be served. For Benjamin, "divine violence" is law-annihilating, pure means that does not advance to an end, never moves to the imposition of a decision. His example is the "general strike," which like an extended miracle nullifies law, "in the determination to resume only a wholly transformed work, no longer enforced by the state, an upheaval that this kind of strike not so much causes as consummates."[74] In this consummation it, too, performs. The idea of such abeyance enables Benjamin in his later work to imagine a form of history that destroys the continuity of historicism (an economy of violence dissembling as progress) through *interruption*, which annihilates from within itself the idea of progress, and from the perspective of "now-time" [*Jetztzeit*] constellates historical events without continuity.[75] Like the general strike, it is a "cessation of happening," combined with "recurrence," and its goal is redemptive. By imagining a form of history that keeps the miracle but shuns decision, Benjamin offers, as is often noted, a radically alternative method of thinking events in time. Its specific potential for connecting with "medieval" events, given its messianic structure and redemptive perspective, is something I pursue in the next chapter. But a brief anecdote might illustrate the difference this perspective offers with regard to periodization.

In his *Imagined Communities*, a book that medievalists have long berated for its uninformed caricature of "the Middle Ages" and its theory of the nation based on temporal exclusion, Benedict Anderson cites Benjamin's *Theses on the Philosophy of History* to support his origin story:

What has come to take the place of the mediaeval conception of simultaneity-along-time is, to borrow again from Benjamin, an idea of "homogeneous, empty time," in which simultaneity is, as it were, transverse, cross-time, marked not by prefiguring and fulfillment, but by temporal coincidence, and measured by clock and calendar.[76]

But Anderson misquotes Benjamin, and his error shuts down precisely the possibility of opening history and attempting to imagine redemption without exclusion, toward which Benjamin strives. Here is what Benjamin says in Thesis fifteen, following his statement in Thesis fourteen that "History is the subject of a structure whose site is not homogeneous, empty time, but time filled by the presence of the now":

The awareness that they are about to make the continuum of history explode is characteristic of the revolutionary classes at the moment of their action. The great revolution introduced a new calendar. The initial day of a calendar serves as a historical time-lapse camera. And, basically it is the same day that keeps recurring in the guise of holidays, which are days of remembrance. Thus the calendars do not measure time as clocks do; they are monuments of historical consciousness.[77]

Anderson's misreading of Benjamin denies both forms of temporality to the Middle Ages, the times of clock and calendar, and collapses the distinction between the two into precisely the homogenized indistinction of the present that Benjamin argues is *not* the structure of history and the "now." The difference between clock and calendar, between the ticks of chronology and an act of present remembrance, between

origin stories that exclude and an openness to the event, is the difference between the sovereign cut of periodization and the abeyance of
that sovereign closure. It is the difference, too, between a Middle Ages
that serves historicism, and a "Middle Ages" that explodes the historical
continuum. At its most radical, it is the difference in the *sense of an epoch.*

Chapter Four
A Political Theology of Time
The Venerable Bede and Amitav Ghosh

Are miracles possible? This question, as I hope the previous chapter demonstrates, is as much political, historical, and philosophical as theological. The potential of the "miraculous" to suspend the limits of a known order—not only the bounds of the "rational," but also the boundaries circumscribing faiths, cultures, sexes, humans, animals—has recently drawn many philosophers to a revised contemplation of "religion" and theology.[1] The potential of such suspense with respect to divisions in time is my interest in this chapter. Whereas my previous chapters study the history and effects of medieval/modern periodization, this chapter studies texts that approach time and periodization differently. They do not perform miracles: ultimately, they periodize. But their contemplations of and encounters with temporal division touch upon, for different reasons and in disparate ways, the possibilities inherent in resisting or *suspending* periodization. Because it moves around the edges of such potential, this chapter, again unlike the previous chapters, is more meditation than argument. The three texts that I study here, Bede's *De temporum ratione* (*The Reckoning of Time*), his *The Ecclesiastical History of the English People*, and Amitav Ghosh's *In an Antique Land*, are in a certain sense immiscible. My interest in this chapter, however, is less in their similarities than in their struggles with time and periodization. I find them suggestive, rather than conclusive, and propose that consideration of temporal division in texts such as these can advance discussion of what it might mean to rethink the political theology of time.

Bede is an obvious choice for many reasons. He was an ambitious and influential historian and theorist of temporality, as well as a powerful synthesizer of previous traditions.[2] His texts periodize, in that they rely on and institutionalize the logic of incarnational time, which medieval/modern periodization both extends and disavows. Yet they do so through a suspension of politics that is in certain ways irreconcilable with this periodization. Bede is also important for the simple reason that he is not Augustine, whose beautiful and complex work on time in *The*

Confessions and *The City of God* exercise magnetic charm, and often over-shadow other "medieval" conceptions of time. Bede of course admired and respected Augustine as a Church father, but to Bede, in subtle distinction from the model of Augustine's two cities, "life in the world, the political and social side of reality, had a value and a function of its own."[3] While Augustine had little need to theorize a place and time for Christian kingship and political history, in eighth-century Britain the very existence of the Church was precarious, and in Bede's estimation it required active kings as much, sometimes more, than monks and monasteries. Bede has more to tell us, then, about a Christian politics of time, and it is no accident that he became the first author to use *anno domini* dating in a political and institutional history, and thus to link—in a way that Augustine does not—the incarnation with political time. He elaborated what we could call a secular theology of time, whereby the necessary, ongoing calculation of time becomes a regulating practice, a way of living that in turn generates the history of the world.

Bede's differences from Augustine, along with the differences of their arguments from many other conceptions of time in the third to the eighth centuries, contravene and to an extent have the potential to undo medieval/modern periodization. As political arguments regarding the temporalization of time they unsettle the contention, which I study at length in the previous chapter, that for thinkers in "the Middle Ages" time was untemporalized, and thus apolitical and ahistorical. Perhaps more important, the political struggles by Bede and others over conceptions of history and temporality *pluralize* "the Middle Ages," and thus undermine the very categories that make medieval/modern periodization possible. There is no single "medieval" conception of time and history.

In Ghosh's *In an Antique Land*, medievalism becomes the method for countering a colonial politics of knowledge precisely because this politics relies upon the medieval/modern divide as a form of territorialization. Through this double-stranded "traveler's tale," Ghosh attempts to stitch occluded "medieval" intercultural affiliations in the twelfth century to tenuous connections and interfaith practices of twentieth-century characters, and strives thereby to open alternative historical trajectories. His narrative traces the Orientalist historiography by which the "secular" and the "religious" became mapped and reified, and his efforts to counter the violence of identity politics both critique and fall prey to periodization. Despite its well-recognized narrative failings, this book does accentuate the strictures and the limits of periodization, and tries to think about how time and politics might be disaggregated. By juxtaposing this text with Bede's, I hope to survey potential contours of such disaggregation.

Calculations

> *In the forty-second year of Caesar Augustus, and the twenty-seventh [year]*
> *after the death of Cleopatra and Antony, when Egypt was turned into a*
> *[Roman] province, in the third year of the one hundred and ninety-third*
> *Olympiad, in the seven hundred and fifty-second from the foundation of the*
> *City [of Rome], that is to say the year in which the movements of all the*
> *peoples throughout the world were held in check, and by God's decree Caesar*
> *established genuine and unshakeable peace, Jesus Christ, the Son of God,*
> *hallowed the Sixth Age of the world by his coming.*[4]

Under the sign of Rome, but with all movement everywhere suspended: this is how Bede describes the incarnation in the world chronicle contained in his *De temporum ratione*, a compendious treatise written in the early eighth century. Bede dates this entry *anno mundi* 3952, a daring and drastic recalculation of the entire *anno mundi* ("year of the world") schema, which he coordinates in this treatise with revisions and explanations of virtually all other temporal systems, from the days of creation, Easter dating, and the Six Ages of man, to the fluctuation of tides, conventional naming of days and months, and imperial dates of indiction. Organized as a comprehensive, exegetical treatment of cyclic and linear time on a universal scale, *De temporum ratione* explicates time as a regulated and regulating system that is integrated with and propelled by the histories of peoples and kings. The result is a political theology of time, not because certain kings are approved by God—although this is important to the historical and typological narrative—but because the calculation as well as the experience of time inherently relies upon political systems.

The political theology that runs through Bede's work on time engages the temporal logic of Christian tradition as he had received it from historical, scientific, and philosophical texts written over many centuries from various, sometimes conflicting, perspectives. Bede pursued this temporal logic and its implications to the minutest detail, and he is the first to combine two genres concerning time, each of which already had encyclopedic and exegetical tendencies: the technical treatise on the measurement of time (often termed *computus*), which centers on the cyclic problem of Easter dating and is thus primarily mathematical and astronomical in focus; and the world chronicle, a linear historical form that had come, with a Roman orientation and some philosophical inconsistencies, primarily from Eusebius of Caesarea, Jerome, Augustine, Orosius, and Isidore of Seville.[5] Bede's later *Ecclesiastical History of the English People*, the first history to use *anno domini* dating and thus to pin its events directly to the incarnation, further extends his method of basing historical argument upon temporal calculation.[6]

Both *De temporum ratione* and the *Ecclesiastical History* engage the questions of secularization and temporality, periodization and sovereignty that I consider throughout this book. Examination of these texts shows just how distorted are the claims, such as those I study in Chapter 3, that in the "Middle Ages" historical time was untemporalized, and "religion" foreclosed any sense of historical agency. Challenging such claims through attention to the operation of time and history in texts such as Bede's is important today, not for the sake of mere empirical correctness but because it exposes the process by which a particular sovereign order proffers its regulative practice as universal. The logic of Bede's texts is not commensurable with the "medieval religious"/"modern secular" binary, and coming to terms with such incommensurability is, I suggest, a prerequisite step in addressing the relation between "religion" and sovereignty as it is manifest in political life today.

Differential Time

Fundamental to Bede's conception of temporality—whether he is discussing Easter dating, the cosmos, or world history—is that time is a function of difference, inextricable from measurement that always requires calculation, and existing meaningfully only insofar as it is ultimately *in*calculable, its futurity open rather than determined. He instantiates this as a mathematical, cosmological, and historical principle drawn from two basic theological tenets: one cannot know the end of time, or more precisely, the "time that remains in this world" (*quae restant saeculi tempora*); and the salvation of the world, as well as of the individual, depends upon both human and divine action.[7] As I explain below, Bede scientifically "hard wires" these principles into cyclic time (the basis of celebrating Easter and thus participating in salvation history), and in a coordinated move, he inscribes them into chronological time by thoroughly revising *anno mundi* dating. He thereby foils attempts to calculate the time of the world's end, which for him would eliminate the possibility of meaningful human action and thus the ground of history. Linked by an ordered cosmos and by the central event of the incarnation, cyclic time and linear time move together but always require interpretation and calculation, and it is upon this necessity that Bede establishes the possibility of regulation and thus politicizes time. In what is apparently his own etymology, he explains: "Times take their name from 'measure'" (*temperamento*, from *tempero*: "to be moderate, to divide, to rule"). He thereby folds temporality, measurement, moderation, and regulation into a single principle.[8]

Bede secures the conception of time as difference within its very beginning, through an unusual account of creation: time began not on the first day when light was created, and when light and dark weighed equally so that "there was no measurement of hours," but on the fourth day with the creation of the sun, moon, and stars: "For He decreed the beginning of time at that point when, upon creating the luminaries, He said, *Let them be for signs and for seasons, and for days and for years.*" Only then did the sun, "rising from the mid-point of the east, with the hours running through their lines by the shadow, inaugurate the equinox."[9] Time comes into existence *as* division, with the movement of the bodies that sign its measure. Later in this chapter Bede again insists upon this beginning for time, with a further emphasis on movement: "But according to the sequence of its initial creation, the beginning of [the Sun's] orbit, and simultaneously the beginning of all time," is the equinox.[10] The choice of the equinox fastens both the beginning and the movement of time to the lunar-solar cycle, which had long been central to controversies over Easter dating. Moreover, as Faith Wallis puts it in her valuable work on Bede's treatise, this choice also necessarily involved "doing violence to astronomical realities," given the incommensurability of the lunar and solar cycles.

By linking the inherent incommensurability of the Easter cycle to the nature of time as differential movement, Bede sets up a situation whereby the necessary, ongoing calculation of time becomes a regulating practice, a way of living that in turn generates the history of the world. According to his presentation, the temporal calculations that produce the liturgical cycle rely upon all three modes of measuring time that he defines early in the treatise: time moves (*decurrit*) according to nature (such as astronomical cycles); according to custom (such as assigning thirty days to a month, or dividing an hour into segments); or according to authority (both human, such as imperial dates of indiction, and divine, such as the command to keep the Sabbath on the seventh day).[11] In this context, the recent suggestion by Andrew Rabin that Bede frames time as a language and affiliates *computus* with Augustinian language theory is persuasive.[12] As a sign system that can only be understood through human interpretation and mediation, time requires the movement from the literal to the figural, which links celestial motion to human order.

This relationship becomes most obvious at the center of Bede's chapter, which emphasizes the importance of humans as historical agents: "Observing the Paschal season [*temporis*] is not without reason [or calculation: *sine ratione*], for it is fitting that through it the salvation of the world both *be figured* and *come to be* [*et figurari et uenire*]."[13] Within the ambit of *ratione*, the reason of Paschal observance merges with the calculation of its time, so that its givenness becomes indissociable from the calculation that defines it and actively presses it into the future. This passive/active combination immediately repeats in the paired verbs of the phrase *et figurari et uenire*, which explicitly insists upon the degree to which humans generate history: as figures *of* the salvation narrative, practicing Christians deliberately bring this salvation into being, with the ratio of time (in the sense of both "reason" and "calculation") acting as the fulcrum of this irreconcilable tension.[14] The cyclic time of liturgy and the linear time of salvation history, both of which lodge within and are driven by concrete political circumstances in Bede's telling, meet at this point of tension. Despite the passive voice of *figurari*, it too conveys a particular sense of the active, since humans—as subjects— must produce themselves *as* figural through intellection and observance. In this sense, *figurari* contracts time within itself, its redemptive performance constellating past, present, and future. Straining away from this representational practice is *uenire*, the "to come," toward which figural practice arcs but around which it cannot close. For Bede, then, human subjects occupy a double position as agents of a world history that is neither fully determined nor fully apprehensible, always in need of calculation and regulation precisely because it is ultimately incalculable.

Salvation history as Bede handles it here clearly does not pit meaningless human action against an already decided providential history, as we have seen suggested by theorists such as Koselleck. In fact, the double involvement of the human subject in the production of history as Bede explains it is one aspect of what Carl Schmitt describes as a "lucid Christian faith in potent historical power" that thwarts "eschatological paralysis of all human events." For Schmitt, the idea of the *katechon*—the imperial "restrainer" who holds off the Antichrist—was the only way such a meaningful human history could have been conceptualized in the Christian Middle Ages.[15] But, like many medieval thinkers, Bede does not need an imperial *katechon*. He certainly knew this concept, which is advocated by Orosius and eschewed by Augustine, who wished to divorce salvation history from the Roman Empire.[16] In Bede's text, however, it is not the *katechon* but the indeterminacy of time itself that guarantees meaningful human history. In a qualitatively different way from that proposed by Schmitt, this approach likewise has implications for empire.[17]

The indeterminacy of time as Bede describes it does bear important functional similarities to the concept of the *katechon* and its links to constituted law and state power. In 2 Thessalonians 2, the biblical source of this concept, Paul describes the *katechon* as restraining the "lawless one" (*anomos*): in its barest terms, the *katechon* is the restraint exerted by the force of law. In his work on this biblical passage, Giorgio Agamben describes the *katechon* as "the force—the Roman Empire as well as every constituted authority—that clashes with and hides . . . the state of tendential lawlessness that characterizes the messianic, and in this sense delays unveiling the 'mystery of lawlessness.'"[18] This structure accords with Bede's handling of time, in that his insistence upon time as differential movement fixed to the incommensurability of the Easter cycle engages the "mystery of lawlessness," but figures it as temporal *incal*culability. The timing of Easter is a "sacred mystery," Bede writes in a later chapter, and its proper celebration "shows outwardly what it holds within by means of the order of time."[19] The proper celebration of Easter, manifested as a lived order through the paradoxical agency of *et figurari et uenire*, requires and executes a regulated order of time. This regulation, which for Bede is not dissociable from politics, holds off the disorder inherent in the ultimate incalculability of time.

As outward display this order constitutes an inhabited practice, and Bede's *Ecclesiastical History*, to which I turn later in this chapter, makes it clear that this temporal observance is intrinsically political, is secured by kings, and is a means of establishing church unity throughout the entire world (*toto orbe*). As Clare Lees describes this process more generally, it "constitutes itself *as* traditional," and in its exercise of authority as social power it attests "the historical dynamism of traditional religious writing."[20] In continuing his chapter on the beginning of time, Bede explicitly states that the Paschal season begins with the equinox so that its observation will *not* pertain "only to God or only to man" (exegetically read as the sun and the moon). The "order of time" pertains to the world, but nonetheless can neither be self-apparent nor self-fulfilling. This is a political theology of time far more complex than that of an imperial *katechon*, which opposes two positive factors—a restraining force and an impending end-time. Bede's conception, by contrast, recognizes that such logic appropriates and at least partially cancels out "mystery" and messianic promise (the "to come" of *venire*), the futurity of which—along with its meaningfulness for each individual—becomes moot when cast as an already determined form. In a movement that does not lend itself to dichotomy, time for Bede calls measure and regulating practice into being as a way of arcing toward an unknown and incalculable, but always promised, future.

These are the terms under which Bede describes the moment of the incarnation as movement "held in check" (*conpressis*, from *comprehendo*, "to bind together, seize, arrest, apprehend"). Here is his world chronicle entry for 3952 again:

In the forty-second year of Caesar Augustus, and the twenty-seventh [year] after the death of Cleopatra and Antony, when Egypt was turned into a [Roman] province, in the third year of the one hundred and ninety-third Olympiad, in the seven hundred and fifty-second from the foundation of the City [of Rome], that is to say the year in which the movements of all the peoples throughout the world [*per orbem*] were held in check [*conpressis*], and by God's decree Caesar established genuine and unshakeable peace, Jesus Christ, the Son of God, hallowed the Sixth Age of the world by his coming.

Not just time, but all political movement is arrested. Bede's emphasis here on "movement" (*motus*: "a motion, moving, change, disturbance, political movement") gathers within its connotations both the celestial movement of cyclic time that guides liturgy, and the linear movement of political events that comprise the world chronicle.[21] These senses already connect, as I have suggested, in the regulation of, and manifestation through, human behavior. As a seizure of history, Christ's entry inaugurates the sixth age—that is, the time that remains to the world—not as a political event, but as an abeyance of politics. With this seizure of movement, the conceivability of community united and bound together *per orbem* occurs through the apprehension of time that begins to end with this coming, a structure that Agamben describes in his interpretation of Paul's letters as "the paradoxical tension between an *already* and a *not yet*," a tension that coincides with the temporality we have seen in Bede's *et figuari et uenire*.[22]

The universalizing effect of the incarnation for Bede results not from political force but from a suspension of history. Even though, like Augustine, Bede has no interest in linking salvation history to the Roman Empire, he intensifies the Roman epitome offered by his sources for this entry. He culls sparingly, selecting and distilling just a few details from the capacious narratives of Rufinus's translation of Eusebius's *Church History* and Orosius's *History Against the Pagans*, and he mentions only dates that funnel into Roman *imperium*, heightening the centralizing effect of the *pax Romana*.[23] The positive valence of this *pax* in Bede comes by way of a double negative, in that it suspends political movement, which in turn marks the impossibility of temporal fixity. The cessation of movement through the momentary annihilation of political difference singularizes temporality, and thus allows for a periodization of world history that corresponds to the event of the incarnation, yet does not attach to a particular sovereign order. From Bede's perspective the incarnation constitutes an *exception*: not an *exception* to a specific legal order, but to the very order that constitutes law and politics.

Bede's chronicle entry posits the incarnation as a qualitative change in universal time and thus periodizes, in a way that can be fiercely hegemonic, but unlike medieval/modern periodization it does not attempt to ground this change by simply evacuating history and politics from the past (as we have seen, for instance, in Koselleck's analysis of "the Middle Ages"). This entry describes what we might call a secular theology of time, irreducible to the "theological" structure of a "timeless exteriority."[24] By keeping history but disallowing possession of it to a particular sovereign order, Bede's passage entails an aspect of the nontranscendence that Agamben finds in his reading of Paul: "For Paul, it is not a matter of 'tolerating' or getting past differences in order to pinpoint a sameness or a universal lurking beyond. The universal is not a transcendent principle through which differences may be perceived—such a perspective of transcendence is not available to Paul. Rather, this 'transcendental' involves an operation that divides the divisions of the law themselves and renders them inoperative, without ever reaching any final ground."[25] Agamben is working here with Paul's undoing of Jewish law, which he interprets not as a supersession of a new law over an old law, but as a division that works within the divisions of the law. Suggesting that Paul divides the fundamental division of the law (Jew/non-Jew) by yet another division, that of flesh/breath (*sarx/pneuma*), Agamben finds that Paul renders the divisions of the law incommensurate and thus inoperative. Bede's entry addresses imperial chronologies and thus deals with a different aspect of political time, but we see in his work too a conception of the incarnation that renders political divisions inoperative. Moreover, for Bede the regulating principle of time is always divided, precisely so that it cannot reach a final ground. Yet, by singularizing the moment at which this alteration of political time occurs, and in recognizing the inexorability of history, Bede both allows for and explicates the process by which political hegemony asserts itself on the grounds of periodization. Later in this chapter I consider how this possibility may also trouble Agamben's formulation of justice in Paul.

TIMELINES

The multiple timelines of world history, as well as their political fates, were graphic and in full color in Bede's sources. In his fourth-century *Chronicle*, the seminal work of this world-chronicle tradition, Eusebius had coordinated multiple timelines by aligning the chronological systems of various peoples in vertical columns, synchronized horizontally, but moving in different patterns according to their own logic. Events and dating systems from a range of sources such as the Bible, regnal lists, and ancient histories appeared embedded in their own chronologies, whether Olympiads, regnal dates, years from a city's foundation, and so on (dating systems that we see configured together in Bede's entry for 3952), with the years from Abraham running in the margin.[26] Gradually these multiple columns reduce to one: Rome. As Wallis describes it: "As peoples and empires appear on the stage of world history, they are granted their own parallel columns within the table; as they are absorbed into the world-empires, these columns gradually disappear, until the Roman empire occupies the entire frame."[27] Eusebius's elaborate tables thus manage both to represent the separateness of histories and to synchronize these histories into a scheme that advances a historical argument: recorded history begins with Abraham, proceeds through a multiplicity of empires, and culminates with Rome and Christianity. It was, as Anthony Grafton and Megan Williams put it, "a visual narrative whose plotline no reader could miss."[28] Translated by Jerome, recopied, and circulated widely, this text offered a visual lesson on the relation between a chronological scheme and the possession of a visible and viable place in history.

Over the centuries between Eusebius and Bede historians recast Eusebius's multiple timelines into synthetic narratives and a single chronology. Orosius's *History Against the Pagans* reshaped the chronicle material into narrative form with an emphasis on Roman *imperium,* and Augustine's *City of God* utterly reconfigured it into the narrative scheme of the Six Ages and two cities, emphatically detaching salvation history from the path of Rome. In the seventh century Isidore of Seville totally recast and distilled the entire Eusebius-Jerome chronicle to a single column, with running *anno mundi* dates.[29] It is in this format that Bede takes it up, integrates it with the logic of time as differential movement, and instantiates the incarnation as a moment of universal periodization associated with sovereignty, but not with a particular sovereign order. True to the chronicle genre's encyclopedic format, any political group can exert legitimate power on the stage of world history (including the English, who enter Bede's chronicle with reference to regnal conversion and Paschal observance), but only in coordination *with* and *as* the regulation of incarnational time.[30] The proper observance of time itself becomes a governing principle, which is dependent upon human practice for its visible meaningfulness and which, in turn, is capable of either legitimating rule or manifesting political instability.

Orthodoxy in Bede's system becomes its own temporality—a highly nuanced, lived relationship of multiple temporal schemes that coordinate *imperia,* salvation history, and church practice throughout the world. Heresy and apostasy, on the other hand, evince instability and a failure to live and practice within this temporal system, a failure that registers in Bede's histories as geographical and historical distention or erasure. This is not to say, however, that heresy and apostasy lack agency. As Jan Davidse observes, Bede's sense of history allowed for discontinuity in time, since forces out of step with Christian salvation still exerted real power in history.[31] Such potential, in turn, is exactly what calls for regulation and thus a politics of time.

It should come as no surprise, then, that Bede combats heresy by recalculating chronological time. Nor is it a surprise that his chief worry was over attempts to calculate the end of time, which could either efface the meaningfulness of human history or put it in the hands of a particular political regime. In order to thwart the idea that one could identify the date of the world's end—long declared a heresy by dominant authorities—Bede thoroughly revises *anno mundi* dating, once again applying mathematics to the reading of scripture and linking cyclic and linear times through their ultimate incalculability, rather than in any positive essence. In so doing he engages a debate that had worried historians since Eusebius, who explicitly combats the efforts of his predecessor Julius Africanus to predict the future on the basis of chronology, and compiled irreconcilable chronographical data to demonstrate the futility of such attempts.[32]

Despite the efforts of Eusebius the debate escalated and grew more complex over the following centuries. In a long and complicated process that I will not elaborate here, the traditions of the "six days of the creation" had combined with that of the "Six Ages" and with that of *anno mundi* dating, which had always placed the incarnation in the sixth millennium. This correspondence gave weight to the idea that each age is a thousand years, and that the end of the Sixth Age, and hence of the world, could be calculated from the point of the incarnation.[33] Powerful theologians and historians, including Augustine and Isidore, had warned against this heresy and attempted to thwart it by arguing that the ages were of varying lengths, not one thousand years each, despite numerical appearances. Bede's intervention erased those appearances. The *anno mundi* had been based on an accounting of the Old Testament generations, as attested in the Greek Septuagint, which sometimes differs in its chronology from Jerome's later Vulgate, a retranslation of the Hebrew directly into Latin. Invoking the Vulgate as the "Hebrew truth," Bede recalculates the generations, sorts the ages into varying lengths, and designates 3952 as the date of the incarnation and the beginning of the Sixth Age, thus dislodging it altogether from millennial calculation.[34] Just as the beginning of time has no point of existence prior to movement and measure, so too for Bede the end of the world is beyond measure: one cannot calculate oneself out of time.

Anno mundi 3952 did not catch on as the date of the incarnation, nor could it break away from recursive battles over heresy.[35] It is perhaps for this reason that Bede abandons the *anno mundi* altogether in his *Ecclesiastical History of the English People*, the first historical narrative to date events according to the *anno domini*. The *anno domini* of course carries the typological relation within itself, and when Bede uses it to political effect it does not divinize typological kings, Augustine's fear, but like the entry for 3952, brings them face to face with typology. This system *literalizes* the incarnation's periodizing function—that is, its interruptive suspension of all movement and its singularization of time—by superseding the movement of "world-time" (*anno mundi*) altogether and incarnating, which is to say secularizing, sacred time. As Karl Löwith phrased it, *Heilgeschehen* merged with *Weltgeschichte* at the point of this division in time.[36] Bede's integration of *anno domini* dating with other dating systems (regnal dates, *ab urbe condite*, imperial indictions, etc.), as I discuss below, both regulates the visibility of peoples in time, and places all temporal reckonings into a *saeculum* with an incalculable future.

Bede's insistence upon human agency in history and upon the openness of futurity certainly defies attempts to evacuate a sense of history from "the Middle Ages," but his interventions have even broader implications for the relationship of periodization and sovereignty in today's struggles over "the now." More telling than his insistence upon incalculability is the fact that his interventions were themselves part of an ongoing political struggle over conceptions of history and its relation to temporality. The prophecies and end-time calculations against which Bede wrote were not, of course, naïve or gullible perceptions of time, any more than is Francis Fukuyama's declaration of the end of history. Apocalyptic claims, as well as those of the more radical millenarianism, are politically freighted bids to control history. In contrast to arguments for a "medieval" eschatological closure that precludes "premodern" politics, we need to understand that Bede, as well as the "heretics" he combats, grasp and contend for time *as* political. As Bernard McGinn puts it, these claims are "better understood as forms of political rhetoric rather than as pre-political phenomena, [and] were as often designed to maintain the political, social, and economic order as to overthrow it."[37] As the term "pre-political" indicates, McGinn is arguing against teleologies such as those in Eric Hobsbawm's *Primitive Rebels*, which oppose the "primitive" and "pre-political" to the "modern" and the "political," categories that align, as I discuss in the previous chapter, with debates over the "religious" and the "secular."

Such arguments by Hobsbawm and similar proponents of a teleological Marxism have long been the target of postcolonial criticism, and it is precisely in combating concepts such as the "pre-political"—as Bruce Holsinger has eloquently demonstrated for subaltern studies—that this criticism has enlisted the Middle Ages as a means of writing an alternate or a disruptive history.[38] In an appropriately ironic reversal, such criticism brings the difference, or the complexity, of the "Middle Ages" to interrupt—or to *suspend*, like a miracle—the hegemony of a "modern" historical trajectory that attempts to foreclose the future. It is the struggle against this foreclosure, dissimulated by medieval/modern periodization and a colonial politics of knowledge, that I want to examine in Amitav Ghosh's *In an Antique Land*.

Memory

> *You wish it were indeed the old Geniza, but it cannot be. It is no higher than*
> *a bare six feet or so while the Geniza of the old Synagogue is known to have*
> *been at least as tall as the rest of the building, some two and a half storeys*
> *high. The old Geniza was probably left standing for a while, after the rest of*
> *the structure was torn down, but it must have perished later.*
>   *Of course, you have no cause to be disappointed. The Synagogue's*
> *location has not altered, whatever the changes in its outer shell. The fact is*
> *that you are standing upon the very site which held the greatest single*
> *collection of medieval documents ever discovered.*[39]

Taking as its point of departure not a void, but the trace of a void made
sentient by desire and incarnated through scholarship, Amitav Ghosh's
In an Antique Land attempts to interrupt contemporary ethnic, religious,
and nationalist violence with life stories from a "medieval" past. True to
this spirit of interruption, the book oscillates between times and
between genres, "in such a way as to make it a constitutively ambiguous
text that can be read as a novel, an autobiography, a traveler's tale, a
quasi-ethnography, and in the final analysis, an intimation of a tragic
philosophy of history."[40] The absent void of what was once the Cairo
Geniza stands in part for the dilemmas of writing a subaltern history,
that of a slave who did not write, and whose life is attested, scrappily and
second-hand, on fragments.

   Central to the linkage between Ghosh's "medieval" and "modern"
narratives is a group of fragments from the Geniza, the story of which
stands as a figure for the movement of history, and in the former space
of which the reader is situated in the passage above. The two main
strands of the book, the Indian narrator's anthropological quest among
rural Egyptian villagers and his reconstructed story of a twelfth-century
Jewish trader and his Indian slave, are linked by a narrative of historical
methodologies—the colonial process of making and effacing a void at
the center of history, and the counterprocess of squeezing an alternate
history out of the colonial archive.

   The history of the Geniza comes to us in the narrator's authoritative,
scholarly voice, one of his many voices that correspond to the book's
play across genres. In the style of the Geniza's foremost scholar, S. D.
Goitein, the narrator explains:

The Synagogue's members followed a custom, widespread at the time, of depos-
iting their writings in a special chamber in the synagogue so that they could be
disposed of with special rites later. This practice, which is still observed among
certain Jewish groups today, was intended to prevent the accidental desecration
of any written form of God's name. Since most writings in that epoch included
at least one sacred invocation in the course of the text, the custom effectively
ensured that written documents of every kind were deposited within the Synagogue. (56)[41]

The Geniza was not an archive. It did not aim at identity or history, was not initiated with documentary intent, was never organized, sorted, or consulted for historical purposes; indeed, it was destined for death without history.[42] Its nonarchival function should of course not be taken as evidence that, as "medieval" and non-European, it is prior to any "real" sense of history, a problem I discuss in the previous chapter. Such an arrogation of history as entirely "modern" and European is a central issue to *In an Antique Land*, and as I discuss below, Ghosh sometimes gets caught in its double bind.

The Geniza was especially rich in documents from the eleventh through the thirteenth centuries, and included everything from marriage contracts, wills, trade records, ordinary correspondence, bills of lading, and deeds of manumission. Ghosh scripts the history of the Geniza's dispersal to libraries and museums throughout Europe and the United States in such a way that its trajectory miniaturizes a colonial and Orientalist politics of knowledge. It accumulated without much notice, he states, until its "discovery" by Europeans: "The visit that first brought the Geniza to the attention of the scholarly world occurred in 1864, and then, soon enough, events began to unfold quietly around it, in a sly allegory on the intercourse between power and the writing of history" (82).[43] Juxtaposed with the story of the removal and dispersal of the Geniza's contents, the figure of its scriptural invocation without historical trajectory centers the book's competing historical methodologies of colonial history and counterhistory.

Ghosh posits this total dispersal as a temporal, cultural, and territorial division, and it is this movement of *division*, rather than any positive action or space, that conjoins the historically produced categories of the medieval, the modern, and the subaltern in his book. The embattled political identities plaguing the story's contemporary scene—Hindu, Jewish, and Muslim—emerge as effects of the effaced links among these groups, in contrast to those that Ghosh finds visible and thriving in the documents from the Middle Ages. He makes the parallel explicit: the emptying of the Geniza is "as though the borders that were to divide Palestine several decades later had already been drawn, through time rather than territory, to allocate a choice of Histories" (95). It is not that what was once one history becomes divided, but rather that division *makes* histories (signified by a capital H), and like a shibboleth, enforces separate identities. Moreover, the point is not that the groups are no longer linked, for the book works hard to argue that they are, but rather that these links have disappeared from the field of official representation, and with only carnivalesque exceptions, their borders are state-patrolled.[44]

The movement of the Geniza's dispersal aligns unequivocally in

Ghosh's telling with the medieval/modern divide. In order to recoup the "Geniza world" Ghosh turns medievalist, and his reconstruction of a thriving Islamic, Jewish, and Hindu tolerance in a cosmopolitan twelfth-century Mediterranean culture fully depends upon "the Middle Ages" as a concept, a period, and an authorizing institutional field. Just as unequivocally he marks the end of the Geniza world with the arrival of Vasco da Gama "on his first voyage to India, on 17 May 1498": "Within a few years of that day the knell had been struck for the world that had brought Bomma, Ben Yiju and Ashu together, and another age had begun in which the crossing of their paths would seem so unlikely that its very possibility would all but disappear from human memory" (286). Medievalism becomes the method for countering a colonial politics of knowledge precisely because this politics instantiates the medieval/modern divide as a form of territorialization. Ghosh does not suggest that this division is utterly successful in its performance—it is not "real": "Within this tornado of grand designs and historical destinies," the narrator-archivist comments, "Khalaf ibn Ishaq's letter seems to open a trapdoor into a vast network of foxholes where real life continues uninterrupted" (15–16). The divide, he suggests, is an effect of dominant historiography and institutionalized categories—categories that persistently get overturned or falsified in his twentieth-century narrative, but that tighten their grip on the imagination as identity politics escalate and as the resources of memory are more intensively policed. However we want to read this book, memory and the ethics of memory are the issues at stake, and periodization is taken as both poison and cure.

Ghosh's medievalism and his "golden age" of the Geniza world have prompted conflicting, sometimes sharp response, the duality of which refracts the political structure of periodization that I have been studying throughout this book. Bruce Holsinger recognizes Ghosh's performance as a medievalist: "Ghosh virtually reinvents himself as a medieval archivist," he writes, "acquir[ing] expertise in medieval codicology, paleography, and philology to excavate a life from the material remains of the premodern archive." He sees Ghosh's methods and his recovery project as attuned to the processes and challenges of medievalists' archival work: "Ghosh's medievalist performance takes place in the service of . . . a project in which a company of past and present medievalists have taught him to sort through the complex web of discourse, obfuscation, and representation that separates Bomma and MS H.6 from 'the stage of modern history.'"[45] Generously read, this performance can be seen as the adoption of a persona, one of the many voices of the book, a performance that can also be understood with reference to Orientalism. Ghosh turns *doppelgänger*, we might say, to the Orientalist scholar, adopting the catachrestic strategy described by Gayatri Spivak as "reversing, displacing, and seizing the apparatus of value-coding.''[46] This scholarly mimesis juts against the narrator's outrage elsewhere in the book at disciplinary "patterns of the Western academy," which, for instance, sort Jewish Egyptian saints and miracles out of "religion" and into "folklore" (342).

The book calls attention to the irony of mimetic performance and the staging of identity, most overtly in those moments of the narrator's discomfiture as, in Ato Quayson's terms, he is "raised to the level of an emblematic stereotype of Indianness" and "his own authority as an ethnographer is constantly undermined by various inversions of the ethnographic gaze."[47] Early in the book, for instance, the narrator ("Amitab" to his Egyptian friends) engages in light self-mocking to redirect the deep cultural implications of stereotypes and religious symbols. After an exasperating exchange with his young friend Jabir, which first made him seem ignorant of "sex" (he was unaware of the idiomatic term), and then revealed that he was not circumcised (hence "impure" in Arabic), he takes an evening walk and comes across Jabir and his young friends. Regaling in his superior position, Jabir announces the ignorance of Amitab, and wishes to demonstrate:

> Taking hold of my elbow he led me to the edge of the canal. "Look at that," he said, pointing at the reflection of the full moon on the water. "What is it? Do you know?"
>
> "Of course I know," I scoffed. "It's Ahmed, Shaikh Musa's son, shining his torch on the water."
>
> There was a hushed silence and Jabir turned to cast the others a triumphant look while I walked on quickly.
>
> "No, ya Amitab," one of the boys said, running after me, his voice hoarse with concern. "That's not so. It's not Ahmed shining his torch in the water—that's a reflection of the full moon." (64)

In an Antique Land is in part a critique of anthropological hubris, and the multiple inversions of such passages—in which "the anthropologist is thought to be primitive by the people he is supposed to be studying,"[48] and in which he in turn mimics the position projected upon him in the doubly convoluted terms of nature and technology—stage the instability of identities and the potential of affect (the boy's concern) to undo institutionalized limits. Chief among these limits is circumcision, to which the book repeatedly turns as the embodied inscription of, as well as the body's conscription in, the intensified order of "religion" and politics. In a manner that resonates, perhaps, with Carolyn Dinshaw's argument for "affective relations across time," the connections that Ghosh-as-medievalist weaves for both his twelfth- and his twentieth-century characters, and that he attempts to cultivate between his readers and the intercultural lives of those characters, depends upon such ironic staging of unstable identity in order to clear space for the already existent, more stable tendency toward affective relations that, the book argues, might counter the violence of narrow identity politics if given mnemonic resources.

It is nonetheless the case, as Kathleen Biddick argues in her trenchant critique of *In an Antique Land*, that Ghosh's "periodization of a medieval Golden Age superseded by modern colonialism" has disturbing implications, particularly with respect to its beneficent vision of "medieval slavery." Biddick observes that "for Ghosh slavery during the Golden age did not demean, but produced links 'that were in some small way ennobling—human connections, pledges of commitment, in relationships that could just as well have been a matter of mere exchange of coinage.'"[49] She also notes the similarity of this presentation of medieval slavery to that of Ghosh's source, S. D. Goitein, "who left Germany in 1923 for Palestine, [and] wrote *Jews and Arabs* for an American audience, during the period of the formation of the Israeli state after World War II. Goitein wished to trace a history of tolerant contact between Jews and Arabs that could serve as a model for future relations in the Middle East."[50] This history links the critical matrix of Ghosh's narrative to that of Goitein's German contemporaries such as Schmitt, Benjamin, and Löwith, as well as Kantorowicz and Auerbach, all of whom were likewise concerned, obviously, with the relation of medieval forms of domination and sovereignty to pre- and postwar politics. It links as well to the narrative of feudal law and slavery that I trace in Chapters 1 and 2. By redeploying Goitein's figure of a golden Middle Ages, Ghosh risks confirming one aspect of colonialism's periodizing logic: the Middle Ages serves as an idealized space of origin for modern identities, an erasure that denies long histories of oppression, and one that medievalists have worked for decades to disrupt. It is also the case, however, that Ghosh's narrative wedges against the other side of periodizations's paradoxical logic: the Middle Ages serves as the despised space of barbarism from which a rational, enlightened modernity could emerge, a historicist model that relegated slavery to a dark, usually "feudal" past, and that effaces slavery from "modern" Europe's civil story. The question becomes whether irony and mimicry can suspend the terms of this double bind.

Several other double binds precede and complicate the histories of Ghosh's narrative. Mark Cohen, a former student of Goitein and a leading Geniza scholar whom Ghosh visited for instruction in deciphering Geniza manuscripts, has detailed the political history of the myth of an "interfaith utopia" under medieval Islam.[51] Used for centuries as a counter to the "lachrymose history" of Jews under Christendom, and in the nineteenth century as a means of "challenging supposedly liberal

Christian Europe to make good on its promise of political equality," this myth went unchallenged until the late 1960s, when it was turned to anti-Semitic effect, in an argument that "Arab hatred and anti-Semitism would end, and the ancient harmony would be restored, when Zionism abandoned both its 'colonialist' and its 'neo-crusader' quest."[52] These versions of "myth and countermyth" as Cohen terms them, continue in virulent strains today, and Ghosh attempts to deal with their complexities and implications in the later sections of the book. As the two strands of the narrative weave tighter and tighter, state violence increasingly weighs on the minds and the lives of his characters as they age: in the 1140s Christian crusaders massacre Jews, and armies of the Almohad dynasty massacre both Christians and Jews; in the late 1980s, Israeli-Palestinian tensions as well as the Gulf war economy constrain and alter the lives of the Egyptian villagers and send many into diaspora. As Biddick observes, there are few Jews in the latter Egyptian narrative, which instead takes the Hindu-Muslim conflict as the vehicle for excavating the difference between interpersonal relationships and violence based on partitions.

Yet another dilemma of periodization surfaces, quite literally, on the back cover of *In an Antique Land*, in a blurb that echoes anthropology at its worst: "Once upon a time an Indian writer named Amitav Ghosh set out to find an Indian slave, name unknown. . . . The journey took him to a small village in Egypt, where medieval customs coexist with twentieth-century desires and discontents." Aside from the obvious "denial of coevalness" in Fabian's sense,[53] this blurb conjures the trope of the "medieval village" superimposed upon colonized peoples, especially by the British in India. In so doing it connects as well to the colonial historiography of early medieval England, which is also integral to the "History" Ghosh accosts. John Ganim explains this lineage:

How could the evidence of the great Indian past be reconciled with the colonial challenge of governing an inferior people and a decadent civilization? . . . Again, the Middle Ages turned out to be a useful metaphor. The deep layers of Indian civilization and its hidden affinities with the West were imagined as medieval, as in the Victorian legal scholar Henry Maine's parallel of the Anglo-Saxon and Indian village. . . . Maine appropriated from Kemble, the great Anglo-Saxonist, an idealization of the Anglo-Saxon village and pointed to similarities with the Indian village. Where the English were in the Middle Ages, so was India in the mid-nineteenth century.[54]

Clearly a gambit for mass-market appeal, the publisher's blurb nonetheless refracts the risks Ghosh takes in stitching the intercultural exchanges between his narrator and the Egyptian villagers to those of his twelfth-century characters, and by emphasizing, at the same time, the inexorable pressures of "modernization" on contemporary Indian and

Egyptian lives. The double bind of periodization precedes and conditions any engagement with this history.

But if we grant that *In an Antique Land* tries both to write a subaltern
history against "History," *and* to work against the trajectory of histories
altogether, in a mode reminiscent of the Geniza's accumulated papers—
bits of many different lives, times, and experiences rustling together
without teleological motive—we might find an attempt at undoing the
strictures that align periodization and "religious" violence. Near the
center of the book, the narrator tells an encrypted story, a sort of Oedi-
pal origin story from his childhood in East Pakistan shortly after the Partition, a story he says he could never bring himself to tell his Egyptian
friend. His father became a diplomat to the new Muslim-majority state,
and his Hindu family moved into a newly built house that "had a large
garden, and high walls ran all the way round it" (206). The garden
would occasionally fill with large groups of people—Hindu refugees,
though the child did not know it—who would stay a few days and then
be gone. The story centers on a night during the 1964 uprisings, when
Hindus filled the garden and an angry mob gathered outside the walls.
Just in time the police arrive, having been alerted by some of the family's
Muslim friends. The "moral" of the story, which is delivered quite
directly, recalls the many prior discussions of circumcision and "purity/
impurity"—first by focusing on "sanity," and then explicitly on circumcision and inscribed bodies, which is also to say the historical division of
law: "I discovered that on the very night when I'd seen those flames
dancing around the walls of our house, there had been a riot in Calcutta
too, similar in every respect except that there it was Muslims who had
been attacked by Hindus. But equally, in both cities—and this must be
said, it must always be said, for it is the incantation that redeems our
sanity—in both Dhaka and Calcutta, there were exactly mirrored stories
of Hindus and Muslims coming to each others' rescue, so that many
more people were saved than killed" (209–10). Where people were
killed the stories were "always the same . . . of women disemboweled for
wearing veils or vermilion, of men dismembered for the state of their
foreskins" (210). What redeems "sanity" here is not religious purity, but
separation from the "purifying" law that partitions: the garden wall separating Hindu and Muslim, the Partition of India, the division of Palestine, and the divisions that divide time as well as territory, "to allocate a
choice of Histories."

In this, Ghosh's passage offers some similarities to Agamben's reading
of Paul, which I discuss above in the context of Bede's work on the temporal politics of the incarnation. In Ephesians 2:14, for instance, Agamben finds Paul suggesting that the " 'wall of separation' that the Messiah
abolished coincides with the 'law of the commandments' [*nomos ton ento-*

lōn], which divided men into 'foreskin' and 'circumcised.'"[55] Whereas
Jewish law had divided Jews from non-Jews, Paul's messianism "divides
the divisions of the law themselves and renders them inoperative."[56]
Despite this similarity in regard to the suspension of laws that partition,
Agamben's and Ghosh's texts operate quite differently with regard to
periodization.

Agamben notes that Paul's rendering "inoperative" of the law on the
basis of the transformative "messianic event" holds similarities to
Schmitt's "state of exception." He argues, however, that because the
state of exception relies upon the distinction inside/outside, and Paul's
division annuls this distinction, Paul's messianic fullness of the law
supersedes the state of exception: "The messianic *plērōma* of the law is
an *Aufhebung* of the state of exception."[57] Agamben does not discuss
"decision" here, for contrary to Schmitt he wants to think an undoing
of law that does not itself become law, does not "decide." The incommensurate divisions for which he argues do not add up to positive law;
however, Agamben works with a formulation that, like Antonio Negri's
discussed above, has "a singular relationship to time," and thereby substitutes a periodizing event for the positive law he wishes to suspend.[58] In
Agamben's case, periodization rests upon the transformative messianic
event, which replaces inside/outside with before/after. Agamben discusses this event in terms of the "transformation that every juridical
status and worldly condition undergoes because of, and only because of,
its relation to the messianic event," by which he wishes to give it a general, not an exclusive, application. Nonetheless he can construe the
terms of this transformation only by demonstrating that Paul renders
inoperative a *particular* law—that is, "Jewish law"—which he works hard
to reify and homogenize as existing a priori.[59] It seems to me that the
transformation Agamben reads in Paul operates as a decision in
Schmitt's sense—a decision that there has been an exception, and that
transforms political life based upon its relation to a homogeneously
identified people. This is a periodizing decision with historical debts and
implications. It is difficult to be rid of Schmitt.

Ghosh's story, at least in part, seems to operate differently, although
I am not suggesting that it tries to offer a comprehensive philosophy,
nor that it ultimately succeeds. Here, the Hindus and Muslims who come
to each others' rescue do not act toward each other on the basis of purifying or "inscribed" law. To the extent that this law would "partition"
them, we could say that they render it inoperative, but not on the basis
of an originary messianic event. Nor do they act toward each other on
the basis of abstract principles of tolerance or universal human rights
(that is, other versions of transcendence or "theology") that come with
origins that regulate time. Rather, like Ghosh's narrator and the Egyp-

tian villagers, and like his twelfth-century characters, they act upon shared experience, a mnemonic basis other than divisive laws engendered in violence. There is nothing idyllic here—the garden is more a refugee camp than an Eden, and rescue means calling the police. But there is the suggestion that together stories and the work of memory can continually undo the partitions of sovereign decision, not the least of which is the medieval/modern divide. "We need histories of transgressive possibility," D. Vance Smith reminds us, "because we need to more fully understand the routes by which and in which things are forgotten, the rhythms of prohibition and pleasure that call us to ourselves in our distant past. . . . To think differently about the Middle Ages may amount to thinking differently about the world."[60]

From the Archive

The Geniza material is replete with information about slaves, many of whom are named in deeds of manumission, sale, and bequest, in court records, and in business transactions made on behalf of their masters or themselves.[61] But Ghosh chooses letters from the archive even though they scarcely mention the slave whose name and life he reconstructs, not only because they allow for a rich interpersonal weave and multiple voices that defy closure, but also because the movement of the letters and the cargo they bring materializes the connections between places and lives. This movement parallels and intersects that of the narrator as he circulates in and out of the archive, from London to Cairo to Philadelphia and back again, pulling threads of stories from institutional entombment and attaching them to the problems, insecurities, and aspirations of men and women in the twentieth-century Middle East.[62] Extracted from the archive, they recontextualize the archive and its story. "There is no political power," as Derrida remarks, "without control of the archive, if not of memory."[63]

For this reason the archive also is crucial to Bede. He gathers many documents for his *Ecclesiastical History of the English People*, including letters from the papal registry in Rome. The principal model for these papal letters is of course the epistolary output of Paul, and despite Paul's insistence upon neutralizing the law of bodily inscription, we must remember that his letters worked through and were dependent upon material inscription and dissemination, and thus in their very emergence they cut back once again through his division of flesh/breath [*sarx/pneuma*], as Agamben describes it.[64] As scripted missives to the Romans, the Corinthians, the Ephesians, and so on, these letters literally incorporated the early church; yet their elevation to biblical status required that they be read spiritually. This *double* movement of letters—

that of their material circulation, and that from their literal to spiritual meaning—is the sine qua non of ecclesiastical expansion over territories, cultures, and people.

Pope Gregory I, another prolific letter writer who learned from Paul, sent the missionary Augustine to Kent in 597, and thus a stream of letters from papal Rome to the English began. Papal letters fill the early pages of Bede's *Ecclesiastical History*, and Bede, of course, would not have missed the parallel between Paul's letters and the letters of popes to English bishops and kings. "Ecclesiastical" in the radical sense (*ek-* out + *kalein*, to call), these letters called upon the English to join the church, to accept its teachings, to get things right. They are also, as Clare Lees and Gillian Overing say of Gregory's letters, "freighted with visions of empire."[65] Papal letters that traveled with the pallium fulfill the double movement I describe above in the most basic sense, in that they conveyed the material effects and the spiritual power to elevate a cleric to a bishop, a city to a see, and, for Bede, Roman over British practices, particularly when it comes to the issue of Easter dating. The emphasis on spatial and temporal movement that we have seen in Bede's work on time becomes narrativized in his *History*, which not only chronicles the material and spiritual growth of the English church, but also writes this church and its people into world history, which, as Bede received it via Eusebius, Jerome, Orosius, and Isidore, as well as from the Old Testament Samuel, meant a history of empires and kings, with empires and kings also providing the matter of exegesis: David is Christ.[66] In setting up a correspondence between the movement of letters and the movement of time, conversion, and exegesis, Bede draws from the archive a means of establishing valid political sovereignty within world order (as he understood it) for a people who lived, as he liked to say, "at the ends of the earth" (*in extremis terrae finibus*), a description that had been applied to Britain by historians and geographers for centuries.[67]

Official, authoritative, and archived from the start, Bede's letters differ fundamentally from the personal correspondence deciphered by Ghosh, yet the epistolary methods of Bede and Ghosh bear similarities with respect to the nature of sovereignty. For Ghosh, the trajectory of the Geniza's dispersal miniaturizes a colonial and Orientalist politics of knowledge that can to a certain degree be countered through an undoing of its spatio-temporal movement. The choice of letters between merchants sets up a double pattern of travel and exchange, whereby the conversation echoes the movement of the letters and the cargo they accompany. Set within a narrative that emphasizes the dependency of colonial politics upon mercantile and epistemological exchange, the attachment of the letters to a new political context demonstrates the impossibility of sovereign closure. From a very different vantage, Bede too relies upon the impossibility of such closure, just as he does with regard to time in *De temporum ratione*, but here again he does so with an interest in regulation and political rule. Both like and unlike Ghosh, who works against a periodizing cut in time that he ultimately reinstates as he writes a counterhistory, Bede balances epistolary movement upon a single spatio-temporal pivot: that of empire.

Empires roil with fluid geographies, multiple chronologies, and conflicting agendas—they neither rise nor fall neatly. Bede's *History*, however, narrows the imperial story and fully aligns the scriptural with the territorial: during the Roman occupation and before the conversion of the English, letters only go out; after the sack of Rome and the arrival of Augustine, letters only come in. Moreoever, as Malcolm Godden has shown, Bede's *History* carefully reorders the chronology of its sources, centers events around the sack of Rome in 410, and neatly correlates this event with Britain's political status. After narrating the treachery of the usurper Constantine III, Bede writes:

Now Rome was taken by the Goths in the eleven hundred and sixty fourth year after its foundation; and after this the Romans ceased to rule in Britain, almost 470 years after Gaius Julius Caesar had come to the island. They had occupied the whole land south of the rampart already mentioned, set up across the island by Severus, an occupation to which the cities, lighthouses, bridges, and roads which they built there testify to this day. Moreover they possessed the suzerainty over the further parts of Britain as well as over the islands which are beyond it.[68]

As Godden remarks of this passage: "Bede's account of British history had begun with the arrival of Julius Caesar in 60 b.c., and he uses the sack of Rome to mark the end of the period of Roman rule, leaving the island open to the next phase of occupation, that of the Anglo-Saxons."[69] Indeed, Bede's rhetoric in this passage seems to depopulate the land entirely, leaving in the Roman wake monuments that speak for themselves, and that monumentalize an imperial past now open for occupation.

Bede frames the plight of the Britons with three accounts of letters sent to the Romans, begging support against invading Picts and Scots. In contrast to the papal *invocations* that will soon arrive for the English, the British letters call out for ultimately futile material aid. The third of these letters has a land-clearing effect more visceral than that of the Roman departure: "In the course of the letter," Bede recounts, "they unfolded their sorrows: 'The barbarians drive us to the sea: the sea drives us back on the barbarians; between them two kinds of death face us: we are either slaughtered or drowned'" (49).[70] The self-damning implications of this letter emerge in the following pages, where, as Andrew Scheil notes, Bede uses a version of the *populus Israhel* mythos to compare the desolation of Britain by the Picts to the destruction of Jerusalem: "It was like the fire once kindled by the Chaldeans which consumed the walls and all the buildings of Jerusalem" (53).[71] The movement of the Britons' letters thus aligns with the narratives of Jewish defeat and exile, and with the conversion of the Old Testament into Christian exegesis. This supersession, combined with the periodization of empire that Bede has already stamped on the landscape—and not unlike the moment of the incarnation in Bede's chronicle—provides the abeyance of politics necessary for the opening of an English temporality that is synchronous, regulatory, and suited to the pattern of world history.

Like the letters of Ghosh's narrative, the movement of the papal letters in Bede's *History* materialize connections between places and lives across time. Bede's narrative preface to the *History* outlines the details of this epistolary history: on his behalf the priest Nothelm "went to Rome and got permission from the present Pope Gregory (i.e., Gregory II, who had previously been secretary of the papal registry) to search through the archives of the holy Roman church, and there found some letters of St. Gregory [Pope Gregory I] and of other popes. On the advice of father Albinus he brought them to us on his return to be included in our *History*" (5).[72] Importantly, then, most of these letters made the same trip twice, once at the time of their posting, and once for the sake of Bede's history via Nothelm, who was the intermediary between Rome and Canterbury, as well as between Canterbury and Bede's Northumbria. Nothelm brings the letters from the papal see of the second Pope Gregory to Archbishop Albinus, who occupies the see of Augustine, to whom they were first sent. Bede emphasizes this correspondence of Gregories, which for his purposes performs spiritual continuity for Rome much as Nothelm's mission relinks English ecclesiastical history—and now also Bede's writing of that history—to the trajectory of a world spiritual and political economy. But by transferring the letters from the registry where they had existed (like the scattered mentions of Britain in the world-chronicle) among letters to Constantinople, Gaul, Sardinia, Egypt, Thessaly, and so on, Bede in a sense undoes the archive.[73] Newly narrativized and contextualized, and for the first time set in *anno domini*, these recirculated letters siphon the power of the archive into a different historical order.

Indeed, the annalistic techniques of the world chronicle now enter into English history, and by drawing upon the periodizations established in both *De temporum ratione* and in his account of the Roman withdrawal in his *History*, Bede configures a chronological scheme for English visibility in world history. This is the case, for instance, as he records the date of the baptism of King Edwin, whose overdetermined conversion process has already occupied many chapters, and to whom he gives unprecedented sway in his list of kings who had held *imperium* over all the kingdoms south of the Humber. Edwin, king of the Northumbrians, "had still greater power and ruled over all the inhabitants of Britain, English and Britons alike, except for Kent only. He even brought under English rule the Mevanian Islands, which lie between England and Ireland and belong to the Britons" (149). This imperial status resonates in the baptismal dating of Edwin and his people: on Easter day, April 12 "in the eleventh year of his reign, that is, in the year of Our Lord 627, and about 180 years after the coming [*aduentu*] of the English to Britain" (187). Here, the date of Easter interchanges with the *anno domini*, embracing the years of Edwin's reign within the movement of cyclic and linear time. The years from the English *adventus* function as dating *ab urbe condite*, monumentalizing an enduring presence, but also a temporal forwardness. We should think here of the paired *"et figurari et uenire"* in Bede's *De temporum ratione* chapter on the "World's First Day." Through a very long, introspective process of conversion, and after taking council with his advisors, Edwin models himself as a *figure* of salvation history through a performance that manifests the coordination of imperial, cyclic time and linear time *per orbem*. In tension with this figuration and its contraction of time is the date of the English *adventus*, the coming and the "to come" [*uenire*], the movement toward a future that is ultimately inapprehensible.

For this reason historiography itself participates in the figural, as both model and meta-model that crafts and manifests temporal regulation. Bede explains how this works in his story of Edwin's successors. After Edwin dies, his kingdom splits and two kings succeed him, Osric and Eanfrith, who had been baptized but turn apostate after gaining kingship. This reversion and its discontinuity with the regulating temporal practice so important to Bede's narrative becomes manifest through their deaths at the hand of the tyrannous British king Caedwalla (*Brettonici Regis tyrannidem*), who kills them, paradoxically, with "unrighteous violence but just vengeance" (*impia manu sed iusta ultione*). The dysfunctional status of both apostasy and British (rather than English) rule registers in the cycles of violence it brings upon the people, and Bede demonstrates that it requires excision from political history: "To this day that year is still held to have been ill-omened and hateful to all good men, not only on account of the apostasy of the English kings who cast aside the mysteries of their faith, but also because of the outrageous tyranny of the British king. So all those who compute the dates of kings have decided to abolish the memory of those perfidious kings and to assign this year to their successor Oswald, a man beloved of God" (215). Bede's strategic rhetoric throughout the *History*, as well as what we have learned from other historical sources, warns of what Allen Frantzen has called Bede's "textual acts of suppression," the silencing of many stories like those of Osric and Eanfrith.[74] Unusual in its metahistorical display, this moment in the *History* gives a glimpse of the process by which a system of temporalization, as Michel de Certeau puts it, "overcomes the difference between an order and what it leaves aside."[75]

This moment is more important, however, for its explication of the relation between historical time and sovereignty. Bede well recognizes sovereign agency, in the sense that a sovereign, who is both inside and outside law, cannot be annulled by law. According to his narrative Osric and Eanfrith do act as sovereigns, particularly in their dissolution of Christian rule. Illegitimate though it is for Bede, their rule exerts historical force, and only an act of sovereignty—in this case by the tyrant Caedwalla—can usurp it. We must remember that for Bede the calculation as well as the experience of time inherently relies for regulation upon political systems, and these three rulers, in contrast to Edwin, do not model themselves as figures of salvation history. To the contrary, their rule disrupts the regulation necessary to generate a successful history for the world, and Bede's comment that chroniclers attempt to abolish their memory recognizes historiography as integral to such regulating practice. Osric and Eanfrith, as José Rabasa remarks with regard to apostasy and dominant historiography, abandon legitimating discourses in a manner that "systematically undoes [their] grammaticity."[76] Inassimilable, apostasy irrupts as violence and laceration: Caedwalla began "ravaging them like a savage tyrant, tearing them to pieces [*dilaceraret*]" (213). Time and scripture are likewise lacerated: Osric and Eanfrith must be *made* to be without history, precisely because historical time is a political argument, not an eschatological given.

In this context I want briefly to consider the imperial dating clauses of the papal letters in Bede's *History*, which often stage the regulating function of the connections between times. Pope Gregory I's well-known letter to King Æthelberht of Kent, for instance, exhorts the king to work hard to convert his subjects, and offers the example of Constantine: "It was thus that Constantine, the most religious emperor [*piisimus imperator*], converted the Roman state from the false worship of idols and subjected it and himself to Almighty God . . . together with the nations under his rule. So it came about that he transcended in renown the reputation of former princes and surpassed his predecessors as much in fame as he did in good works" (113). The letter closes with a traditional dating clause registering the imperial year of another most religious ruler, "Mauricio Tiberio *piisimo* Augusto," in the ninth year of his reign, eighteenth year after his consulship, and in the fourth indiction. A small detail, but Gregory's echoed *piisimus imperator* links the time of imperial conversion with that of his own Rome, and describes the terms for entering into the trajectory of this imperial history by holding up its terms and spoils to Æthelberht. Set in Bede's *History*, the letter's physical movement from Rome to Kent materializes this link even as it mimics the historical movement of *imperium*, understood to have converged in and then emanated from Rome.

The most striking example of this process is a triplex of letters from Pope Honorius: one sent to King Edwin; one to the newly appointed archbishop Honorius; and one to the *genti Scottorum*, the people of the Irish, who have refused to comply with Roman Paschal dating, which for Bede is key to unified temporal practice *per orbem*. Edwin's letter follows immediately upon Bede's description of this king's Augustus-like peaceful reign (a mother with babe could traverse the entire kingdom unmolested). It opens with a reminder that his kingship comes from God, then announces that the pope is sending two pallia, one each to bishop Paulinus and Archbishop Honorius, "on account of the sincerity of [the king's] faith" (195). The doubled *pallia*, intended to allow consecration of new archbishops without the difficult travel to Rome, explicitly acknowledge the geographical distance between Rome and the English: the *pallia* come "because of the great extent of the provinces . . . that lie between us and you." In one move, an English *imperium* is acknowledged as within Christian purview and as separate—both geographically and in the sense that it has a degree of independent Christian power.

The immediately following letter from Pope Honorius to Archbishop Honorius forms a pair with the Edwin letter in that its subject is also the double *pallia*. This letter, the only one in Bede's history that reflects upon letter-exchange itself, opens with the salutation, *Dilectissimo fratri Honorio Honorius* (thus accenting the mirrored names), then begins: "Among the many good gifts which the Redeemer in his mercy deigns to bestow upon his servants, his munificent bounty and kindness grants that through brotherly interchange we can show our mutual love, as though in contemplation face to face (*alternis aspectibus*)" (197). The geographical distance emphasized only a few lines above suddenly vanishes, and like the genealogical tie of a namesake, the binding power of letters dissolves space, bringing the distant correspondents face to face. This distilled moment, tied to salvation history by virtue of Christ's mercy, suspends time and space in a manner not unlike the chronicle entry for Christ's birth. This letter also crosses the political and spiritual, referencing the issue of *pallia* as "in accordance with your request and that of the kings our sons" (199). The problem of the distance to Rome is then repeated, this time in terms of land and sea (*longa terrarum marisque interualla*). The letter ends with a complex imperial dating clause, and then Bede adds, as he does for no other letter, the *anno domini*, thus simultaneously bringing the Roman and English church, imperial time and ecclesiastical time, into a position of perfect interchange—face to face, as it were.

Not so for the recalcitrant Irish who refuse to follow the Roman dating for Easter, and thus fall hopelessly out of time. Bede's introduction to their letter (which immediately follows the *anno domini* dating of Bishop Honorius's letter) makes clear that there are different ways of living *in extremis terrae finibus*. The Irish, Bede summarizes, are urged "not to consider themselves, few as they were and placed on the extreme boundaries of the world, wiser than the ancient and modern churches of Christ throughout the earth [*per orbem*]" (199). On the heels of this summary, Bede excerpts a letter to the Irish from Pope John I, which reveals that their earlier letter of inquiry regarding Easter dating had arrived to a dead pope. Infelicitously timed, theirs is a dead letter. After a gap in time their letter is opened and read, and they are warned of heresy and threatened with damnation—in other words, permanent exclusion—in sharp contrast to the immediately preceding mirror image of the English Church and Roman Church firmly lodged in the interchange of imperial and salvation time.

Bede held no grudge against the Irish who lived "properly" in time, as is well known. My point here is that this contrast between the English, who live at the ends of the world but within the embrace of history, and the resistant Irish, who live at the edge of exclusion and in a gap in time, depends upon the logic of Bede's periodization, and as such it schematizes the spatio-temporal nature of laws that partition. Bede's periodization does, like Schmitt's decision and like medieval/modern periodization, establish forms of homogeneity, laying claim to a *nomos* of the earth, a territorialization of world and time. Bede's grasp of historicity and temporal incommensurability, however, evinces an openness that is irreconcilable with periodization that is based upon a particular political order—or in the case of medieval/modern periodization, as a claim to the beginning of politics itself. Indeed, this openness is precisely what requires the political arguments that Bede wages in a bid for the territorialization of the Church *per orbem*.

The messianic *event* as Bede describes it is of course a "miracle": it both suspends and is unrecognizable to all existing norms, and—in the details of its structure at least—it does not revert to the interests of a state, as does Schmitt's *decision*. This difference in the structure of periodization, which for thinkers such as Bede attaches not to a political event but to an abeyance of politics, is a crucial aspect of what has drawn philosophers to reconsider the potential of "religion" and theology in the face of current ethical and political dilemmas. This philosophical discussion, however, has not considered the potential of the *event* in terms of periodization, which so often aligns temporal division with violent identity politics; nor has it considered the complicating factor of medieval/modern periodization, which puts a fold in the concepts under discussion, and which dissembles the process by which the historicity of these concepts is made to disappear. How a suspension of political order might occur or be recognized at all without reconstituting a political regime remains the enduring problem. I offer no answers here, but instead suggest that excavating the fold constituted by medieval/modern periodization is a prerequisite to asking such questions, and attempting to reimagine what "the now" might be.

Epilogue

On the morning of June 18, 2007, National Public Radio aired the following:

Pakistan, a key U.S. ally in the war on terrorism, has looked increasingly unstable in recent weeks, with discontent over President Gen. Pervez Musharraf's rule spilling into the streets. . . . Nowhere have the anti-Musharraf protests been more vociferous than in the city of Lahore, regarded as Pakistan's cultural and intellectual heartland. However, a close look at the social undercurrents in Lahore reveals that unrest in Pakistan is fueled not only by religion and politics, but also by an ancient system of feudalism and privilege. . . . .

"One of the weaknesses of the struggle for democracy in Pakistan has been precisely that we have not done away with feudalism," said Rashid Rahman, executive editor for *The Post* newspaper and a staunch critic of Musharraf. Feudalism exists largely in Pakistan's southern Punjab and Sindh provinces.

Rahman said over the years, governments have introduced land reforms intended to reduce the power of the feudals but without much effect. "Land is the source of power still for the overwhelming majority of our legislators," he said. "They are therefore large landowners with very strong, vested interests in retaining that system and keeping millions and millions of the peasantry enslaved economically, politically, socially and in every other way."

Among those playing a leading role in the anti-Musharraf protests are political parties led by two previous prime ministers, Benazir Bhutto and Nawaz Sharif. Yet corruption thrived when those two leaders held power in Pakistan, and they didn't manage to end the undemocratic grip that feudalism has on Pakistani politics.[1]

"Feudalism," apparently, is a story with more work to do. Pakistan has lately strained the categories of U.S. diplomacy and media coverage. Its status as "a key U.S. ally in the war on terrorism" vies with stories of "rogue" nation behavior: President Musharraf's dictatorial rule, intensifying "religious extremism," and political and economic corruption. These negative characteristics are precisely those that the United States would prefer to associate either with "developing" nations that it monitors and aids, or that it invades and occupies, and to keep safely distant from reports of its own problems with political and economic corruption, "religious extremism," and presidential behavior. No mere slur in this context, "feudalism" solves the problem by putting temporal distance between modern democracy and rogue nation behavior. It does so with remarkable exactitude, precisely calibrated to the history of the concept as it was mapped on Europe's past and an Indian present, always as a marker of what must be left behind. Today, after the Partition and under very different circumstances, its political clout is still well understood by the Pakistanis interviewed, who, for the benefit of the American press at least, take up the rhetoric of "feudalism" for new agendas.

In this NPR report, the difference between a potentially stable Pakistan that could act as an ally, and a dangerously unstable Pakistan that could become a full-fledged enemy, is described in terms of its inability to overcome its own past. Were it not for this temporal distancing, the problems related to Pakistan's "ancient system of feudalism and privilege" could sound eerily familiar to U.S. listeners: unchecked political power results in presidential interference with the judiciary, and kinship bonds abet election-rigging. Pakistan must successfully overcome this "ancient" past by making the transition from feudalism, "a system where money and muscle matters," to democracy, "a presidential system like that in the United States." There seems to be no irony intended.

Conditions in Pakistan and the United States are of course quite different, but "feudalism" monitors the history of this difference as well. It allows reports such as this to deflect recent political events, and to attribute current problems in nations such as Pakistan simply to "ancient," ostensibly endemic, cultural factors. This story of an "ancient system of feudalism" forgets, remarkably enough, the reorganization of land under the East India Company and centuries of colonial rule, as well as colonialism's parting gift of the Partition that caused massive migration and constituted India and Pakistan as political entities and religious enemies.

"Feudalism"—the story of a past that kept "millions and millions of the peasantry enslaved," a story written as a means of placing slavery in Europe's past and elsewhere so that Europe's, and then America's, story of rising political freedom and democracy could unfold as antithetical to that slavery and subjugation, even though the history of this democracy has developed hand in hand with the enslavement and economic oppression of millions and millions of people—continues to do its job.

So too does "secularization," which also turns political difference into temporal distance. Its performance today is more complex, volatile, and ubiquitous than that of "feudalism," primarily because its narrative has come under direct fire. When it can be boldly stated that "secularism is a name Christianity gave itself when it invented religion, when it named its other or others as religions," the gig is up, so to speak.[2] Such a statement could only come after Christianity's claim to secular, universal principles has been met with real force, a circumstance that has so changed the world political terrain that response on all sides must come—and ever more intensively does come—in the language of "religion."

The political currency of feudalism and secularization returns us to the question "Where is the Now?" which, I have suggested, is the appropriate question to be asked about medieval/modern periodization. The assumption that "the Middle Ages" actually existed as a meaningful entity, and that it was "religious" and "feudal," bulwarks the persistent determination to ignore the historicity of fundamental political categories. The problem with the "grand narrative" of the West is not simply one of linearity and the myth of "progress." More crucially, it is a problem of the formation of concepts in conjunction with periodization, a process that retroactively reifies categories and erases their histories. If the future is to be open, rather than already determined, then periodization must come undone.

Notes

Introduction

1. Bede, *De temporum ratione*, ed. Charles W. Jones, 274. Tr. Faith Wallis, *The Reckoning of Time*, 13. For the distinctiveness of Bede's etymology, see Wallis's note to this passage. According to the *Oxford Latin Dictionary*, *tempere* derives from *tempus*.

2. For discussion of the history of etymological practice prior to Bede, see the introduction to Isidore's *The Etymologies of Isidore of Seville*, 11.

3. For discussion of Bede and the idea of the *anno domini*, see Deliyannis. In his world chronicle included in *De temporum ratione*, Bede uses *anno mundi* dating, but his *Ecclesiastical History of the English People* uses the *anno domini*. The point is not that Bede was the first to conceptualize *anno domini* dating, which had occasionally been used in charters, but rather the importance of its use in a political narrative. Bede relies heavily upon divisions of time for his arguments about ecclesiastical and political dating, which I discuss at length in Chapter 4.

4. Versions of this argument, which I will examine in more detail below, can be found in Kosseleck, *Futures Past*, Certeau, *The Writing of History*, and Osborne, *The Politics of Time*.

5. One fairly recent foundation for this common argument is that of Jacques Le Goff in his well-known essays "Merchant's Time and Church Time in the Middle Ages" and "Labor Time in the 'Crisis' of the Fourteenth Century," *Time, Work, and Culture in the Middle Ages*, 29–42 and 43–52. Although Le Goff often nuances his argument and warns against exaggeration, he provides a neat template for strict periodization between an ecclesiastical, agrarian, providentially oriented Middle Ages and a secular, commercial, and humanist modern age. His scheme has been taken up as shorthand for validating simple divisions between "medieval" and "modern" conceptions of time.

6. Johannes Fabian, *Time and the Other*, xl.

7. Fabian, *Time and the Other*, 11–12.

8. Fabian, *Time and the Other*, 26. At this point in his argument Fabian recognizes but dismisses in a note Kenelm Burridge's argument in *Encountering Aborigines*, and comments that "where I see breaks and discontinuity, he [Burridge] regards the Christian conception of otherness as the main continuous source of anthropological curiosity. This leads him to ascribe a fundamental role to missionary practice as a model for anthropology."

9. This phrase comes from the description of Fabian's argument by Matti Bunzl, in his foreword to the second edition of *Time and the Other*, x.

10. Masuzawa, *Invention of World Religions*, 20. For further, detailed discussion of this process, see Perkins, *Christendom and European Identity: The Legacy of a Grand Narrative Since 1789*; see also Lila Abu-Lughod, "The Debate About Gender, Religion, and Rights."

11. I discuss the temporal implications of this relationship with "democracy" in the Epilogue to this book.

12. See, for example, Wallace, *Premodern Places* and "Periodizing Women"; Holsinger, *The Premodern Condition*; Davis, "National Writing in the Ninth Century"; Lampert, "Race, Periodicity and the (Neo)Middle Ages"; Fuchs and Baker, "The Postcolonial Past"; Ingham and Warren, *Postcolonial Moves*. A recent special issue of the *Journal of Medieval and Early Modern Studies* on the topic of "Medieval/Renaissance: After Periodization," ed. Jennifer Summit and David Wallace, offers rich discussions of this topic, although it appeared too late for me to engage them here.

13. Dipesh Chakrabarty, *Habitations of Modernity*, xix–xx. Chakrabarty has been criticized within postcolonial studies for appearing to suggest that non-Western societies exhibit traces of the past, and for valuing the time of "gods and spirits" in a way that plays into the hands of religious extremism. As I discuss in Chapter 3, both sides of this argument are caught up in binaries instituted through periodization.

14. As Julia Reinhard Lupton notes, this supersessionary structure is one of the "foundational principles of modern periodization per se." *Afterlives of the Saints*, 23. See also Biddick, *The Typological Imaginary*. I address this issue at length in Chapter 4.

15. We find, for example, both mass-market textbooks and postcolonial novels adopting this organization. See *The Longman Anthology of World Literature*, ed. David Damrosch, which divides all world literature into two volumes and six sub-categories: Volume 1: *The Ancient World, The Medieval Era* (fourth through the fourteenth centuries), *The Early Modern Period*; Volume 2: *The Seventeenth and Eighteenth Centuries, The Nineteenth Century*, and *The Twentieth Century*. For the interrelation of medievalism and Orientalism, see Ganim, *Medievalism and Orientalism*.

16. Fabian, *Time and the Other*, 31.

17. Lowe and Lloyd, *The Politics of Culture in the Shadow of Capital*, 1.

18. This is the case even though a globalized Middle Ages can also, conversely, offer a means of narrating a resistant participation in those forms. For examples of resistant uses of medievalism in colonies and former colonies, see Davis and Altschul, *Medievalisms in the (Post)Colony*.

19. As Le Goff has recently phrased it, periodization is a way of "controlling time," and of "defining and assigning a date to the construction of a meaningful identity." See his "Maîtriser le temps," *Temps et Histoire*, 2 (2004), 19, 20.

20. Chakrabarty, "Where Is the Now?" The question "When Was the Middle Ages?" was the topic of a plenary session of the meeting of the Medieval Academy of America, Toronto, 2007. The main focus of the panel was the assignment of certain dates for the beginning and end of the Middle Ages.

21. See especially Donald R. Kelley, "De Origine Feudorum: The Beginnings of an Historical Problem"; J. G. A. Pocock, *The Ancient Constitution and the Feudal Law*. Susan Reynolds has questioned this historiography, and briefly analyzes it in her *Fiefs and Vassals: The Medieval Evidence Reinterpreted*.

22. As an adjective, "feudal" had been current since at least the tenth century, but it had no corresponding noun. See Marc Bloch, *Feudal Society*, vol. 1; J. Q. C. Mackrell, *The Attack on "Feudalism" in Eighteenth-Century France*.

23. See especially Benjamin's "Storyteller," in *Illuminations*, 89.

24. Reynolds, *Fiefs and Vassals*. See especially her introduction.

25. For discussion of the denomination of "feudal*ism*," see R. J. Smith, *The*

Gothic Bequest: Medieval Institutions in British Thought, 1688–1863. In France, *féodal-ité* was coined in the late eighteenth century. See Bloch, *Feudal Society*, vol. 1; Mackrell, *The Attack on "Feudalism" in Eighteenth-Century France.*

26. Schmitt, *Political Theology*, 7. I discuss Schmitt at length in Chapter 3.

27. See for instance, Holsinger, *The Premodern Condition*; Dinshaw, *Getting Medieval*; Ganim, *Medievalism and Orientalism*; Frantzen, *Desire for Origins*; Smith, *The Household Imaginary*; Cole, "What Hegel's Master/Slave Dialectic Really Means." In her forthcoming *Memory's Library*, Jennifer Summit discusses the "double effort of rejection and recovery" underlying the formation of early modern libraries in the context of building a new national identity.

28. Holsinger, *The Premodern Condition*, 4, 6.

29. For discussion in a different context of the retrospective writing of a narrative for the "rise of the West" and its relation to periodization, see Janet Abu-Lughod, "On the Remaking of History: How to Reinvent the Past."

30. Scholars who have tried to approach the history of the concept of the Middle Ages through study of terms such as "medieval" and its Latin and various vernacular cognates have declared surprise at the paucity of information such a study yields. See Robinson, "*Medieval*, the *Middle Ages*," Gordon, "*Medium Aevum* and the Middle Age," as well as Mommsen, "Petrarch's Conception of the 'Dark Ages.'"

31. Typical of this argument, for instance, is Peter Burke's *The Renaissance Sense of the Past*, and Koselleck's *Futures Past*, which I discuss at length in chapter 3 below. Other examples of this pervasive tendency are Ferguson, *The Renaissance in Historical Thought*; Ferguson, *The Articulate Citizen and the English Renaissance*; and Kemp, *The Estrangement of the Past: A Study in the Origins of Modern Historical Consciousness.*

32. Talal Asad, *Formations of the Secular: Christianity, Islam, Modernity*, 1.

33. For recent discussion, see, in addition to Asad, Needham and Rajan, eds., *The Crisis of Secularism in India*; De Vries and Sullivan, eds., *Political Theologies*; Bhargava, ed., *Secularism and Its Critics*; Viswanathan, *Masks of Conquest.*

34. Asad, *Formations of the Secular*, 25.

35. Ibid., 255.

36. He finds in a self-consciously "modernizing" judicial reform in nineteenth- century Egypt, for instance, the argument for religious disciplinary ritual as the intellectual prerequisite for a moral judge. He proposes a resemblance and perhaps a genealogical tie between this embodied practice and the "concept of *habitus*," traced through Pierre Bourdieu and Marcel Mauss to medieval Christian discourse and to the Aristotelian tradition that it shared with Islam. These reforms, nonetheless, marked "revolutionary change" in the legal system on behalf of "secularization and modernization." Asad, *Formations of the Secular*, 250–53. For an extended discussion of Bourdieu's "medievalism" with regard to his theory of *habitus*, see now Holsinger's *The Premodern Condition*, 94–113.

37. Asad, *Formations of the Secular*, 13.

38. Ibid., 15–16.

39. Schmitt, *Political Theology*, 36.

40. Schmitt, *Roman Catholicism and Political Form*, 17.

41. However, as I discuss in Chapter 3, Löwith had many fundamental disagreements with Schmitt regarding other issues.

42. Koselleck, *Futures Past*, 7.

43. This is an important consideration for Osborne in his *Politics of Time*, which I address in Chapter 3.

44. Masuzawa, *The Invention of World Religions*, 19.

45. Simpson, *Reform and Cultural Revolution*, 1.

46. Ibid., 12. Simpson grants that his focus is almost exclusively English, but, as I argue in Chapters 3 and 4, this political and juridical pattern holds as well for sixteenth-century France, Germany, and Italy, at least.

47. Certeau, *The Writing of History*, 6–7.

48. Ibid., 7.

49. Ibid., 5. See also 15, note 14, where Certeau suggests that the cause of this historiographical difference could be traced back "to the slow transformation of history produced toward the end of the Middle Ages by the emancipation of cities, subjects of power, and the autonomy of jurists, technicians, thinkers, and functionaries of this power," which does not undo his periodization, but rather integrates it into a narrative context.

50. See especially Foucault's *Archeology of Knowledge*, which considers the sovereign subject with respect to juridical sovereignty and ("modern") disciplinary power. As Giorgio Agamben intimates, Foucault resists a unitary theory of power by separating a juridico-institutional model of power from that of a totalizing biopolitics along temporal lines that conceal rather than analyze the nucleus of sovereign power. See *Homo Sacer: Sovereign Power and Bare Life*, 4–7.

51. See Bartlett, "Foucault's 'Medievalism'"; Lochrie, "Desiring Foucault"; Lees, "Engendering Religious Desire: Sex, Knowledge, and Christian Identity in Anglo-Saxon England"; Biddick, *The Typological Imaginary*; and Dinshaw, *Getting Medieval*, 200. With regard to Foucault's elision of colonialism, Ann Laura Stoler remarks that "Foucault's selective genealogical attention to the dynamics of internal colonialism within Europe by and large positioned the racial formations of Europe's imperial world outside his epistemic field and off his analytic map," *Race and the Education of Desire: Foucault's History of Sexuality and the Colonial Order of Things*, 91. For further critique of Foucault's chronologies and their elision of the colonial site of race, see Bhabha, "'Race,' Time and the Revision of Modernity," in *Location of Culture*, especially 247–48.

52. Both Dinshaw and Holsinger deal extensively with the work of Foucault. Dinshaw has traced a "liberatory potential" as well as a disruptive rhetorical strategy in Foucault's medievalism, which, she finds, uses "conventional historical markers" to critique conventional history, thus allowing him "strategically to clear a space" for his own project of disaggregating identity (*Getting Medieval*, 196–97). In his investigation of medievalism's centrality to French theory, Holsinger links this strategy in Foucault, along with some of his attitudes toward the juridical subject, to the influence of the medievalism of Georges Bataille, particularly with regard to the latter's work on sovereignty and sexuality (*The Premodern Condition*, 52–56, and chapter one generally). The pattern found in theorists such as Foucault of both cordoning off and identifying with an alternative "Middle Ages" is a symptom, I suggest, of periodization *already* at work in the structures of sovereignty with which they grapple.

53. Simpson, *Reform and Cultural Revolution*, 558–59.

54. Bruno Latour, *We Have Never Been Modern*, 76.

55. Simpson, *Reform and Cultural Revolution*, 558, my emphasis.

56. I use "performative" here in the sense of J. L. Austin's speech act theory in *How to Do Things with Words*, and as extrapolated by theorists such as Jacques Derrida and Judith Butler. See particularly Derrida's "Signature Event Context" in *Margins of Philosophy*, and Butler, *Bodies that Matter*.

57. Wallace, "Periodizing Women," 403.

58. The threat of such a counter-reading to the "modern" and to the categories dependent upon its integrity are evident in the shape of resistance to it, discernable, for instance, in works such as Constantin Fasolt's recent *The Limits of History*, which studies the linkage of history and law in order to prove that "all history is modern [read, "modern European"] history," and that "histories of the Middle Ages are condemned to oscillate between irreverent incomprehension and reverent idealization—or lose their meaning" (228). Fasolt claims to circumscribe his "history" as "one particular limited and modern form of understanding that is itself a party to the historical proceedings it describes" (223), but this caveat does not mitigate his sorting of evidence in order to argue for an historical break in "history" itself. Read against the grain, work like Fasolt's is nonetheless instructive for its demonstration of the exclusions upon which an intact modernity relies, and for its slippage between an insistence upon history's unknowability and, at the same time, an insistence upon the empirical status of "modern" novelty. Fasolt is surely right, however, to consider periodization in terms of political and legal history.

59. Some of the salient works by medievalists addressing this topic are Biddick, *Shock of Medievalism*; the essays in *The Postcolonial Middle Ages*, ed. Cohen; *Postcolonial Moves*, ed. Ingham and Warren; Ingham, *Sovereign Fantasies*; *Postcolonial Approaches to the Middle Ages*, ed. Kabir and Williams; Lampert, "Race, Periodicity, and the (Neo-) Middle Ages"; Spiegel, *The Past as Text*, and "Epater les Médiévistes"; Holsinger, "Medieval Studies, Postcolonial Studies, and the Genealogies of Critique"; Wallace, *Premodern Places: Calais to Surinam, Chaucer to Aphra Behn*, as well as his "Carving up Time and the World: Medieval-Renaissance Turf Wars; Historiography and Personal History"; Warren, *History on the Edge: Excalibur and the Borders of Britain*. Works by postcolonial theorists that engage the relationship of the Middle Ages and colonialism include Chakrabarty, *Provincializing Europe: Postcolonial Thought and Historical Difference*; Rabasa, "Franciscans and Dominicans Under the Gaze of a Tlacuilo," "*Without* History? Apostasy as a Historical Category," "Decolonizing Medieval Mexico," and *Inventing A-M-E-R-I-C-A: Spanish Historiography and the Formation of Eurocentrism*.

Chapter 1. Sovereign Subjects, Feudal Law, and the Writing of History

1. For discussion of the different uses of the term *imperium* from the time of the Roman Empire through the eighteenth century, see Anthony Pagden, *Lords of All the World: Ideologies of Empire in Spain, Britain, and France, c. 1500–c.1800*, 14–19 (which also discusses the implications of these uses in a colonial context); Skinner, *Foundations of Modern Political Thought*, vol. 1; Fuchs, *Mimesis and Empire: The New World, Islam, and European Identities*. I discuss the issue of *imperium* more fully below. My epigraph from Noam Chomsky comes from "Homi Bhabha Talks with Noam Chomsky," in a special issue of *Critical Inquiry* on Edward Said.

2. See Berman, *Law and Revolution II*, especially chapter 3, for discussion of this generation of humanist jurists, which he calls the "second phase" or the "principled stage of humanist legal science."

3. *Feudalism*, of course, has long moderated debates over the history and development of modes of power, whether these battles rage among medieval historians interested in military, dynastic, and state formations, or among Marxists disputing the history of modes of production. The scholarship is far too vast to document, but as samples of the former one could consider the exchange in *Past and Present* 142 (1994): 6–42; 152 (1996): 196–223; and 155 (1997): 177–95.

Examples of the latter can be found in *The Brenner Debate: Agrarian Class Structure and Economic Development in Pre-Industrial Europe.*

4. On the cry to abolish *la féodalité*, see Otto Brunner, "Feudalism: The History of a Concept," 32–61; Bloch, *Feudal Society*, xvii–xviii; and Mackrell, *The Attack on "Feudalism,"* 1–16.

5. Resistance to the idea that a "feudal society" (in a Marxist sense) is "backward" and must necessarily lead to a more "advanced" stage of capitalism is recent, and is a function of postcolonial criticism. An early, although sometimes problematic, example is Ranajit Guha's *Elementary Aspects of Peasant Insurgency in Colonial India.* More recent critiques of developmental historicism, however, take aim at the idea of "precapitalist" forms, and avoid the term *feudal*. See Lisa Lowe and David Lloyd's introduction to *The Politics of Culture in the Shadow of Capital*; and María Josefina Saldana-Portillo's "Developmentalism's Irresistible Seduction."

6. For the importance of these scholars and their relation to other scholars working on feudal law, see Donald Kelley's "*De Origine Feudorum*": The Beginnings of an Historical Problem."

7. See Kelley, "*De Origine Feudorum.*" Kelley argued forty years ago that medievalists should take an interest in this origin story, and although I disagree with his approach, which is laden with periodizing assumptions, his work has been invaluable to this project.

8. However, serfs sometimes did own property. Indeed, none of the categories typically arranged under "feudalism" can be applied without complication to the time and space labeled the "European Middle Ages." For an example of a nuanced discussion of personal and property relations without distortive reduction by feudal terminology, see Cheyette, *Ermengard of Narbonne*, especially chapters 7 and 8.

9. See, for example, the important case discussed by Walter Ullmann in "Arthur's Homage to King John." For a general discussion of the *Libri feudorum* and its history, see the works cited in note 11 below. Despite the plural grammatical form of its title, scholars typically refer to the *Libri* in the singular.

10. Polemics over the definition, essence, or the existence of feudalism have consumed generations of scholars, and I am not going to enter that fray. I am interested, rather, in the space of ambivalence marked not only by this persistent debate and its irresolution, but also by the enormous range of meanings covered by *feudalism*, and by the repeated confessions of historians that, while *feudalism* is a misleading and improper term, they must use it anyway. In a useful survey of the concept of feudalism from the eighteenth through the mid-twentieth century, Otto Brunner, "Feudalism: The History of a Concept," observes that its uses range from a technical legal sense, to the many analyses of feudalism as a social or economic system, to the vague, popular sense of political leadership by the nobility or by landed proprietors. Susan Reynolds also analyzes feudalism's wide range of meanings with a trenchant critique of recent historiography in the introduction to her *Fiefs and Vassals*. The *locus classicus* for historians' confessional despair over the inadequacy of *feudalism* is F. W. Maitland's in Pollock and Maitland, *The History of English Law before the Time of Edward I*, 1:66–67.

11. Kelley, "*De Origine Feudorum*," 228. See also J. G. A. Pocock, *The Ancient Constitution and the Feudal Law*, 1–29; and Kelley, *Foundations of Modern Historical Scholarship: Language, Law, and History in the French Renaissance.*

12. The *Libri*'s relations to canon law were never entirely distinct, as illustrated, for instance, by the insertion of a number of treatises from *Gratian's Decre-*

tum (a compilation of canon law), including an eleventh-century letter by Bishop Fulbert on obligations of fidelity, into the *Libri* in the twelfth century.

13. Three recensions of the *Libri feudorum* edited by Karl Lehmann are collected in Eckhardt, ed., *Consuetudines Feudorum*. Lehmann describes 139 manuscripts of the *Libri*, most from the thirteenth and fourteenth centuries. Mario Montorzi includes a facsimile of a glossed text in *Diritto feudale nel Basso medioevo*. For an excellent discussion of the *Libri feudorum*'s popularity, the thirteenth-century commentaries, and their use in legal practice, see Ryan, "*Ius Commune Feudorum* in the Thirteenth Century." For general discussion of the *Libri* and its commentary tradition, see Reynolds, *Fiefs and Vassals*, 215–30; Kenneth Pennington, "Law, Feudal" and "*Libri Feudorum*"; and Kelley, "*De Origine Feudorum*."

14. Pennington, "*Libri Feudorum*," 324, 325.

15. Pennington, "*Libri Feudorum*," 325; Reynolds, *Fiefs and Vassals*, 5–10 and 181–257.

16. Scholars (mainly Italian and German legal scholars) have only recently undertaken detailed study of the *Libri* in its historical context (see the citations listed in Pennington, "*Libri Feudorum*"; and Ryan, "*Ius Commune Feudorum*"). It would reward literary study to focus on this text, which deals with inheritance laws (including the problem of women's ability to inherit a fief), the relations of fidelity between lord and vassal, and offenses deserving forfeiture of a fief (for example, desertion of one's lord in battle, revealing his secrets, seducing or attacking his wife or daughter). Reynolds is mainly concerned with the work of historians, but her observations pertain as well to literary studies, which often presuppose a fuzzy, homogenizing sense of "feudal society" (as well as "feudal loyalties," "feudal honor" or the even less judicious "feudal mentality" or "feudal world"), which inhibits a nuanced approach to historical and cultural difference. Reynolds's tough polemic has inspired resistance, but perhaps Fredric Cheyette's rich and much admired *Ermengard of Narbonne and the World of the Troubadours*—which discusses shifting complexities of property-holding, social status, and oaths of fidelity without grinding them against generic terms like "feudal" or "feudalism"—will have more success as a model for thinking about such issues.

17. Ryan, "*Ius Commune Feudorum*," 63, 57–59.

18. "Le moins que l'on puisse dire c'est que ces données chronologiques et géographiques ne correspondent pas toutes à ce que l'on sait—ou que l'on croit savoir?—des institutions féodales et de leur importance à l'époque médiévale." Gérard Giordanengo, "Consilia Feudalia," 151; my translation.

19. Reynolds, *Fiefs and Vassals*. See her introduction, especially 4–14, which also briefly discusses the sixteenth-century historiography of feudal law.

20. David Lloyd, *Ireland After History*, 37.

21. Cited in Ryan, "*Ius Commune Feudorum*," 63. Tellingly, the question "Quid sit feudum?" is in the subjunctive, and might better be rendered "What might a fief be?" Ryan provides a fascinating account of the legal flexibility of the term *fief* in the thirteenth century, which he reads through the implicit contradiction of a rubric in the *Libri feudorum*: "De feudo non habente propriam naturam feudi."

22. "Ausus etiam sum, barbarica illorum librorum scriptione offenses, in libello quondam observationum scribere, ingeniorum illam carnisicinam esse, et Augiae stabulum, in quo expurgando altero Hercule opus esset." François Hotman, *De Feudis Commentatio Tripartita*, 1. In his dedicatory letter to Caspar Sedlitz, Hotman discusses his work on feudal law in the context of his teaching

in Germany, which had officially "received" Roman civil law. As a Huguenot whose politics were too extreme even for Calvin, Hotman twice had to flee France, and barely escaped the St. Bartholomew's massacre. For his career, see Kelley, *François Hotman: A Revolutionary's Ordeal.*

23. On the desire to purge nonclassical elements from the Roman legal corpus, see Kelley, *Foundations of Modern Historical Scholarship*, 19–50; Pocock, *Ancient Constitution and the Feudal Law*, 8–11; Ralph E. Giesey, "When and Why Hotman Wrote the *Francogallia*"; Julian Franklin, *Jean Bodin and the Sixteenth-Century Revolution in the Methodology of Law and History*. See also Kelley, "Law"; and with specific reference to Ulrich Zasius, Steven Rowan, *Ulrich Zasius: A Jurist in the German Renaissance, 1461–1535*. All feudists were not the same, of course. Those who put feudal law to work in their juridical projects were reacting in part to scholars such as Jacques Cujas, who produced a valuable edition of the *Libri feudorum*, but insisted on its purely antiquarian status. His stance did not prevent his opponents from using his work, however, and his investigations became part of the feudal narrative.

24. Kelley, "Law," 76. *Accursiani* refers to Accursius, author of the thirteenth-century *Glossa ordinaria*, taken by humanists as the prototype of a glossing practice that obfuscated the text.

25. See Berman, *Law and Revolution II*, 104–8.

26. I am here citing Peter Osborne's representation of the commonplace understanding of medieval/Renaissance periodization in his *Politics of Time*, 9–10. See also Reinhart Koselleck, *Futures Past: On the Semantics of Historical Time.*

27. Hotman, *De Feudis*, 1–2. Hotman's comment regarding the grammarian purists is cited in Kelley, "*De Origine Feudorum*," 209.

28. See generally Giesey's introduction to his edition of François Hotman, *Francogallia*, 20–37; Kelley, "Law," "*De Origine Feudorum*," and *Foundations of Modern Historical Scholarship*; and Pocock, *Ancient Constitution and the Feudal Law*, 1–29. On the transformed idea of the "old civilian formula" of the *mens legum* in particular, see Kelley's "Law," 90.

29. Giesey, "Introduction," 32.

30. Hotman discusses the Germanic origin of feudal law in *De Feudis*, 1–6 and in his dedicatory letter to Caspar Sedlitz (unpaginated). Hotman's plans for legal reform and its relation to feudal law (as it was attested in the *Libri* and as he culled it from historical documents) and to French customaries is too complex for full discussion here. See especially Giesey, "When and Why Hotman Wrote the *Francogallia*"; as well as Pocock, *Ancient Constitution and the Feudal Law*, 77–79; David Baird Smith, "François Hotman"; and Kelley, *François Hotman.*

31. Tribonian's efforts were part of an earlier attempt at classical revival. When Justinian became emperor (of the Eastern Empire) in 527, he initiated a program to restore the ancient glory of the Roman Empire, in part through revival of classical Roman law. His *Digest* (or *Pandects*) is an anthology of extracts arranged in fifty books. See Stein, "Roman Law," 42–47. Justinian's *Digest* was "rediscovered" in Italy in 1070, accelerating a revival of the study and practice of Roman civil law. See Luscombe and Evans, "The Twelfth-Century Renaissance," 310–16.

32. Giesey, "When and Why Hotman Wrote the *Francogallia*," 608. See also Kelley, *François Hotman*, 179–204.

33. Hotman, *Antitribonian*, 36. I am grateful to Bill Jordan for assistance in understanding and translating Hotman's technical terms.

34. Pocock, *Ancient Constitution and the Feudal Law*, 14.

35. Rabasa, *Writing Violence on the Northern Frontier*, 245. For discussion of the historiographical association of the massacres, see chapter 6, especially 230–34. On the struggle between the French and Spanish in Florida more generally, see Hoffman, *The Spanish Crown and the Defense of the Caribbean 1535–1585*. I thank José Rabasa for generous conversation on these points, and Joseph Patrouch for advice and for suggesting Hoffman's work.

36. David Wallace, "Carving up Time and the World: Medieval-Renaissance Turf Wars; Historiography and Personal History."

37. Mignolo, *The Darker Side of the Renaissance: Literacy, Territoriality, and Colonization*, 430–33; and see esp. 20 and his afterword, 315–34.

38. Kelley, "*De Origine Feudorum*," 216–17. In the following discussion I am greatly indebted to the works of Donald Kelley already cited, as well as his "Civil Science in the Renaissance."

39. The *Libri* itself included a brief synopsis of the development of feudal tenure: it was at first held at the lord's pleasure, later for the term of the vassal's life, and eventually became heritable. See the discussion in Pocock, *Ancient Constitution and the Feudal Law*, 70–90; and Reynolds, *Fiefs and Vassals*, 229.

40. Andreas Alciato, cited in Kelley, "Law," 77. For discussion of the deployment of this phrase in colonial logic, see Pagden, *Lords of All the World*; Rabasa, "Decolonizing Medieval Mexico."

41. Kelley, *Foundations of Modern Historical Scholarship*, 53–85; McNeil, *Guillaume Budé and Humanism in the Reign of Francis I*.

42. Kelley, *Foundations of Modern Historical Scholarship*, 63, 60.

43. Guillaume Budé, *Annotationes priores et posteriors . . . in pandectas*, fol. 192v, cited in translation in Kelley, "*De Origine Feudorum*," 218.

44. Some French feudists, most notably Jacques Cujas, repeated the Roman client-patron theory, though with some discomfort, while others, like François Le Douaren, distanced the *Libri feudorum* from the empire by insisting that its origin was Lombard, even as they denied its authority in France or over the French king. Kelley, "*De Origine Feudorum*," 221; and *Foundations of Modern Historical Scholarship*, 106, 189.

45. Zasius, Budé, and the Italian Andreas Alciato were known as the "triumvirate" of jurists who spearheaded the revision of civil law. A contemporary view of this self-conscious renovation is well shown by their contemporary Étienne Pasquier in his *Recherches sur la France*: "Le siècle de l'an mil cinq cens . . . nous apporta une nouvelle estude de loix qui fut de faire un marriage de l'estude du droict avec les letters humaines par un langage latin net et poly: et trouve trois premiers entrepreneurs de ce nouveau mesnage, Guillaume Budé, François enfant de Paris, André Alciat, Italien Milanois, Udaric Zaze, Alleman né en la ville de Constance." Pasquier has been detailing the history of French universities, and gives pride of place in the new study of law to his compatriot Budé. *Les oeuvres d'Estienne Pasquier*, 1:999. For a critique of the "triumvirate" conception and its historical distortions, as well as of the German "reception" of Roman law, see Rowan, *Ulrich Zasius*, 206–13 and 6–13, respectively.

46. Zasius, *Usus feudorum epitome*, vol. 4, col. 243; hereafter cited by volume and column numbers.

47. Ibid., 4:244. Zasius does not, however, credit Budé. Zasius and Budé were personal rivals, although Zasius respected Budé's work on Roman law. When Budé accused Zasius of plagiarizing him on another point, Zasius reminded him that he was not the only person in Europe with a Latin library. See Rowan, *Ulrich Zasius*, 92–122, esp. 106.

48. "Verisimile est, cum Romani in provinciis Gallia, Germania, et alibi victricia signa circumtulissent, bonaque pars militum Romanorum in provinciis remansisset, ipsos cum multum eis esset agri, vicinos pro clientulis invitasse, eisque agros et fundos nominee clientelae concessisse, atque ita temporis, quod omnia variat, processu, feuda, caeterasque id genus emersisse concessiones" (*Usus feudorum epitome*, 4:244).

49. "Hae consuetudines feudales autoritatem habent legalem, et ita allegari possunt; nec enim frustra in corpus Iuris Civilis inserte sunt. . . . Habent ergo legis vicem usus feudorum, non solum in foro seculari, sed etiam ecclesiastico" (ibid., 4:243–44).

50. Rowan, *Ulrich Zasius*, 92–122.

51. Du Moulin, Commentarii in Parisienses . . . consuetudines (Cologne, 1613), 7.

52. Kelley, "*De Origine Feudorum*," 224.

53. Du Moulin, *Comentarii*, 3.

54. "A quibus Francis primum inuectum est in Galliam. Deinde dimanauit in Insubres, et in utranque Siciliam, Apuliam, et plerasque alias regions. Verum est Longobardos Insubriam ingressos anno Christi 572" (ibid., 5).

55. Ibid., 7, 25.

56. The friendship between these two polemical figures, however, did not survive the political and religious strife that was their medium. For a discussion of their relationship and its political relevance, see Giesey, "Introduction," 8–26; Kelley, *François Hotman*. Hotman follows Du Moulin in forwarding his Germanist thesis for the origin of fiefs in his *De Feudis*.

57. Du Moulin, *Commentarii*, 26.

58. Giesey, "Introduction," 32.

59. See Gilmore, *Argument from Roman Law in Political Thought, 1200–1600*; Skinner, *Foundations of Modern Political Thought*, 2:129–30 for Zasius, and 261–64 for Du Moulin.

60. Rowan, *Ulrich Zasius*, 87. Rowan is quoting from an early manuscript of the *Usus feudorum epitome*.

61. "Et certe quia obligatio feudalis vasalli ad dominum, et domini ad vasallum, est reciproca: unde ad ea quae iurat vasallus, et quae fidei sunt, securitatis et defensionis, ad ea etiam dominus vasallo tenebitur" (Certainly the feudal obligation of the vassal to the lord, and the lord to the vassal, is reciprocal: wherefore, to those things that the vassal swears, which are loyalty, security, and defense, the lord also is held by the vassal) (*Usus feudorum epitome*, 4:278). For discussion of Zasius's decision as a magistrate in a case that found against the emperor's ability to surpass the bonds of this reciprocal relation, see Rowan, *Ulrich Zasius*, 194–95.

62. The *locus classicus* on the *merum imperium* is Gilmore, *Argument from Roman Law*. Gilmore, however, argues for a steady teleological development, whereby medieval "feudal" forms gradually give way to concepts of private property and the national state. On the *merum imperium*, see also Franklin, *Jean Bodin and the Rise of Absolutist Theory*; Skinner, *Foundations of Modern Political Thought*; Lloyd, "Constitutionalism."

63. Carl Schmitt, *Political Theology*, 7.

64. Giorgio Agamben, *Homo Sacer: Sovereign Power and Bare Life*, 32.

65. Rowan, *Ulrich Zasius*, 86–87, 100–101; Skinner, *Foundations of Modern Political Thought*, 129–30; Gilmore, *Argument from Roman Law*, 57–61. Both Rowan and Skinner find that Zasius bases his argument on the restriction of the emper-

or's power and the location of the *merum imperium* upon his theory of the contractual relation of the fief.

66. See Tuck, *Natural Rights Theories: Their Origin and Development*; Kelley, "Law"; for Zasius on the *ius gentium*, see Rowan, *Ulrich Zasius*, 99–101.

67. Kelley, "Law," 86, referring to Bodin's *Methodus ad facilem historiarum cognitionem* and his *Les six livres de la République*.

68. Du Moulin, *Commentarii*, 144. This famous passage is on page 128 of the 1681 edition of Du Moulin's *Opera Omnia*, the most commonly cited edition of his *De Feudis*. I have adopted the translation of this passage from Gilmore's *Argument from Roman Law*, 64.

69. I take these examples from Skinner, *Foundations of Modern Political Thought*, 263–64. They are typical, however, of the reception of Du Moulin and the feudists' work generally.

70. Thomas Craig, for instance, recommended the adoption of feudal law to James VI and I, to whom he dedicated his *Jus Feudale* in 1603, writing: "for, no matter how far the subdivision of the soil of Britain were carried, every acre would be held of Your Majesty in fee (to use our legal expression), and the possession of every holding would carry with it the obligations of a faithful servant." Craig, *Jus Feudale*, I, x.

71. Perry Anderson, *Lineages of the Absolutist State*, 24.

72. Ibid., 18–29, emphasis in original. Even though Anderson takes the phrase "feudal Absolutism" from the *Communist Manifesto*, he finds that generally Marx and Engels did not fully grasp the logic of the feudal nature of the Absolutist state (see 23 n. 12).

73. For a subtle, classic discussion of Petrarch and his contemporaries in this regard, see Mommsen, "Petrarch's Conception of the 'Dark Ages.'" Jacques Le Goff provides a history of the terms *antique, modern,* and their variants in "Antique (Ancient)/Modern." Wallace Ferguson provides useful (though heavily periodizing) discussion in *The Renaissance in Historical Thought: Five Centuries of Interpretation*.

74. Orlando Patterson, *Slavery and Social Death: A Comparative Study*.

75. Du Moulin, *Commentarii*, 142–43: "homagium tripliciter accipitur, primo ratione servitutis, vel quasi ipsiusmet personae. Secundo, ratione simplicis iurisdictionis. Tertio, ratione feudi. Primo modo proprie dicitur, secundo et tertio modis improprie et metaphorice" [Homage is received in three ways: first, by way of servitude, or virtually of one's own personal station. Second, by way of simple jurisdiction. Third, by way of a fief. The first is described in a proper sense, the second and third improperly or metaphorically].

76. Tuck, *Natural Rights Theories*; and Pagden, *Lords of All the World*.

77. Du Moulin, *Commentarii*, 143–46. Du Moulin gives as one example the evidence that churchmen may not give homage, since homage is exclusive and a pledge of fidelity to one against all others, and would therefore be a violation of their vows.

78. I discuss this passage in my consideration of Bodin below.

79. Du Moulin, *Commentarii*, 60. See Lloyd's discussion in "Constitutionalism" of Du Moulin's view that the king was an administrator, not proprietor, of jurisdictions.

80. Du Moulin, *Commentarii*, 90.

81. See Susan Buck-Morss, "Hegel and Haiti." I discuss this essay further below.

82. See Peter Osborne, *Politics of Time*, 70–81; and Andrew Cole, "What Hegel's Master/Slave Dialectic Really Means."

83. Osborne, *Politics of Time*, 72.

84. In the *Philosophy of History*, Hegel discusses a *Feudal System*, which he thinks of, like the feudists, in terms of the distribution of rights/power. Private power, which precluded a "sense of universality" (and hence the state), amounted to "the severest bondage" (344). When he speaks of serfs as slaves, it is not in the context of the "feudal system," although he associates the entire period (ninth through fifteenth centuries) with "the terrible struggle and discipline of slavery," through which humanity was emancipated into a third phase of self-consciousness (405–7). Thus he confirms the sixteenth century's sense of its universalizing, supersessionary project. For a discussion of Hegel's position in the history of the concept of feudalism, see Brunner, "Feudalism: The History of a Concept."

85. Cole, "What Hegel's Master/Slave Dialectic Really Means." I want to thank Professor Cole for allowing me to see this essay before publication. It seems to me that the "feudal" connection of these terms would derive primarily from their long history in law and philosophy, part of which I have been tracing here.

86. Buck-Morss, "Hegel and Haiti," 850.

87. On the interrelation of freedom and slavery in the rise of democracy, see Cadava, "The Monstrosity of Human Rights"; Hamacher, "One 2 Many Multiculturalisms."

88. Jean Bodin, *Les six livres de la République*,; trans. Richard Knolles, *The Six Bookes of a Common-weale*, 99, 106. Further citations are to this edition and translation. As Julian Franklin explains in his introduction to *On Sovereignty*, Bodin composed a French version of *Les six livres* (1576), which he several times revised, then later produced a Latin version (1586) that differs from the French in many respects. There is no edition that takes both versions into account. In his 1606 translation, however, Knolles did work with both the revised French and the Latin texts, and Franklin points out that his "judgment is generally excellent" (*On Sovereignty*, xxxvii). An edition or translation such as Franklin's, which takes recent work on Bodin into account, would have been preferable, but Franklin translates only a few chapters. Bodin often cites Du Moulin, but almost always in a claim to refute him. As Franklin notes, "Bodin perhaps is a little unfair to Charles Du Moulin, whom he calls, nonetheless, 'my colleague, the glory of all the jurists'. . . . Du Moulin's position on the use of Roman law was much the same as Bodin's." Franklin, in Bodin, *On Sovereignty: Four Chapters from The Six Books of the Commonwealth*, 132 n. 55. They do differ, however, in regard to the exclusiveness of the feudal oath.

89. *Six Bookes of a Commonweale*, 114; *Six livres de la République*, 1:229: "le droit des fiefs, usitez par toute l'Europe et l'Asie, et plus encor en Turquie qu'en lieu du monde."

90. Hotman, *Francogallia*, 297. Heller, "Bodin on Slavery and Primitive Accumulation," argues that for most of Bodin's contemporary Frenchmen, the Turks were a negative symbol of tyranny and oppression, an Orientalist counterexample of a strong monarchy.

91. *Six Bookes of a Commonweale*, 114; *Six livres de la République*, 1:230: "Parquoy il est besoin d'esclaircir ceste question, qui tire apres soy le poinct principal de la souveraineté." Knolles stipulates in his marginalia that "These Vicarii were slaves commanded by other slaves." See McRae's notes to this line, *Six Bookes of a Commonweale*, 114 nn., as well as Patterson, *Slavery and Social Death*, 300. The couplet is from Martial's *Epigrams* II, 18.

92. In his *Premodern Places: Calais to Surinam, Chaucer to Aphra Behn*, David Wallace offers another angle on the relationship of medieval/modern periodization, slavery, and colonialism (esp. 239–302).

93. See especially *Six Bookes of a Commonweale*, 40–41. Bodin considers the lack of freedom to marry and to leave the lord's land, for instance, as characteristics of this bondage.

94. Bodin makes this point vivid by telling the story of a slave who rapes his master's wife, throws his children from an upper story of the house to their deaths, and causes him to cut off his own nose and thus entirely and permanently to lose his honor (ibid., 45).

95. In the eighth and ninth centuries, Bodin relates, the slaves under the Franks rebelled, inspired by the liberty given to Arab slaves if they would enlist in the wars. Likewise, Lothair "called the slaues vnto his aid with promise of libertie" (ibid., 39). Thus, slavery aligns with civil disruption, and emancipation with national strength. Henry II's enfranchisement of manumitted men in 1549 was "done in the great fauour of libertie" (41). In book 3, Bodin suggests that slavery was returning with the civil unrest of his time (see 387–88).

96. Ibid., 34.

97. Ibid., 43–44.

98. Ernst Renan, "What Is a Nation?"

99. *Six Bookes of a Commonweale*, 44.

100. *Six Bookes of a Commonweale*, 119; *Six livres de la République*, 1:238: "Par ainsi nous conclurons, qu'il n'y a que celuy absoluëment souverain qui ne tient rien d'autruy: attendu que le vassal pour quelque fief que ce soit, fust-il Pape ou Empereur, soit service personnell à cause du fief qu'il tient. Car combien que ce mot de Service en matiere des fiefs, et en toutes les coustumes, ne face aucun prejudice à la liberté naturelle du vassal, si est-ce qu'il emporte droits, devours, honneur et reverence au seigneur feodal, qui n'est point une servitude realle, ains elle est annexee, et inseparable de la personne, et n'en peut estre affranchi sinon en quittant le fief."

101. See *Six livres de la République*, 1:243, cf. 1:240–41; *Six Bookes of a Commonweale*, 120–21. This Orientalist strain in "feudalism" will continue, in Voltaire for instance, and will become a factor in colonial logic, particularly in India. For discussion of the reconceptualization of Turks in the fifteenth and sixteenth centuries, see Bisha, *Creating East and West: Renaissance Humanists and the Ottoman Turks*.

102. See the discussion of Bodin and subsequent theorists of sovereignty in Kriegel, "The Rule of the State and Natural Law."

Chapter 2. Feudal Law and Colonial Property

1. John Selden, *Titles of Honor*, 2nd ed. (1631), dedication to Edward Heyward, unpaginated.

2. See *The Essential Codex Mendoza*, ed. Berdan and Anawalt, xi–xii. The subjects of the codex called themselves "Mexica" and are now commonly called "Aztec." The codex is named for the Spanish viceroy Antonio de Mendoza, who commissioned the manuscript at the request of the king. Peter Mason, in "The Purloined Codex," suggests that the codex may not be the same one commissioned by Mendoza for Charles V. The remainder of the codex's history is uncontroversial. Woodcuts from the codex were used for Purchas's *Purchas, his Pilgrimes*, 1625.

3. For a full discussion of Selden's *Jani Anglorum*, its position in the debates on constitutionalism, and Selden's innovations in situating England's sovereignty debates in the terms that had been prevalent on the continent, see Christianson, *Discourse on History*, especially chapter 1. No discussion of "feudal law" occurs in English writing, to the best of my knowledge, until Selden's 1610 *Jani Anglorum*.

4. Selden's early work *Analecton Anglobritannicon*, "a historical account of the governance of ancient Britain and England," was modeled on Hotman's *Francogallia*. See Christianson, *Discourse on History*, 13–14. His debt to Hotman, as well as to other French feudists and to Bodin, extended throughout his career.

5. François Hotman, *De Feudis Commentatio Tripartita*, 661. The glossary *De Verbis Feudalibus* is one of the three parts of Hotman's commentary on fiefs. Hotman discusses Littleton's *Tenures* under the entry for "feodum," probably reacting to Littleton's definition: *"feodum idem est quod haereditas"* (*"feodum* is the same that inheritance is"), cited and translated in Coke's *The First Part of the Institutes of the Laws of England*, book 1, chapter 1, 1a. With "inconcinnè scriptum" Hotman no doubt refers to Littleton's old law French. Hotman's criticism was often reprinted and well known among legists. It aroused Coke's ire. See Charles Butler's preface to the thirteenth edition of Coke's *Institutes of the Laws of England*, reprinted in the fifteenth edition, xiii–xv.

6. Spelman, "The Original of the Four Terms of the Year," *Reliquiae Spelmannianae*, 99. The difference between legal traditions in England and on the continent has long been described in terms of the insularity of England's "common law" mind (as discussed by Pocock, for instance) and to the dominance of the Inns of Court over the universities in everyday legal business. Scholars have been revisiting this history. See Ian Maclean, *Interpretation and Meaning in the Renaissance*, 181–86.

7. In the first edition of *Titles of Honor* Selden proposes: "Out of the [Carolingian] Empire, by imitation, it seems, or by generall consent of Nations, most part of *Europe* took their forms of Feudall possessions." *Titles of Honor*, 1st ed. (1614), 297. By the 1631 edition he was more emphatic: To "those Northern Nations which overran the most of all *Europe*, about the time of the declining Empire . . . we may more fitly attribute the Original of the common use of Feuds through all the Western and Southern part of *Europe*." *Titles of Honor*, 2nd ed., 274. Compare the arguments of Hotman and Du Moulin, chapter 3 above.

8. John Ganim, *Medievalism and Orientalism*, 64. For lengthy discussion of Selden and Cotton, see David Berkowitz, *John Selden's Formative Years: Politics and Society in Early Seventeenth-Century England*.

9. Some of Selden's later texts were extremely ambitious in scope. They need more study, but it seems that they are fairly even-handed in their comparative study of societies. For discussion of his oeuvre, see Berkowitz, *John Selden's Formative Years*.

10. Frantzen, *Desire for Origins*, 151–52.

11. Spelman's works, particularly *Feuds and Tenures*, are cited by historians from Blackstone to Pocock as fundamental to the historiographical understanding of English feudal law. Blackstone relies heavily upon Spelman and cites him repeatedly in *Commentaries on the Laws of England*. See, for example, his introduction in volume 1. For Pocock, see *The Ancient Constitution and the Feudal Law*, 119, and more generally Chapter 5 (titled "The Discovery of Feudalism: Sir Henry Spelman").

12. Henry Spelman, *Feuds and Tenures*, in *Reliquiae Spelmannianae*, 24.

13. Spelman, *Feuds and Tenures*, 5. Spelman argues that these practices spread as the Normans "planted" them in "the multitude of their Colonies," ibid.

14. For contemporary discussion of Spelman's response to the case, see Gibson's preface to *Reliquiae Spelmannianae*; for discussion of the background and political motivations of the case, which sought to undermine the security of land tenures in Ireland not maximally beneficial to the crown, see Paul Christianson, *Discourse on History, Law, and Governance in the Public Career of John Selden, 1610–1635*, 297–98. For discussion of the Commission on Defective Titles and its political and economic ambitions more generally, see Aidan Clarke, *The Old English in Ireland, 1625–42*, 111–24.

15. As Aidan Clarke explains: "The term old English, or *sean-Ghaill*, was commonly used in the early seventeenth century to denote the descendants of those who had colonized Ireland from the period of the Norman invasion to, approximately, that of the reformation. Later colonists, and their descendants, who were for the most part differentiated from their predecessors by the profession of forms of the protestant religion, were distinguished by the term new English." *The Old English in Ireland*, 15.

16. Clarke, *The Old English in Ireland*, 113.

17. Selden's historical claim for the existence of English feudal law from the time of the Saxons allowed the judges to invalidate the argument that the land grant in question was separable from its tenure (already judged "defective"), and thus wholly to void the holder's patent, "both to the Lands and to the Tenure." "The Case of Tenures Upon the Commission of Defective Titles," in William Molyneux, *The Case of Ireland's Being Bound by Acts of Parliament in England, Stated*, 228. The commission began with the presupposition that the original land grant by James I required tenure-in-capite (the tenure most profitable to the king) rather than the common tenure by socage by which it was held. The patent was therefore considered defective in its tenure, and the question became whether the grant of land was divisible from the tenure by which it was held.

18. Sir Thomas Craig, *Jus Feudale*, I, x. "Nam si tota Britannia in partes vel minutisisimas secetur, nulla erit, quae non in Feudo de M.T. teneatur (ut in foro loqui solemus) nulla quae non fidem debeat." Epistola Nuncupatoria, *Jus Feudale*, ed. Luther Mencken (Leipzig: Johan Gleditsch, 1716), preface unpaginated. Craig had studied feudal law in Paris, and his preface to James VI and I encouraged a unification of English and Scottish law. His understanding of feudal law as monarchial and centralized may now seem odd, but it was a prevalent view at the time of his writing, as I discuss in Chapter 1.

19. Christianson, *Discourse on History*, 297.

20. See Christianson, ibid., passim for discussion of Selden's attempts to limit crown power, and especially chapter 2 for his active role in the debates over the Petition of Right; see also Berkowitz, *John Selden's Formative Years*.

21. "The Case of Tenures," 201.

22. Corinne C. Weston, "England: Ancient Constitution and Common Law," 379–85; Pocock, *The Ancient Constitution and the Feudal Law*, 299–302.

23. For discussion of Suárez, see Tuck, *Natural Rights Theories: Their Origin and Development*, 54–57; Pagden, *Lords of All the World: Ideologies of Empire in Spain, Britain and France, c. 1500–1800*, 97–100; Tully, *A Discourse on Property: John Locke and His Adversaries*; Quentin Skinner, *The Foundations of Modern Political Thought*, vol. 2, chapter 6; Howell A. Lloyd, "Constitutionalism," 292–97.

24. Mason quotes Suárez in support of the contention that a king is bound

by former statutes and regnal agreements: "I hope it is as lawful for me to cite a Jesuit as it is for Dr. Maynwaring to falsify him." Suárez, in his first book, *De Legibus, cap.* 17, delivers his opinion in these words: "Amplitudo et restrictio potestatis regum circa ea quae per se mala vel injusta non sunt . . . pendet ex arbitrio hominis et ex antiqua conventione vel pacto inter reges et regnum" ("The fullness and restriction of the power of kings with respect to those things which are of themselves neither evil nor unjust depends on the judgment of man and the ancient agreement or compact made between kings and the realm") *Commons Debates 1628,* ed. Robert C. Johnson et al., vol. 3, 528. The editors note that the quotation is from book 5, chapter 17. See also pages 536, 540, and 549–50.

25. Schmitt, *Political Theology,* 7.

26. *Commons Debates 1628,* ed. Johnson, vol. 3, 528.

27. Agamben, *Homo Sacer: Sovereign Power and Bare Life,* 32.

28. "atque ita etiam ille modus quodamodo includit consensum reipublicae, vel exhibitum, vel debitum." Francisco Suárcz, *De Legibus ac Deo legislatore,* vol. 1, 207; trans. Gladys L. Williams et al., vol. 2, 385. Suárez argues that only "just war" can confer valid dominion, but since he considered successful just wars as punishment for a state's wrongdoing, war could validate itself retroactively, especially if waged for a Christian cause. The conquered state is then "bound to obedience and acquiescence in such subjection" ("tunc ipsa tenetur parere, et consentire subiectioni"). Ibid.

29. As early as 1901 F. W. Maitland observed the complex relation between English and continental legal traditions and the issuance of colonial charters, although not in the spirit of my argument here. As he notes, in 1632 Maryland was granted to Lord Baltimore, as was Pennsylvania to William Penn, "To have and to hold in free and common socage as of the castle of Windsor"; in 1620 the grant to the Council of New England, in 1669 the charter granted to the East India Company for the port and island of Bombay, and in 1670 the charter to the Hudson Bay Company were granted "as of the manor of East Greenwich in the county of Kent, in free and common soccage and not in capite nor by knight's service." *English Law and the Renaissance,* 32 and 93–94 (notes 68–70). For an informative discussion of these tenures and their legal history (although it deals with them in terms of "outworn feudalism") see Viola Florence Barnes, "Land Tenure in English Colonial Charters of the Seventeenth Century," 4–40. Pagden briefly discusses colonial arguments over this feudal status in the eighteenth century, *Lords of All the World,* 132–36. The relationship between Selden's astute use of feudal historiography and his other works, particularly *Mare Clausum,* a treatise on natural law in defense of England's rights to "ownership of the sea," requires more investigation. A poem entitled "Neptune to the Common-Wealth of England," annexed by Marchamont Nedham to his translation of *Mare Clausum,* directly addresses England's lag behind the Spanish and Belgians in the East Indies and looks toward glory and wealth through "North-West discoveries." *Ownership of the Sea.*

30. "translata potestate in regem, per illam efficitur superior etiam regno, quod illam dedit, quia dando illam se subiecit, et priori libertate privavit, ut in exemplo de servo, servata proportione, constat. Et eadem ratione non potest rex illa potestate privari, quia verum illius dominium acquisivit." *De Legibus,* vol. 1, 208; tr. vol. 2, 387.

31. Sir John Davies, *A Discovery of the True Causes Why Ireland Was Never Entirely Subdued,* 217. For a discussion of Davies and the establishment of the Commis-

sion on Defective Titles, see Hans S. Pawlisch, *Sir John Davies and the Conquest of Ireland: A Study in Legal Imperialism*. The conceptual link between the Norman Conquest in England and the English conquest of Ireland had already been drawn by Edmund Spenser, whose 1596 *View of the State of Ireland* argues for imposition of English common law in Ireland by right of conquest on the basis of Norman precedent.

32. Davies, *A Discovery of the True Causes*, 219.

33. Ibid., 224.

34. Spelman, *Feuds and Tenures*, 38, 46.

35. Pocock, *The Ancient Constitution and the Feudal Law*, 66. Pocock's characterization of common lawyers as insular and unhistorical has been roundly criticized, and he has defended and refined his views of this and of his discussion of historiography in his 1987 Retrospect. He does not, however, revise his statements regarding Spelman and "feudalism." In addition to the criticism that Pocock addresses in his retrospect, see Paul Christianson, "Young John Selden and the Ancient Constitution, ca. 1610–1618," *Proceedings of the American Philosophical Society* 128 (1984): 271–315; Pawlisch, *Sir John Davies and the Conquest of Ireland*; and Harold J. Berman, "The Origins of Historical Jurisprudence: Coke, Selden, Hale."

36. Ibid., 64. Pocock titles two of his chapters "The Discovery of Feudalism"—one on French and Scottish historians and the other on Spelman.

37. Pocock is in good company, of course. Virtually every historian of this topic writes "feudal" and "feudalism," used loosely and with many loaded assumptions, back over the discussion of the feudists' texts, in a manner that obfuscates the performance of their historiography.

38. Certeau, *The Writing of History*, 3–4.

39. H. V. Bowen, *Revenue and Reform: The Indian Problem in British Politics, 1757–1773*, 63. Also at issue was whether parliament or the law courts should finally pronounce a decision on this point. For a detailed account of the struggle, see Bowen's chapter 4, on which much of my summary is based; see also Lucy Sutherland, *The East India Company in Eighteenth-Century Politics*, chapter 6. For a brief summary of the debate on April 14, see "Parliamentary Diaries of Nathaniel Ryder, 1764–7," *Camden Miscellany* XXIII, ed. P. D. G. Thomas, 338–40. Blackstone's speech was apparently not recorded. For accounts of the East India Company's acquisition of this territory, from the battle of Plassey in 1757 to the assumption of the Diwani, see Bowen, chapter 1; Walter K. Firminger, *Affairs of the East India Company: The Fifth Report from the Select Committee of the House of Commons*, vol. L, introduction, chapter 1; Sutherland (cited above, this note), chapter 8.

40. After years of military and diplomatic struggle, the company received the Diwani from the Mogul Emperor, in return acknowledging the emperor's de jure sovereignty and guaranteeing an annual payment of tribute. Cited in Bowen, *Revenue and Reform*, 10.

41. East Indian affairs came into the spotlight as a national and economic issue in the mid-eighteenth century, and took up an enormous amount of parliamentary time between the company acquisition of the *Diwani* in 1765, and the trial of Warren Hastings (1787–95)—on the same issues of property and sovereignty that rested, in domestic politics, upon the theorization of feudalism. See Robert Travers, *Ideology and Empire in Eighteenth-Century India*. Frederick Whelan notes that India consumed more parliamentary time than any other issue in the 1780s. *Edmund Burke and India: Political Morality and Empire*, 4. Many historical

accounts of eighteenth-century politics efface the substantial importance of East Indian Affairs in the 1780s. The important and influential work of Pocock particularly exhibits a blind spot to Indian affairs, although he discusses empire at length in terms of the American colonies.

42. For a contemporary discussion of these intertwined issues, see David Hume's essay "Of Public Credit." For a discussion of the debates and their terms, see Pocock, *Virtue, Commerce, and History* (though Pocock never discusses the East India colonial context). For a discussion of these issues in Hume's "Of Public Credit" and "On the Balance of Power," which, as Ivstan Hont remarks, "could equally have merited the title 'Of Universal Empire,'" see Hont, "The Rhapsody of Public Debt," 321–48. Good examples of the logic employed by the various factions in Parliament as these arguments developed can be found in the 1783 debates on William Pitt's Motion for Reform in Parliament, on Charles Fox's Motion on his East India Bills, and on the West Indies Slave Trade, *The Parliamentary History of England*, vol. 28, 826–75; 1187–213; and 711–14, 1207–1210.

43. The first edition of Blackstone's four-volume *Commentaries* came out from 1765 to 1769; it went through eight editions before his death in 1780. See David Lieberman, *The Province of Legislation Determined: Legal Theory in Eighteenth-Century Britain*, 31.

44. William Blackstone, *Commentaries on the Laws of England*, 4th ed., vol. 1, 70. I will cite from this edition by volume and page number.

45. Lieberman, *The Province of Legislation Determined*, see generally chapter 1; quotation on 49. Lieberman points out that Blackstone's readers often find him inconsistent regarding the relation between natural and historical law (49). His self-distancing from natural law could have in part resulted from resistance to radical theorists who invoked natural law and original contracts. My point here, however, is that Blackstone *needed* both nature and history, even though he could not reconcile them.

46. These debates were also caught up in the question of the American colonies. See Pocock, "Political Thought in the English-speaking Atlantic, 1760–1790: The Imperial Crisis." Reasons for condemning conquest varied. Hume, for example, was against imperial wars of conquest, stating economic reasons: war increased the national debt to the degree that it damaged commercial growth. See his "Of Public Credit" and "Of the Balance of Power." *The Philosophical Works of David Hume*. Similarly, many others considered commercial domination, without the military and administrative expense entailed in territorial acquisition, the soundest economic policy. See the discussion in Bowen, *Revenue and Reform*.

47. For the longstanding debate over the Norman Conquest, including whether it was actually a conquest at all, see Pocock, *Ancient Constitution and the Feudal Law*, especially chapters 2 and 7; Smith, *The Gothic Bequest*; Klein, "The Ancient Constitution Revised."

48. V. G. Kiernan, "Marx and India," in Marxism and Imperialism, 169.

49. "Legal fiction" is a term of art, not of course Blackstone's term. As Lieberman explains, this "was a standard device used by the courts to adapt the historic forms of common law to altered social circumstances." *Province of Legislation Determined*, 47.

50. Kathleen Biddick, *The Shock of Medievalism*; see her chapter "Gothic Ornament and Sartorial Peasants."

51. Spivak, *A Critique of Postcolonial Reason: Toward a History of the Vanishing Present*, 82.

52. Cited in Bowen, *Revenue and Reform*, 68, from British Library Add. MSS 18469, f.77.

53. Cited in Bowen, *Revenue and Reform*, 69, from British Library Eg. MSS 218, f. 134.

54. See Sutherland, *The East India Company in Eighteenth-Century Politics*. See also Travers, *Ideology and Empire in Eighteenth-Century India*; Bowen, *Revenue and Reform*; Frederick Whelan, *Edmund Burke and India: Political Morality and Empire*, chapter 1.

55. Guha, *A Rule of Property for Bengal: An Essay on the Idea of Permanent Settlement*, 12. Guha provides the text of the 1793 proclamation by Lord Cornwallis on his page 11. For a discussion of the settlement, its misunderstanding of and effects on the changing state of property rights, particularly in Bihar, see Gyan Prakash, *Bonded Histories: Genealogies of Labor Servitude in Colonial India*, especially chapter 3; Firminger, *Affairs of the East India Company*, introduction.

56. For a discussion of this point, see Jon Wilson, "Governing Property, Making Law: Land, Local Society, and Colonial Discourse in Agrarian Bengal, c. 1785–1830." Much study has been done on the difference between Francis's plan and the settlement implemented in 1793. My concern here, however, is with the logic of Francis's plan and its reading by Guha.

57. Bruce Holsinger, "Medieval Studies, Postcolonial Studies, and the Genealogies of Critique."

58. Guha, *A Rule of Property*, 9. For a similar project that focuses mainly on the nineteenth century, see Eric Stokes, *The English Utilitarians and India*.

59. Guha, *A Rule of Property*, 21, 19.

60. The details of this historiography were recognized well over a century ago. As the nineteenth-century legal historian Frederic Maitland famously quipped, one answer to the question "what was the feudal system?" would be "an early essay in comparative jurisprudence," and to the question "when did the feudal system attain its most perfect development?" he would respond "about the middle of the last century." Such recognition, of course, posed no barrier to the historical development of the concept, which continued unabated in the work of Maitland and others. Frederic William Maitland, *The Constitutional History of England*, 142. Elizabeth A. R. Brown builds upon Maitland's cynicism toward "feudalism" in her groundbreaking "The Tyranny of a Construct: Feudalism and Historians of Medieval Europe," 1064. For a brilliant and sympathetic reading of Maitland's thinking about the history of the Middle Ages, see Maura B. Nolan, "Metaphoric History: Narrative and New Science in the Work of F. W. Maitland." As Marc Bloch acknowledges in his introduction to *Feudal Society*, vol. 1, "feudal*ism*" emerged in France as a function of the political moment: the noble apologist Boulainvilliers first applied *féodalité* to a state of society, and on his heels Montesquieu's *Spirit of the Laws* popularized the idea of the *lois féodales* as the distinguishing characteristic of medieval Europe. *Feudal Society*, xvii–xviii.

61. Guha, *A Rule of Property*, 102.

62. Ibid., 13. "The concept of the fief," Reynolds argues in her *Fiefs and Vassals*, "is essentially post-medieval: it is a set of ideas or notions about the essential attributes of pieces of property that historians have defined as fiefs, some of which may not appear in the sources under any of the words that we translate as fief" (12). Elsewhere she notes, "Most of what is known about fiefs and benefices before the twelfth century comes from records that were made in great churches in order to safeguard their property" (62–63)—in other words, spe-

cifically located, interested sources that cannot be used to infer a generic meaning for holdings construed to be fiefs or benefices. She argues throughout *Fiefs
and Vassals* that fief and *bénéfice* (two of her primary targets) cannot meaningfully
be discussed in any general way, or be applied to something called "feudal society," since they have been conceptualized by modern historians, generically distributed over time and space, and often read back into documents in which they
never appear. This argument runs throughout Reynolds's book, but see especially chapter 3.

63. Guha, *A Rule of Property*, 101. Guha is quoting from *Sir Philip Francis's Minutes on the Subject of a Permanent Settlement for Bengal, Behar and Orissa*, ed. Romesh
C. Dutt (Calcutta, 1901). I will be citing from Philip Francis, *Original Minutes of
the Governor-General and Council of Fort William on the Settlement and Collection of the
Revenues of Bengal*. At the point in question Francis writes, "When he [the sover-
eign] grants Jaguires, or lands for religious purposes, his order is addressed to
the Zemindars, Chowderies, and Talookdars. The land continues to be deemed
a part of the Zemindary; the sovereign only grants the revenue of it" (72).
According to Gyan Prakash's valuable glossary in his *Bonded Histories*, a "jagir"
was "a Mughal tenure that gave the state's share of the land revenue to its
holder"; a "Zemindar" was, "under the Mughals, the collector of revenue;
under the British, landowner" (229–30). Guha quotes the following passage
from Voltaire's *Essai sur l'Histoire Générale*, which Francis also appends to his plan:
"Donner des terres et en jouir sont deux choses absolument différentes. Les
Rois Européens qui donnent tous les Bénéfices Ecclésiastiques, ne les possèdent
pas. L'Empereur dont le droit est de conférer tous les Fiefs d'Allemagne et d'Italie quand ils vaquent faute d'héritiers, ne recueille pas les fruits de ces Terres."
Vol. 4 (Geneva: 1761), 188.

64. Pocock, *The Ancient Constitution and the Feudal Law*; R. J. Smith, *The Gothic
Bequest: Medieval Institutions in British Thought, 1688–1863*, especially chapters 2
and 3. For a revision and extension of some of Pocock's arguments, see William
Klein, "The Ancient Constitution Revisited."

65. The revision of attitudes toward peasant rebel consciousness is the project
of Guha's *Elementary Aspects of Peasant Insurgency*. For a study of the potential and
implications of Guha's challenge to Marxist readings of peasant behavior or consciousness as "prepolitical," see Chakrabarty, *Provincializing Europe*, introduction, especially 11–16. Chakrabarty notes that Guha's work is extremely
important, even foundational, to his own interrogation of history. See also Prakash, "Subaltern Studies as Postcolonial Criticism."

66. For these and other writings by returning company servants, see Guha, *A
Rule of Property*, chapter 2; Bowen, *Revenue and Reform*, 28–29, 95–96; A. Bayly,
*Empire and Information: Intelligence Gathering and Social Communication in India,
1780–1870*, 53–54.

67. Guha, *A Rule of Property*, 100. Guha refers to Voltaire, *Fragments sur l'Inde*
(Paris, 1773), 34–37.

68. The political immediacy of Indian detail for Voltaire is indicated by his
comment upon Bernier's letter to Colbert: "Ç'eût été une imprudence bien
dangereuse de parler ainsi à l'administrateur des finances d'un Roi absolu."
Guha, 100.

69. Henry Pattullo, "Essay upon the Cultivation of the Lands, and Improvements of the Revenues, of Bengal," 5.

70. Karl Marx, *Theories of Surplus Value*, chapter 6, especially page 54.

71. As Guha points out, talk of the country's "ancient constitution" (refer-

ring to Hindu law before the Mughal conquest), with its obvious echo of contemporary English politics, had become almost "a matter of convention" for writers on East Indian affairs. *A Rule of Property*, 25. See also Hastings and Barwell's "Plan for a Future Settlement of the Revenues," in Francis, *Minutes*, 13.

72. Francis pitted his theory against the short-term revenue farming administered under Warren Hastings. For a discussion of the farming system as a recurrent issue of company policy, see Guha, *A Rule of Property*, 52–60. Guha also notes the strong influence of Blackstone on Francis.

73. Robert Travers, *Ideology and Empire in Eighteenth-Century India*, 174–75. I thank Professor Travers for allowing me to read a portion of his work prior to its publication.

74. Francis, *Minutes*, 37.

75. Guha, *A Rule of Property*, 103. Guha evidences here a number of unpublished letters from the *Francis MSS*. He makes note of Francis's reliance upon Blackstone's idea of crown-sovereignty (which is apparent throughout the *Minutes*) on 96.

76. Francis appends several sets of answers to questions posed by the Council to various Indian officials. To the question: "Whether lineal descent conveys an absolute right to the succession, independent of government, or whether an act of Government is necessary to establish that right?" the "pundits" Roy Royan and Canongoes responded that a zemindary traditionally devolved to the son, even though ownership ultimately resided in the king; the son should repair to the king for a new *Sunnud* [a grant; or official document conveying a grant], without which he could not be acknowledged as zemindar. Francis, *Minutes*, 73–75.

77. Francis, *Minutes*, 72. This is the same passage, discussed above, in which Guha finds Francis echoing Voltaire.

78. Sudipta Sen, *Empire of Free Trade: The East India Company and the Making of the Colonial Marketplace*, 132.

79. Guha, *Rule of Property*, 94, citing *The Francis Mss* 53 (49) 17, January 22, 1776 (unpublished).

80. I am working here with Bhabha's essay "Of Mimicry and Man: The Ambivalence of Colonial Discourse," *The Location of Culture*, 85–92, quotation 86.

81. Francis, *Minutes*, 19–20.

82. In his *Tableau Économique*, an inaugural text for the physiocrats, François Quesnay seems to favor large-scale cultivation (vi). In his "Essay upon the Cultivation of the Lands, and Improvements of the Revenues, of Bengal," Henry Pattullo, whom Francis probably follows, argues for the benefits of small estates (11–12). Jon Wilson argues that the relative productivity of large and small estates "were unsettled issues of debate in England at the very moment the permanent settlement was being framed." See his "Governing Property, Making Law," 8–9.

83. Francis, *Minutes*, 59.

84. David Hume, *The History of England, from the Invasion of Julius Caesar to the Revolution in 1688*, vol. 2, 30.

85. For a discussion of the role of Hume's *History of England* (which quickly became a bestseller) in political and philosophical debates on government and authority, see Nicholas Phillipson, "Propriety, Property and Prudence: David Hume and the Defence of the Revolution." See also Smith, *The Gothic Bequest*, chapter 3; Phillips, *Society and Sentiment*, chapter 1.

86. Walter Benjamin, "The Storyteller," *Illuminations*, 87.

Chapter 3. The Sense of an Epoch

1. I discuss this narrative of secularization and its correlative mapping through anthropology and Orientalism in my introduction above. For discussion of the history of "religion," see Masuzawa, *The Invention of World Religions*; Asad, *Genealogies of Religion*. For recent approaches to secularism, see Asad, *Formations of the Secular*; Needham and Rajan, *The Crisis of Secularism in India*, and Anidjar, "Secularism." For a historical account of an earlier and different "disembedding" of "religion" from culture in the early years of Christianity, see Schwartz, *Imperialism and Jewish Society, 200 B.C.E. to 640 C.E.*

2. Anidjar, "Secularism," 62. This is not to say, of course, that "religion" in its ostensibly privatized form did not remain important. Nor is it to say, as Anidjar notes, that "formations of the secular did not occur in other cultures, or that other cultures . . . are incapable of progress" (59); but these postulations already assume the limits of the division religious/secular, the history of which is the question here. For discussion of the genealogy of "religion" as a term, see Derrida, "Faith and Knowledge," and Jean-Luc Nancy, "Church, State, Resistance." Anidjar's discussion is in part set in the context of ongoing debate regarding "secularism" and its meaning in the work of Edward Said. See Mufti, "Auerbach in Istanbul: Edward Said, Secular Criticism, and the Question of Minority Culture" and "Critical Secularism: A Reintroduction for Perilous Times"; Robbins, "Secularism, Elitism, Progress, and Other Transgressions: On Edward Said's 'Voyage In.'"

3. De Vries, introduction to de Vries and Sullivan, *Political Theologies*, 2.

4. Carl Schmitt, *Roman Catholicism and Political Form*, 17; first published as *Römischer Katholizismus und politische Form* (Hellerau: Jakob Hegner Verlag, 1923). Ulmen's translation is based on the third German edition of the treatise, itself a reprint of the "improved" second edition published in 1925. See Ulmen's comments, xil. For discussion of Schmitt's historical and theoretical relation to Weber, see David Dyzenhaus, *Legality and Legitimacy*, and his "Legal Theory in the Collapse of Weimar"; John P. McCormick, *Carl Schmitt's Critique of Liberalism*; and for a different view, Catherine Colliot-Thélène, "Carl Schmitt versus Max Weber: Juridical Rationality and Economic Rationality," in Mouffe, ed., *The Challenge of Carl Schmitt*. For discussion of the relationship between *Roman Catholicism and Political Form* and *Political Theology*, see the introduction to the former by Ulmen. As Ulmen observes, the first edition of *Political Theology* "contains a note indicating that Schmitt's four chapters on the theory of sovereignty were written together with an essay titled 'The Political Idea of Catholicism,'" xxxi. See also Dyzenhaus, *Legality and Legitimacy*, and McCormick, *Carl Schmitt's Critique of Liberalism*. Gopol Galakrishnan makes the odd suggestion that these two texts are "almost diametrically opposed" (based, it seems to me, on a narrow reading of *Roman Catholicism*). See *The Enemy: An Intellectual Portrait of Carl Schmitt*, 51, and 53–65.

5. Menke, *Reflections of Equality*, 179. For a discussion of the importance of recognizing "an unutilized desire to celebrate community," with some reference to Schmitt, see Nancy, "Church, State, Resistance."

6. See Dyzenhaus, "Legal Theory in the Collapse of Weimar."

7. Benjamin sent a letter to Schmitt, enclosed with a copy of his *The Origin of German Tragic Drama*, in which he expresses his debt to Schmitt's "presentation of the doctrine of sovereignty." Samuel Weber includes its text in his "Taking Exception to Decision: Walter Benjamin and Carl Schmitt," an important essay

on the differences between the thinking of these two men. On the difference between Schmitt and Benjamin on the point of the exception, see also Werner Hamacher, "Afformative, Strike: Benjamin's 'Critique of Violence'" in Benjamin and Osborne, eds., *Walter Benjamin's Philosophy*.

8. Lupton, *Citizen-Saints: Shakespeare and Political Theology*, 2; see generally her introduction, as well as her arguments in *Afterlives of the Saints*. Lupton's investigations in *Citizen-Saints* are in many ways compatible with my interests here. However, whereas she focuses on the possibility, in contradistinction to Marx's negative assessment of religion in civil society, "that religious particularizations, and the laws that protect such diversity can also offer sites for reconceiving the universal being of humanity from within civil society, outside of or in response to the abstract mediations of the state" (9), I am more interested in the processes and assumptions that produce the dichotomy of religion and state, and the dilemma that it generates for politics and history.

9. Balibar, *We, the People of Europe?* 135. For Schmitt's popularity with the left early in his career, and his similarities to the Frankfurt School, see Ellen Kennedy, "Carl Schmitt and the Frankfurt School"; for opposing views, see the response in the same volume by Ulrich K. Preuss, "The Critique of German Liberalism: Reply to Kennedy," and Martin Jay's more polemical, "Reconciling the Irreconcilable? Rejoinder to Kennedy." Schmitt's connections to Strauss are both personal and theoretical; most obviously, Strauss provided "Notes" to Schmitt's *The Concept of the Political*, which, translated by Harvey Lomax, are appended to the English edition, ed. Schwab. For Schmitt's personal assistance to Strauss and their correspondence, see Meier, *Carl Schmitt and Leo Strauss*. For various views of the relatedness of their theories, see ibid.; Smith, *Reading Leo Strauss*; McCormick, *Carl Schmitt's Critique of Liberalism*.

10. Schmitt, *Political Theology*, 6 (my emphasis).

11. Ibid., 31–32.

12. Ibid., 36.

13. Ibid., 38.

14. Ibid., 36.

15. Benjamin, "Critique of Violence." Benjamin's example of such suspension is the general strike, which is "beyond all legal systems, and therefore beyond violence," and which he contrasts to legal violence, 292–300 and passim. For a thorough analysis of "Critique of Violence," see Judith Butler, "Critique, Coercion, and Sacred Life in Benjamin's 'Critique of Violence.'" The most famous response to Benjamin's "Critique" is Derrida's "Force of Law."

16. Benjamin, *The Origin of German Tragic Drama*, 62 (translation modified).

17. Ibid., 65.

18. Ibid., 56.

19. Ibid., 69, 71. See Weber's "Taking Exception to Decision."

20. Benjamin, *The Origin of German Tragic Drama*, 70. One might note here a similarity to Ernst Kantorowicz's discussion of "the king's two bodies," which also resonates with arguments by Schmitt, as in the following discussion of the priesthood being made into an office: "The fact that the office is made independent of charisma signifies that the priest upholds a position that appears to be completely apart from his concrete personality. Nevertheless, he is not the functionary and commissar of republican thinking. In contradistinction to the modern official, his position is not impersonal, because his office is part of an unbroken chain linked with the personal mandate and concrete person of Christ." *Roman Catholicism and Political Form*, 14. Kantorowicz, who had fled Ger-

many during the war, acknowledged but also distanced the connections of his book to "some of the idols of modern political religions," which, he asserts, were not its inspiration. Nonetheless: "Such as it now stands, this study may be taken among other things as an attempt to understand and, if possible, demonstrate how, by what means and methods, certain axioms of a political theology which *mutatis mutandis* was to remain valid until the twentieth century, began to be developed during the later Middle Ages." *The King's Two Bodies: A Study in Mediaeval Political Theology*, xviii.

21. Karl Löwith, *Meaning in History: The Theological Implications of the Philosophy of History*. Löwith had been a pupil of Heidegger, and was himself a teacher of Reinhart Koselleck, whom I discuss below.

22. Löwith, *Meaning in History*, 191. Löwith also discusses Vico, whom he treats, of course, as an exception to this pattern.

23. I discuss this aspect of Certeau's theory in my introduction above, 17–19.

24. Löwith, *Meaning in History*, 1–2.

25. Löwith had bitterly critiqued Schmitt's theory of the "decision" in an earlier essay, "The Occasional Decisionism of Carl Schmitt." For discussions of Löwith, and the relation of his work to "secularization" and to Schmitt, see Richard Wolin's introduction to *Martin Heidegger and European Nihilism*; Chantal Mouffe, *The Return of the Political*; for discussion of Löwith in relation to Benjamin, see Julia Reinhard Lupton, *Afterlives of the Saints*, 30–32.

26. Auerbach, it is worth noting, shared with Schmitt a background in German legal training: Schmitt received his doctorate in jurisprudence from the University of Strassburg in 1910; Auerbach received his from the University of Heidelberg in 1913.

27. Carl Schmitt, *Roman Catholicism and Political Form*, 18–19. For discussion of Schmitt's theory of political representation and its implications, see Weber, "'The Principle of Representation': Carl Schmitt's *Roman Catholicism and Political Form*."

28. Löwith, *Meaning in History*, 225 n. 2. Löwith further discusses the destructive, imperial trajectory of secularized messianism on 202–3.

29. Ibid., 190.

30. For Löwith's discussion of "incalculability," see ibid., 199–200.

31. Schmitt's alignment of sovereign decision with the friend/enemy distinction, which I do not have space to elaborate here, is the topic of his *The Concept of the Political*.

32. Blumenberg chose the term "legitimacy" to counter the "illegitimacy" attributed to secularization, particularly since "the 'Final Resolution of the Reichstag's Special Commission' [*Reichsdeputationshauptschluss*] of 1803 established the term 'as a concept of the usurpation of ecclesiastical rights, as a concept of the illegitimate emancipation of property from ecclesiastical care and custody'" (*The Legitimacy of the Modern Age*, 20).

33. Ibid., 119.

34. Ibid., 18–21. Blumenberg sometimes tries to validate his periodizing claims with the familiar narrative of a modern age (*Neuzeit*) that self-legitimates by proclaiming the "legitimacy" of knowledge, in contrast to the "medieval" rejection of *curiositas* (the claim for such an overarching "medieval" rejection of curiosity and knowledge is, of course, not only reductive but ludicrous). For him the modern age constitutes not a "transformation" of medieval, theological forms, but a "reoccupation" of their place by a "new consciousness of nature and the world," and "the legitimacy of the new, free endowment of meaning."

Unsurprisingly, Petrarch furnishes the liminal, exemplary case, and his gaze from the heights of Mont Ventoux explicitly literalizes the *spatio*-temporal stakes of periodization: "The description of the ascent of Mont Ventoux exemplifies graphically what is meant by the 'reality' of history as the reoccupation of formal systems of positions" (342). This description comes at the end of a chapter (325–42) on medieval scholasticism, which (according to Blumenberg) had the opportunity with Siger of Brabant to accept a "consciousness of reality," but rejected it in favor of Augustine's condemnation of *curiositas*.

35. Ibid., 99.

36. Koselleck, *Futures Past: On the Semantics of Historical Time*. My pagination refers to the first edition. The second edition includes a new introduction by the translator, Keith Tribe, to which I sometimes refer below.

37. See the discussion in my introduction above, pp. 5–6.

38. See Keith Tribe's "Translator's Introduction" to the 1985 edition of *Futures Past* (ix). Koselleck was also heavily influenced by his relationships with Hans Georg Gadamer and Hans Robert Jauss, and to a lesser degree (personally) by Martin Heidegger, all of whom were colleagues at some point in his career. He was also a student of Karl Löwith.

39. Koselleck, *Critique and Crisis: Enlightenment and the Pathogenesis of Modern Society*, 5.

40. Ibid., 9.

41. Blumenberg, *The Legitimacy of the Modern Age*, 32.

42. It must also be noted, although I cannot address it here, that Heidegger's contemplation of time followed upon his *Habilitationsshrift* on scholastic medieval theology. For discussion of this as well as the reliance of other German philosophers upon study of the Middle Ages, see Bruce Holsinger's introduction to *The Premodern Condition*, as well as Ethan Knapp's "Heidegger, Medieval Studies and the Modernity of Scholasticism."

43. Osborne, *The Politics of Time*, 113–14. As the most notable example of this "all-too-common charge," Osborne cites Löwith's *Meaning in History*.

44. Koselleck, *Futures Past*, preface, xxii–xxiii.

45. Koselleck's translator, Keith Tribe, comments in his "Notes on Translation and Terminology" in the 1985 edition that *Vergangene Zukunft* might be better translated as "The Bygone Future," xix. In his first note to "Modernity and the Planes of Historicity," Koselleck refers to the use made of *vergangene Zukunft* by R. Aron, *Introduction to the Philosophy of History* (London, 1961), 39ff.

46. Schmitt, *Political Theology*, 46.

47. In discussing the title of Schmitt's postwar book *The Nomos of the Earth*, Balibar provides a useful explanation of Schmitt's idea of world order as a form of incarnation accomplished through territorialization: "In its *abstract* aspect, this refers to the principle of territorialization of the life of men and of right, incarnated in 'original juridical acts' Schmitt calls *Landnahmen*: occupation of land, founding of cities and colonies, conquests and alliances, and the like. In its *concrete* aspect it refers to a certain centrality of Europe, from the sixteenth until the twentieth century, in the determination of the regions and borders that 'map' the world. Passing over a number of complex transitions, we can say that territorialization allows the secularization of the state-form characteristic of modernity by subordinating religion (*cujus regio ejus religio*, the principle of the Treaty of Westphalia) and organizing the 'domestication of war.'" Balibar, *We the People*, 138.

48. For further discussion, see my introduction above.

49. In his 2004 revised introduction to *Futures Past*, Keith Tribe works to distance Brunner's involvement in the dictionary project, in part perhaps because of his strong past association with the National Socialist party (an association he treats delicately), and in part perhaps to claim the achievement primarily for Koselleck (xi-xiv). In this revised introduction, Tribe also discusses more extensively Koselleck's debts to Gadamer, Schmitt, Jauss, and Heidegger, and fends off suggestions (following the translation's initial publication) that Koselleck was influenced by the "Cambridge School" of history, to which he has some similarities.

50. Otto Brunner, cited in Howard Kaminsky and James Van Horn Melton, translator's introduction to *Land and Lordship*, xx. *Land and Lordship* was first published as *Land und Herrschaft. Grundfragen der territorialen Verfassungsgeschichte Österriechs im Mittelalter* in 1939. Kaminsky and Van Horn Melton translate from the fourth (1959) edition, Brunner's final revision. Brunner argued that the basic German structure of political association (*Volksstaat*) endured despite the interruption of the un-German, French-derived bourgeois *Rechsstatt* (xxi), although he excised this discussion in the fourth, 1959 edition of *Land und Herrschaft*. An indirect link between German *Landesgeschichte* and the *Annales* school is often noted. Kaminsky and Van Horn Melton cite the suggestion that the French movement may have derived from "the experience of Marc Bloch and Lucien Febvre at the University of Strasbourg after 1918, when the French took over a German university with a seminar and library of *Landesgeschichte* that had no equivalent elsewhere in France." In 1972, Fernand Braudel suggested: "Is it by chance that Henri Berr, Lucien Febvre, Marc Boch, and myself all came from eastern France? That the *Annales* began at Strasbourg, next door to Germany and to German historical thought?" (ibid., xxv–xxvi). I discuss Brunner's theory of Germanic continuity further with regard to feudal law above in Chapter 1.

51. Brunner's probing for historical roots and for a narrative of transition between "Old Europe" (*Alteuropa*, as he called it following Burckhardt) and a new world order must be understood, as his translators argue, within a historic and historiographical framework that includes not only the scholarship of "Marc Bloch, [and] the philosophy of Martin Heidegger but also of Georg Lukács, the social science of Carl Schmitt but also of Max Horkheimer." Translator's introduction to *Land and Lordship*, xxvii.

52. Koselleck, quoted in translator's introduction, xi.

53. Koselleck, "Modernity and the Planes of History" in *Futures Past*, 4–5. Hereafter cited in the text by page number.

54. Biddick, *The Typological Imaginary*, 1. Biddick also attends to the role of Altdorfer's architectural etchings in the encryptment of "Jews within the tomb of the typological imaginary at the same time that it fabricates a writing surface constitutive of a new graphic regime of 'scientific' representation" (65). The typology of Altdorfer's etchings could be productively read against that of the *Alexanderschlacht*.

55. The difference between this potent historical sensibility and an eschatological emptying-out of history is one topic of Agamben's *The Time that Remains*. Working with the texts of Schmitt and particularly Benjamin and Paul, Agamben re-labels this time "the time of the now," which is to say "messianic" time, a contraction of past and present never reducible to unitary chronology, and associated, structurally and juridically, with Schmitt's "exception." See Agamben, *The Time that Remains*, especially 59–87; 104–12. I discuss Agamben's text further in Chapter 4.

56. Carl Schmitt, *The Nomos of the Earth in the International Law of the Jus Publicum Europaeum*, 60.

57. Schmitt, *Political Theology*, 36, 49.

58. Antonio Negri, *Insurgencies: Constituent Power and the Modern State*, 11, 8.

59. Negri, *Insurgencies*, 8.

60. Schmitt, *Political Theology*, 12.

61. This is the main basis of Derrida's critique of Schmitt in *The Politics of Friendship*.

62. Negri, *Insurgencies*, 11.

63. Asad, *Formations of the Secular*, 255. Asad is here discussing the process of "secularization" in colonial Egypt. See generally his chapter 7.

64. Negri, *Insurgencies*, 23.

65. For this discussion of Certeau, see the introduction above, pages 17–19.

66. Chakrabarty, *Provincializing Europe*, 107, 14.

67. Dipesh Chakrabarty, *Provincializing Europe*, 15–16. See also the collected essays in Bhargava, ed., *Secularism and Its Critics*, and Needham and Rajan, eds., *Crisis of Secularism in India*.

68. Chakrabarty, *Provincializing Europe*, 15, 23. See generally the introduction and chapter 4. For the noncontemporaneity of the present with itself, Chakrabarty relies on Derrida's *Spectres of Marx: the State of the Debt, the Work of Mourning, and the New International*. I take the full quotation regarding noncontemporaneity from *Spectres of Marx*, xix.

69. Chakrabarty, *Provincializing Europe*, 96, 108.

70. This debate is the topic of Chakrabarty's "Radical Histories and Question of Enlightenment Rationalism: Some Recent Critiques of *Subaltern Studies*." He responds especially to the accusations by Tom Brass and Sumit Sarkar. See Tom Brass, "A-way with Their Wor(l)ds: Rural Labourers through the Postmodern Prism"; and Sumit Sarkar, "The Fascism of the Sangha Parivar." Chakrabarty also cites the failure of the "Christian Enlightenment" to account for its own contradictions as it insisted upon eradicating Indian, particularly Hindu, "superstition and magic."

71. Gyan Prakash, "Writing Post-Orientalist Histories of the Third World: Perspectives from Indian Historiography"; see also Partha Chatterjee, *The Nation and Its Fragments*.

72. Chakrabarty, "The Time of History and the Times of Gods," 52. Ellipsis in original.

73. Schmitt, *Political Theology*, 31.

74. Benjamin, "Critique of Violence," 291–92.

75. See Buck-Morss, *Dialectics of Seeing*, 442 n. 24.

76. Benedict Anderson, *Imagined Communities*, 24.

77. Benjamin, *Theses on the Philosophy of History*, in *Illuminations*, 261–62.

Chapter 4. A Political Theology of Time

1. For a few examples of this diverse and expanding discussion, see Derrida and Vattimo, eds., *Religion*; Agamben, *The Time That Remains*; Badiou, *Saint Paul*; Žižek, Santner, and Reinhard, eds., *The Neighbor: Three Inquiries in Political Theology*; Vries and Sullivan, eds., *Political Theologies*.

2. The popularity and influence of Bede's *De temporum ratione* has been much discussed. For a synopsis, see Rabin, "Historical Re-Collections: Rewriting the World Chronicle in Bede's *De Temporum Ratione*," 1. It would be difficult to over-

state the influence of the *Historia*, which for centuries was, and in many ways still is, the taproot of English historiography and strains of English nationalism. For discussions of its importance during the early Middle Ages, see Goffart, *The Narrators of Barbarian History*, 235–36; J. E. Cross, "Bede's Influence at Home and Abroad: An Introduction"; George Hardin Brown, *Bede the Venerable*; Joyce Hill, "Carolingian Perspectives on the Authority of Bede."

3. Jan Davidse, "The Sense of History in the Works of the Venerable Bede," 689.

4. Bede, *De temporum ratione*, 495; trans. Faith Wallis, *The Reckoning of Time*, 195.

5. For discussion of the encyclopedic and exegetical tendencies of *computus* as Bede received it, particularly in the Irish tradition, see Faith Wallis's "Introduction" to *The Reckoning of Time*, especially xxii–xxvi. The chronicle tradition was always encyclopedic: Eusebius's *Chronological Canons* culled from as many prior sources as available. See Aldan A. Mosshammer, *The Chronicle of Eusebius and Greek Chronographic Tradition*, 15–16. Jerome's translation and continuation of Eusebius intersperses new material within Eusebius's entries and continues the history where Eusebius left off. In his preface, Jerome situates his additions to Eusebius within the logic of translation and *translatio*, areas that are, of course, of great interest to him: "For it must be known that I performed in part both the function of a translator and an author, because I both expressed the Greek very faithfully and added some things which seemed to me omitted, especially in the Roman history, of which Eusebius, the original author of this book, was not as uninformed as he was knowledgeable, but it seems to me that since he was writing in Greek, he found it necessary to provide only a cursory treatment for his own countrymen. Therefore . . . I have very carefully excerpted from Tranquillus and other illustrious historians." See Malcolm Drew Donaldson, *A Translation of Jerome's Chronicon with Historical Commentary*, 1. Isidore and Bede, however, as Walter Goffart puts it, "compiled entirely new chronicles, using Eusebius-Jerome as a source rather than as a trunk to be developed." See his *The Narrators of Barbarian History (A.D. 550–800)*, 9. See also Allen, "Universal History 300–1000: Origins and Western Developments," 33. The *computus* section of Bede's *De temporum ratione* is the first to integrate cosmology (that is, discussion of solstices and equinoxes, the zodiac, seasonal variations, tides, etc.) with calculation of the Easter calendar. By fusing this combination with the chronicle from a theological perspective, as Faith Wallis observes, Bede encompasses both liturgy and providential history (*The Reckoning of Time*, lxvii). I discuss the details of the chronicle in more detail below.

6. The *anno domini* had been a feature of Easter tables, and had been sporadically used in English charters since the seventh century. See Deliyannis, "Year-Dates in the Early Middle Ages," 5–22; Kenneth Harrison, *The Framework of Anglo-Saxon History to A.D. 900*, especially chapter 4 for dating prior to Bede, and chapter 5 for Bede's history. Bede twice refers to the *anno domini* within chronicle entries in *De temporum ratione*, once in reference to the beginning date of the Dionysian Paschal tables (*anno mundi* 4518), and once to mark the conversion of the Ionian Irish to Roman Easter dating (*anno mundi* 4670).

7. Bede discusses the "time that remains" in chapter 67, "The Remainder of the Sixth Age," Jones, 535–37; Wallis, *Reckoning of Time*, 239–40. I discuss his emphasis on the human and divine participation in salvation below.

8. "Tempora igitur a 'temperamento' nomen accipiunt," *De temporum ratione*, 274.

9. "ibi namque temporis initium statuit qui luminaribus conditis dixit, *ut sint in signa, et tempora, et dies, et annos*. Nam praecedens triduum, ut omnibus uisum est, absque ullis horarum dimensionibus, utpote necdum factis sideribus, aequali lance lumen tenebrasque pendebat; et quarto demum mane sol a medio procedens orientis, horis umbratim suas per lineas currentibus, aequinoctium quod annuatim seruaretur inchoauit." *De temporum ratione*, 291; trans. Wallis, *Reckoning of Time*, 24.

10. "Iuxta uero primae suae conditionis ordinem xxii kalendarum [i.e., March 21, the equinox] suprascriptarum initium sui circuitus et omnium simul temporum caput attolit," *De temporum ratione*, 294, trans. Wallis, *Reckoning of Time*, 27. In her discussion of this point, Wallis suggests that for Bede time began with the universe, and that the sun and moon were only the signs of time, and that on the fourth day it was the measurement of time, rather than time itself that was created. This seems to controvert Bede's very direct statements on the matter, however. See her statements in *The Reckoning of Time*, lxvii, and in "*Si Naturam Quaeras*: Reframing Bede's 'Science,'" 83.

11. "trimoda ratione computum temporis esse discretum: aut enim natura, aut consuetudine, aut certe aucotritate decurrit," *De* temporum ratione, 274.

12. Rabin, "Historical Re-Collections," 30. Rabin suggests that Bede's three modes of time reckoning correspond to the criteria of classical and patristic rhetorical theory, popularized for the Middle Ages by Victorinus and Augustine. For a detailed discussion of Bede's use of classical literature, the relation of his exegetical approach to language theory, and the grammatical tradition, especially as developed by Augustine, see Martin Irvine, *The Making of Textual Culture: 'Grammatica' and Literary Theory, 350–1100*, 272–97.

13. "Neque enim sine ratione paschalis obseruantia temporis, qua mundi salutem et figurari et uenire decebat," *De temporum ratione*, 292; Wallis, *Reckoning of Time*, 26 (my emphasis; translation modified).

14. In his study of the "sense of history" in Bede, Jan Davidse makes a strong argument for human agency in Bede, countering the suggestion that the centrality of the incarnation to history cancelled the possibility of meaningful difference between moments in time, past and present, and also notes an "irreconcilable tension" between monastic withdrawal and worldly politics. Writing under circumstances much changed from the time of Augustine, he argues, Bede knows that the Church relies upon kingship for expansion. "The Sense of History in the Works of the Venerable Bede," 647–95.

15. See the discussion of Schmitt and the *katechon* in Chapter 3 above. Schmitt's focus was on the empire-seeking German kings, for whom the concept of an imperial *katechon* did help to mediate the notion of *translatio imperii.*

16. See McGinn, *Visions of the End: Apocalyptic Traditions in the Middle Ages*, 83–84; Allen, "Universal History," 26–32. For the multiplicity of views on eschatology and the apocalypse, see Bynum and Freedman, *Last things: Death and the Apocalypse in the Middle Ages.*

17. This indeterminacy of the future has been discussed by Jean-Claude Schmitt, who notes that, "In medieval Latin, 'future' is usually a plural noun: *futura*," which is a "recognition of the future's complexity." He also observes the tensions in the duality of Christian representations of historical time, which is linear and cyclical, religious and mythical. "Appropriating the Future," 5–6. Despite some nuanced readings of "medieval" senses of the future, including the point that "Providence had not fixed the course of things once and for all," and his recognition that "The future is a matter of power," Schmitt ultimately

repeats, in extremely reductive terms, the medieval/modern divide as stipulated by Koselleck (whom he cites early on), and based on Weber's "disenchanted world." For discussion of complex later medieval conceptions of the future, including "a future which stretched on without end," see Ian P. Wei's essay "Predicting the Future to Judge the Present: Paris Theologians and Attitudes to the Future," 9–36.

18. Giorgio Agamben, *The Time That Remains*, 110–11. As Agamben notes, Paul does not mention the Antichrist.

19. "Etiam temporis ordine foras quid intus habeat ostendat," *De* temporum ratione, 456.

20. Clare Lees, *Tradition and Belief: Religious Writing in Late Anglo-Saxon England*, 5, 7. Emphasis mine.

21. Charlton Lewis's *An Elementary Latin Dictionary* lists "caeli signorumque motus" as well as "repentini Galliae motus" as exemplary usages of "motus," 519.

22. Agamben, *The Time That Remains*, 69.

23. See Rufinus, 1.5.2 (p. 45); and Orosius, *Historiarum adversos paganos libri quinque*, book 6, chapter 22. Orosius also emphasizes "a single peace," but segues quickly to adulation of Augustus.

24. This phrase is from Osborne, *The Politics of Time*, 113–14. I discuss Koselleck at length in Chapter 3 above.

25. Agamben, *The Time that Remains*, 52. Agamben is here countering Badiou's formulation that "The production of equality and the casting off, in thought, of differences are the material signs of the universal. . . . *The production of the Same is itself internal to the law of the Same.*" See Badiou's *Saint Paul: The Foundation of Universalism*, 109 (emphasis in original).

26. See Mosshammer, *The Chronicle of Eusebius*,15–16; Grafton and Williams, *Christianity and the Transformation of the Book*, 137 and chapter 3 more generally, which provides expansive discussion of the background, context, and production of Eusebius's chronicle and his dating scheme; see also Brian Croke, "The Origins of the Christian World Chronicle"; Allen "Universal History," 20–23.

27. Wallis, *Reckoning of Time*, 355.

28. Grafton and Williams, *Christianity and the Transformation of the Book*, 173.

29. Walter Goffart, *Narrators of Barbarian History*, 247; Michael Allen, "Universal History 300–1000," 33.

30. Andrew Rabin analyzes the inclusion of the English in Bede's chronicle in his "Historical Re-Collections," but with a different emphasis than mine here. He also makes the excellent observation that Bede refers seven times in his chronicle to the history of *computus*, and suggests that "if *computus* makes possible a unified understanding of world history, then the *DTR* [*De temporum ratione*], which brings together the history of *computus*, contributes crucially to the progress of Christian historiography" (33).

31. Davidse, "The Sense of History in the Works of the Venerable Bede."

32. Grafton and Williams, *Christianity and the Transformation of the Book*, 150–56.

33. If one placed the incarnation at 5,500 years from Creation, for instance, and calculated one's own time as 300 years after the incarnation, then the world would end in 200 years. For historical details and discussion of attempts to calculate an end-time as well as the struggles against such calculation, see Bernard McGinn's introduction to *Visions of the End*, 1–36; Richard Landes, "Lest the Millenium Be Fulfilled: Apocalyptic Expectations and the Pattern of Western Chronography, 100–800 C.E."; and Allen, "Universal History, 300–1000."

34. By invoking the Vulgate as the "Hebrew truth," Bede follows Jerome. See "Jerome's Letter to Pammachius." Bede intersperses his recalculations throughout his world-chronicle, and frequently comments upon the translation gap, calling upon Jerome and Augustine as authorities. See, for instance, the entries for *anno mundi* 874, 1656, 1693, 2453, 2519, 2790, 3310, and 3341 in *De temporum ratione*, chapter 66.

35. Bede was apparently accused of heresy after using the 3952 date of the incarnation in his shorter version of the world chronicle included in his earlier *De temporibus*. The charge was based on thousand-year ages, and accused Bede of suggesting that Christ did not come in the sixth age. Our evidence for this exchange is one-sided, however, in that it comes from Bede's comments in *De temporum ratione*, and from his "Letter to Plegwin," in which he renounces the accusation and explains his position. Wallis discusses the critical history of this accusation and includes a translation of the Letter to Plegwin in *The Reckoning of Time*, xxx–xxxi, 405–15.

36. For discussion of Löwith, see Chapter 3 above.

37. McGinn, *Visions of the End*, 30.

38. See Holsinger, "Medieval Studies, Postcolonial Studies, and the Genealogies of Critique," for a thorough discussion of the engagement of subaltern studies with the Middle Ages and medievalism on this topic. He suggests that this engagement amounts to "a revisionist theory of *periodization*," 1218. The classic argument against the "pre-political" is Ranajit Guha's *Elementary Aspects of Peasant Insurgency in Colonial India*.

39. Amitav Ghosh, *In an Antique Land: History in the Guise of a Traveler's Tale*, 59. Hereafter cited from this edition by page number.

40. Ato Quayson, *Calibrations*, 11. The multiple genres, and the multiple voices, of *In an Antique Land* are important to my argument; therefore, contrary to common practice in discussion of Ghosh's book, I will refer to the narrative voice as "the narrator" or as "Amitab," as he is called by many of the other characters. Assuming that the "I" of the book can simply be equated with Ghosh himself flattens many of the narrative's effects. Similarly, I do not term the book a "novel," which reduces its multiple genres.

41. See the historical description of the Geniza in the introduction to S. D. Goitein, *A Mediterranean Society*, 9–10. Goitein's five-volume *Mediterranean Society* has provided the foundation for scholarship on Geniza documents, much of it by Goitein's students, including Mark Cohen, whose personal advice Ghosh weaves into his story. See the foreword by Lassner to the volume cited above.

42. See Lassner's introduction to Goitein's *A Mediterranean Society*, 12.

43. Here is how Lassner describes its dispersal: "The history of the transfer of the Cairo Geniza to the libraries of Europe and America explains the scattered state of this material today. Under these circumstances, it is not surprising that pages of one and the same book, indeed, fragments of the very same document, may be found in such distant places as St. Petersburg, Cambridge, and New York" (11).

44. Gaurav Desai rightly points out that Ghosh sometimes simplifies and even reverses the roles of popular syncretism and the state: sometimes it is the "people" who are the "enforcers of History." See "Old World Orders: Amitav Ghosh and the Writing of Nostalgia," 130.

45. Holsinger, "Medieval Studies, Postcolonial Studies, and the Genealogies of Critique," 1213. Holsinger's discussion largely concerns Ghosh's article in *Subaltern Studies* 7 (1992), "The Slave of MS.H.6," which preceded *In an Antique Land*.

46. Cited in Prakash, *American Historical Review*, 1476. Desai, in "Old World Orders," also finds Ghosh's irony both effective and productive, despite historical problems.

47. Quayson, *Calibrations*, 12. See also the discussion in James Clifford's *Routes: Travel and Translation in the Late Twentieth Century*, 1–6.

48. The quotation is from Quayson, *Calibrations*, 15.

49. Kathleen Biddick, *The Typological Imaginary*, 97, quoting Ghosh, 263. Biddick also states that Ghosh compares medieval slavery to "the yardstick of early modern plantation systems" (ibid.). This comparison is found in Goitein's *Jews and Arabs*, which Biddick quotes, but I have not found it in Ghosh, who writes, interestingly, that the relationship of the merchant Ben Yiju and his slave (for whom Ghosh reconstructs the name "Bomma") "was probably more that of patron and client than master and slave, as that relationship is now understood. If this seems curious, it is largely because the medieval idea of slavery tends to confound contemporary conceptions, both of servitude and of its mirrored counter-image, individual freedom. . . . In the Middle Ages institutions of servitude took many forms, and they all differed from 'slavery' as it came to be practised after the European colonial expansion of the sixteenth century" (259).

50. Biddick, *Typological Imaginary*, 97.

51. Cohen, *Under Crescent and Cross*. Ghosh tells the story of his meeting with Cohen on page 104 of *In an Antique Land*.

52. Cohen, *Under Crescent and Cross*, 4–6.

53. I refer here to Johannes Fabian's work in *Time and the Other*, in which he describes the refusal to allow "othered" cultures the status of a contemporary—or a "coevalness" in time.

54. Ganim, "Native Studies: Orientalism and Medievalism," 127.

55. Agamben, *The Time That Remains*, 47.

56. Ibid., 52. For other discussion of Paul's letters and his relation to the law, see John Gager, *Reinventing Paul* and chapter 1 of Lupton's *Citizen-Saints*. The recent scholarship on Paul is vast, and I cannot engage it here.

57. Ibid., 108.

58. For discussion of Negri on periodization, sovereignty, and the "exception" see Chapter 3 above, 96–98.

59. Agamben, *The Time That Remains*, 22, and 44–53. See especially 46–47.

60. Smith, "Irregular Histories: Forgetting Ourselves," 178.

61. See Goitein, *Mediterranean Society*, ed. Lassner, 240–47.

62. Ghosh foregrounds the image of the archival tomb. In describing the location of Ben Yiju's final letter, for instance, he writes: "The documents are kept in the Institute's rare book room, a great vault in the bowels of the building. . . . Within the sealed interior of this vault are two cabinets that rise out of the floor like catafalques. The documents lie inside them, encased in sheets of clear plastic, within exquisitely crafted covers" (348).

63. Derrida, *Archive Fever*, 4 n. 1.

64. See Agamben's chapter 3 in *The Time That Remains*.

65. Clare Lees and Gillian Overing, "Signifying Gender and Empire," 10.

66. Bede's regnal typology is a complex issue that I cannot fully engage here. For discussions of his exegesis on 1 Sam. (also known as 1 Kings), see Judith McClure, "Bede's Old Testament Kings"; and George Hardin Brown, "Bede's Neglected Commentary on Samuel." For discussion of Bede's treatment of Christian kingship, see N. J. Higham, *An English Empire: Bede and the Early Anglo-Saxon Kings*.

67. See Lavezzo, *Angels at the Edge of the World*, chapter 1; Nicholas Howe, "Rome: Capital of Anglo-Saxon England."

68. *Bede's Ecclesiastical History of the English People*, 41. Citations are by page number from this edition. Translations are from this text unless otherwise noted.

69. Malcolm Godden, "The Anglo-Saxons and the Goths," 50.

70. Bede takes the beginning of this letter from Gildas's *The Ruin of Britain*.

71. Andrew Scheil, *The Footsteps of Israel: Understanding Jews in Anglo-Saxon England*, 108–9. *Bede's Ecclesiastical History*, 53.

72. *Bede's Ecclesiastical History*, 5. For Gregory's registry and Bede, see Paul Meyvaert, "The Registrum of Gregory the Great and Bede."

73. The letters of the papal registry are edited in T. Mommsen, *Liber Pontificalis, Monumenta Germaniae historica*.

74. Allen Frantzen, *Desire for Origins*, 141. Bede's highly selective memory and choices, as well as his presentation of details, have been the subject of much controversy. For discussion of the absence of women in Bede, see Clare Lees and Gillian Overing, *Double Agents: Women and Clerical Culture in Anglo-Saxon England*, 15–39. With regard to whether Bede favored a Northumbrian, Canterbury, or more widely English history, see Walter Goffart, "Bede's History in a Harsher Climate," as well as his *Narrators of Barbarian History*; Patrick Wormald, "Bede, the *Bretwaldas* and the Origins of the *Gens Anglorum*."

75. Certeau, *The Writing of History*, 89.

76. José Rabasa, "*Without* History? Apostasy as a Historical Category," unpublished paper.

Epilogue

1. Philip Reeves, "Pakistanis Criticize Influence of Feudal Families," *Morning Edition*, June 18, 2007 unpaginated.

2. Anidjar, "Secularism," 62, discussed in Chapter 3 above.

Works Cited

Abu-Lughod, Janet. "On the Remaking of History: How to Reinvent the Past." *Remaking History*. Ed. Barbara Kruger and Phil Mariani. Seattle: Bay Press, 1989. 111–29.

Abu-Lughod, Lila. "The Debate About Gender, Religion, and Rights: Thoughts of a Middle East Anthropologist." *PMLA* 121:5 (2006): 1621–30.

Agamben, Giorgio. *Homo Sacer: Sovereign Power and Bare Life*. Trans. Daniel Heller-Roazen. Stanford, Calif.: Stanford University Press, 1995.

———. *State of Exception*. Trans. Kevin Attell. Chicago: University of Chicago Press, 2005.

———. *The Time That Remains: A Commentary on the Letter to the Romans*. Trans. Patricia Dailey. Stanford, Calif.: Stanford University Press, 2005.

Allen, Michael I. "Universal History 300–1000: Origins and Western Developments." *Historiography in the Middle Ages*. Ed. Deborah Mauskopf Deliyannis. Leiden: Brill, 2003. 17–42.

Anderson, Benedict. *Imagined Communities: Reflections on the Origin and Spread of Nationalism*. Rev. 2nd ed. London: Verso, 1991.

Anderson, Perry. *Lineages of the Absolutist State*. London: Verso, 1974.

Anidjar, Gil. "Secularism." *Critical Inquiry* 33 (2006), 52–77.

Asad, Talal. *Genealogies of Religion*. Baltimore: Johns Hopkins University Press, 1993.

———. *Formations of the Secular: Christianity, Islam, Modernity*. Stanford, Calif.: Stanford University Press, 2003.

Aston, T. H., and C. H. E. Philpin, eds. *The Brenner Debate: Agrarian Class Structure and Economic Development in Pre-Industrial Europe*. New York: Cambridge University Press, 1985.

Auerbach, Erich. *Mimesis: The Representation of Reality in Western Literature*. Princeton, N.J.: Princeton University Press, 1953. Reprinted 2003.

———. "Figura." *Scenes from the Drama of European Literature: Six Essays*. Gloucester, Mass.: Peter Smith, 1959. Reprinted 1973.

———. "Philology and *Weltliteratur*." Trans. Edward Said and Marie Said. *Centennial Review* 13 (1969), 1–17.

Austin, J. L. *How To Do Things With Words*. Cambridge, Mass.: Harvard University Press, 1975.

Badiou, Alain. *Saint Paul: The Foundation of Universalism*. Trans. Ray Brassier. Stanford, Calif.: Stanford University Press, 2003.

Balakrishnan, Gopol. *The Enemy: An Intellectual Portrait of Carl Schmitt*. London: Verso, 2000.

Balibar, Étienne. *We, the People of Europe? Reflections on Transnational Citizenship*. Trans. James Swenson. Princeton, N.J.: Princeton University Press, 2004.

Barnes, Viola Florence. "Land Tenure in English Colonial Charters of the Seventeenth Century." *Essays in Colonial History Presented to Charles McLean Andrews.* New Haven, Conn.: Yale University Press, 1931. 4–40.

Bartlett, Anne Clark. "Foucault's 'Medievalism.'" *Mystics Quarterly* 20 (1994): 10–18.

Bataille, Georges. *The Accursed Share,* vol 3. Trans. Robert Hurley. New York: Zone Books, 1993.

Bayly, A. *Empire and Information: Intelligence Gathering and Social Communication in India, 1780–1870.* Cambridge: Cambridge University Press, 1996.

Bede, The Venerable. *Bede's Ecclesiastical History of the English People.* Ed. and trans. Bertram Colgrave and R. A. B. Mynors. Oxford: Clarendon, 1969.

———. *De temporum ratione.* Ed. Charles W. Jones. *Corpus Christianorum Series Latina* 123B. Turnhout: Brepols, 1977. Trans. Faith Wallis as *The Reckoning of Time.*

Benjamin, Walter. *Illuminations.* Trans. Harry Zohn. Ed. Hannah Arendt. New York: Schocken, 1968.

———."Critique of Violence." *Reflections: Essays, Aphorisms, Autobiographical Writings.* Trans. Edmund Jephcott. Ed. Peter Demetz. New York: Schocken, 1978. First published as "Zur Kritiz der Gewalt," *Schriften,* Band I. (Frankfurt: Suhrkamp Verlag, 1955). 277–300.

———. *The Origin of German Tragic Drama.* Trans. John Osborne. London: Verso, 1998. First published as *Ursprung des deutschen Trauerspiels* (Frankfurt: Suhrkamp Verlag, 1963).

Berdan, Frances F., and Patricia Rieff Anawalt, eds. *The Essential Codex Mendoza.* Berkeley: University of California Press, 1997.

Berkowitz, David. *John Selden's Formative Years: Politics and Society in Early Seventeenth-Century England.* Washington, D.C.: Folger Shakespeare Library, 1988.

Berman, Harold J. "The Origins of Historical Jurisprudence: Coke, Selden, Hale." *Yale Law Journal* 5:1 (1994): 1651–738.

———. *Law and Revolution II.* Cambridge, Mass.: Harvard University Press, 2003.

Bhabha, Homi. *Location of Culture.* London: Routledge, 1994.

Bhargava, Rajeev, ed. *Secularism and Its Critics.* Delhi: Oxford University Press, 1998.

Biddick, Kathleen. *Shock of Medievalism.* Durham, N.C.: Duke University Press, 1998.

———. *The Typological Imaginary.* Philadelphia: University of Pennsylvania Press, 2003.

Bisaha, Nancy. *Creating East and West: Renaissance Humanists and the Ottoman Turks.* Philadelphia: University of Pennsylvania Press, 2004.

Blackstone, William. *Commentaries on the Laws of England,* 4th ed. Oxford: Clarendon, 1770.

Bloch, Marc. *Feudal Society.* Trans. L. A. Manyon. London: Routledge, 1961. Vol. 1.

Blumenberg, Hans. *The Legitimacy of the Modern Age.* Trans. Robert M. Wallace. Cambridge, Mass.: MIT Press, 1983; first published as *Die Legitimität der Neuzeit* (Frankfurt: Suhrkamp Verlag, 1966).

Bodin, Jean. *Les six livres de la République.* Ed. Christiane Fremont, Marie-Dominique Couzinet, and Henri Rochais. 6 vols. Paris: Fayard, 1986.

Bowen, H. V. *Revenue and Reform: The Indian Problem in British Politics, 1757–1773.* Cambridge: Cambridge University Press, 1991.

Brass, Tom. "A-way with Their Wor(l)ds: Rural Labourers Through the Postmodern Prism." *Economic and Political Weekly* 28:23 (1993), 1162–68.

Brooks, Nicholas. *Bede and the English.* 1999 Jarrow Lecture. Jarrow, Durham: St. Paul's Church, 1999.

Brown, George Hardin. *Bede the Venerable.* Boston: Twayne, 1987.

———. "Bede's Neglected Commentary on *Samuel.*" In DeGregorio, ed., 121–42.

Brunner, Otto. "Feudalism: The History of a Concept." Trans. Miriam Sambursky. *Lordship and Community in Medieval Europe.* Ed. Fredric L. Cheyette. New York: Holt, 1968.

———. *Land and Lordship: Structures of Governance in Medieval Austria.* Trans. Howard Kaminsky and James Van Horn Melton. Philadelphia: University of Pennsylvania Press, 1992.

Buck-Morss, Susan. *The Dialectics of Seeing: Walter Benjamin and the Arcades Project.* Cambridge, Mass.: MIT Press, 1989.

———. "Hegel and Haiti." *Critical Inquiry* 26 (2002): 821–65.

Budé, Guillaume. *Annotationes priores et posteriors . . . in pandectas.* Paris, 1556.

Burke, Peter. *The Renaissance Sense of the Past.* New York: St. Martin's, 1969.

Burns, J. H., ed. *The Cambridge History of Medieval Political Thought, c. 350–c. 1450.* Cambridge: Cambridge University Press, 1988.

———. *Cambridge History of Political Thought: 1450–1700.* Cambridge: Cambridge University Press, 1991.

Burrow, J. A., and Ian P. Wei, eds. *Medieval Futures: Attitudes to the Future in the Middle Ages.* Woodbridge: Boydell, 2000.

Butler, Judith. *Bodies that Matter: On the Discursive Limits of "Sex."* New York: Routledge, 1993.

———. "Critique, Coercion, and Sacred Life in Benjamin's 'Critique of Violence.'" In Vries and Sullivan, 201–19.

Bynum, Caroline Walker, and Paul Freedman, eds. *Last Things: Death and the Apocalypse in the Middle Ages.* Philadelphia: University of Pennsylvania Press, 2000.

Cadava, Eduardo. "The Monstrosity of Human Rights." *PMLA* 121.5 (2006): 1558–565.

Certeau, Michel de. *The Writing of History.* Trans. Tom Conley. New York: Columbia University Press, 1988.

Chakrabarty, Dipesh. "The Time of History and the Times of Gods." In Lowe and Lloyd, eds., 35–60.

———. "Radical Histories and the Question of Enlightenment Rationalism: Some Recent Critiques of *Subaltern Studies.*" *Economic and Political Weekly* 30:14 (1995): 751–59. Reprinted in Vinayak Chaturvedi, ed., *Mapping Subaltern Studies and the Postcolonial.* London: Verso, 2000. 256–80.

———. *Provincializing Europe: Postcolonial Thought and Historical Difference.* Princeton, N.J.: Princeton University Press, 2000.

———. *Habitations of Modernity: Essays in the Wake of Subaltern Studies.* Chicago: University of Chicago Press, 2002.

———. "Where Is the Now?" *Critical Inquiry* 30:2 (2004): 458–62.

Chatterjee, Partha. *The Nation and Its Fragments: Colonial and Postcolonial Histories.* Princeton, N.J.: Princeton University Press, 1993.

———. "Secularism and Tolerance." *Secularism and Its Critics.* Ed. Rajeev Bhargava Delhi: Oxford University Press, 1998. 345–79.

Cheyette, Fredric L. *Ermengard of Narbonne and the World of the Troubadours.* Ithaca: Cornell University Press, 2001.

Chomsky, Noam. "Homi Bhabha Talks with Noam Chomsky." *Critical Inquiry* 31, no. 2 (2004): 419–24.

Christianson, Paul. "Young John Selden and the Ancient Constitution, ca. 1610–1618." *Proceedings of the American Philosophical Society* 128 (1984): 271–315.

———. *Discourse on History, Law, and Governance in the Public Career of John Selden, 1610–1635.* Toronto: University of Toronto Press, 1996.

Clifford, James. *Routes: Travel and Translation in the Late Twentieth Century.* Cambridge, Mass.: Harvard University Press, 1997.

Cohen, Jeffrey Jerome, ed. *The Postcolonial Middle Ages.* New York: Palgrave, 2000.

Cohen, Mark. *Under Crescent and Cross.* Princeton, N.J.: Princeton University Press, 1994.

Coke, Sir Edward. *The First Part of the Institutes of the Laws of England: or, A Commentary upon Littleton* (15th edition). London: E. and R. Brooke, 1794.

Cole, Andrew. "What Hegel's Master/Slave Dialectic Really Means." *Journal of Medieval and Early Modern Studies* 34 (2004): 577–610.

Cole, Andrew, and D. Vance Smith. *The Legitimacy of the Middle Ages.* Durham: Duke University Press, forthcoming.

Colliot-Thélène, Cathrine. "Carl Schmitt Versus Max Weber: Juridical Rationality and Economic Rationality." *The Challenge of Carl Schmitt.* Ed. Chantal Mouffe. London: Verso, 1999. 138–54.

Craig, Sir Thomas. *Jus Feudale.* Trans. James Avon Clyde. Edinburgh: William Hodge, 1934.

Croke, Brian. "The Origins of the Christian World Chronicle." *History and Historians in Late Antiquity.* Ed. Brian Croke and Alanna M. Emmett. Sydney: Pergamon, 1984. 116–31.

Cross, J. E. "Bede's Influence at Home and Abroad: An Introduction." *Beda Venerabilis: Historian, Monk, and Northumbrian.* Ed. L. A. J. R. Houwen and A. A. MacDonald. Groningen: Egbert Forsten, 1996. 17–29.

Damrosch, David, ed. *The Longman Anthology of World Literature,* 2 vols. New York: Longman, 2003, 2004.

Davidse, Jan. "The Sense of History in the Works of the Venerable Bede," *Studi Medievali* series 3, 23:2 (1982): 647–95.

Davies, Sir John. *A Discovery of the True Causes Why Ireland Was Never Entirely Subdued.* Ed. James P. Myers. Washington, D.C.: Catholic University Press, 1988.

Davis, Kathleen. "National Writing in the Ninth Century: A Reminder for Postcolonial Thinking About the Nation." *Journal of Medieval and Early Modern Studies* 28.3 (1998): 611–37.

Davis, Kathleen, and Nadia Altschul, eds. *Medievalisms in the (Post)Colony.* Baltimore: Johns Hopkins University Press, forthcoming.

DeGregorio, Scott, ed. *Innovation and Tradition in the Writings of the Venerable Bede.* Morgantown: West Virginia University Press, 2006.

Deliyannis, Deborah Mauskopf. "Year-Dates in the Early Middle Ages." *Time in the Medieval World.* Ed. Chris Humphrey and W. M. Ormrod. York: York Medieval Press, 2001. 5–22.

Derrida, Jacques. *Margins of Philosophy.* Trans. Alan Bass. Chicago: University of Chicago Press, 1982.

———. "Force of Law: The 'Mystical Foundation of Authority.'" *Deconstruction and the Possibility of Justice.* Ed. Drucilla Cornell, Michel Rosenfeld, and David Gray Carlson. London: Routledge, 1992. 3–67.

———. *Spectres of Marx: the State of the Debt, the Work of Mourning, and the New International.* Trans. Peggy Kamuf. New York: Routledge, 1994.

———. *The Politics of Friendship.* Trans. George Collins. New York: Verso, 1997.

———. *Archive Fever: A Freudian Impression.* Trans. Eric Prenowitz. Chicago: University of Chicago Press, 1998.

———. "Faith and Knowledge: Two Sources of 'Religion' at the Limits of Reason Alone." Trans. Samuel Weber. *Religion.* Ed. Jacques Derrida and Gianni Vattimo, 1–78.

Derrida, Jacques, and Gianni Vattimo, eds. *Religion.* Stanford, Calif.: Stanford University Press, 1998.

Desai, Gaurav. "Old World Orders: Amitav Ghosh and the Writing of Nostalgia." *Representations* 85 (2004): 125–48.

Dinshaw, Carolyn. *Getting Medieval: Sexualities and Communities, Pre- and Postmodern.* Durham, N.C.: Duke University Press, 1996.

Donalson, Malcolm Drew. *A Translation of Jerome's Chronicon with Historical Commentary.* Lewiston, N.Y.: Mellen University Press, 1996.

Du Moulin, Charles. *Commentarii in Parisienses . . . consuetudines.* Cologne, 1613.

Dyzenhaus, David. *Legality and Legitimacy: Carl Schmitt, Hans Kelsen and Hermann Heller in Weimar.* Oxford: Clarendon, 1997.

———. "Legal Theory in the Collapse of Weimar: Contemporary Lessons?" *American Political Science Review* 91:1 (1997): 121–34.

Eckhardt, Karl, ed. *Consuetudines Feudorum.* Aalen, Germany: Scientia Verlag, 1971.

Fabian, Johannes. *Time and the Other: How Anthropology Makes Its Object.* New York: Columbia University Press, 1983; 2nd ed., 2002.

Fasolt, Constantin. *The Limits of History.* Chicago: University of Chicago Press, 2004.

Ferguson, Arthur B. *The Articulate Citizen and The English Renaissance.* Durham, N.C.: Duke University Press, 1965.

Ferguson, Wallace. *The Renaissance in Historical Thought.* New York: Houghton Mifflin, 1948.

Firminger, Walter K. *Affairs of the East India Company: The Fifth Report from the Select Committee of the House of Commons, vol. L.* Delhi: Neeraj Publishing House, 1812. Reprinted in 1985.

Foucault, Michel. *The Archaeology of Knowledge.* Trans. A. M. Sheridan Smith. New York: Pantheon, 1972.

Francis, Sir Philip. *Original Minutes of the Governor-General and Council of Fort William on the Settlement and Collection of the Revenues of Bengal.* London, 1782.

———. *Sir Philip Francis's Minutes on the Subject of a Permanent Settlement for Bengal, Behar and Orissa.* Ed. Romesh C. Dutt. Calcutta, 1901.

Franklin, Julian. *Jean Bodin and the Sixteenth-Century Revolution in the Methodology of Law and History.* New York: Columbia University Press, 1963.

———. *Jean Bodin and the Rise of Absolutist Theory.* Cambridge: Cambridge University Press, 1973.

Franklin, Julian, ed. and trans. *On Sovereignty: Four Chapters from The Six Books of the Commonwealth.* Cambridge: Cambridge University Press, 1992.

Frantzen, Allen. *Desire for Origins: New Language, Old English, and Teaching the Tradition.* New Brunswick, N.J.: Rutgers University Press, 1991.

Fuchs, Barbara. *Mimesis and Empire: The New World, Islam, and European Identities.* Cambridge: Cambridge University Press, 2001.

Fuchs, Barbara, and David J. Baker. "The Postcolonial Past." *Modern Language Quarterly* 65:3 (2004): 329–40.

Gager, John G. *Reinventing Paul.* Oxford: Oxford University Press, 2000.

Ganim, John. "Native Studies: Orientalism and Medievalism." In Jeffrey Jerome Cohen, 123–34.

———. *Medievalism and Orientalism.* New York: Palgrave, 2005.

Ghosh, Amitav. *In An Antique Land: History in the Guise of a Traveler's Tale.* New York: Vintage, 1994.

Giesey, Ralph E. "When and Why Hotman Wrote the *Francogallia*," *Bibliothèque d'Humanisme et Renaissance* 219 (1967): 581–611.

———. Introduction to Hotman, *Francogallia.*

Gilmore, Myron Piper. *Argument from Roman Law in Political Thought, 1200–1600.* Cambridge, Mass.: Harvard University Press, 1941.

Giordanengo, Gérard. "Consilia Feudalia." *Legal Consulting in the Civil Law Tradition.* Ed. Mario Ascheri, Ingrid Baumgärtner, and Julius Kirshner. Berkeley: University of California Press, 1999.

Godden, Malcolm. "The Anglo-Saxons and the Goths." *Anglo Saxon England* 31 (2002): 47–68.

Goffart, Walter. *The Narrators of Barbarian History (A.D. 550–800).* Princeton, N.J.: Princeton University Press, 1988.

———. "Bede's History in a Harsher Climate." In DeGregorio, ed., 203–26.

Goitein, S. D. *A Mediterranean Society: An Abridgment in One Volume.* Rev. and ed. Jacob Lassner. Berkeley: University of California Press, 2003.

Gordon, George. "*Medium Aevum* and the Middle Age," SPE Tract 19. Oxford, 1925.

Grafton, Anthony and Megan Williams. *Christianity and the Transformation of the Book: Origen, Eusebius, and the Library of Caesarea.* Cambridge, Mass.: Harvard University Press, 2006.

Guha, Ranijit. *A Rule of Property for Bengal: An Essay on the Idea of Permanent Settlement.* Paris: Mouton, 1963.

———. *Elementary Aspects of Peasant Insurgency in Colonial India.* Delhi: Oxford University Press, 1983. Reprinted Durham, N.C.: Duke University Press, 1999.

Hamacher, Werner. "Afformative, Strike: Benjamin's 'Critique of Violence.'" *Walter Benjamin's Philosophy: Destruction and Experience.* Ed. Andrew Benjamin and Peter Osborne. London: Routledge, 1993. 110–38.

———. "One 2 Many Multiculturalisms." *Violence, Identity, and Self-Determination.* Ed. Hent de Vries and Samuel Weber. Stanford, Calif.: Stanford University Press, 1997. 284–325.

Harrison, Kenneth. *The Framework of Anglo-Saxon History to A.D. 900.* Cambridge: Cambridge University Press, 1976.

Hegel, G. W. F. *Philosophy of History.* Trans. J. Sibree. Amherst, N.Y.: Prometheus, 1991.

Heller, Henry. "Bodin on Slavery and Primitive Accumulation." *Sixteenth Century Journal* 25 (1994): 53–65.

Higham, N. J. *An English Empire: Bede and the Early Anglo-Saxon Kings.* Manchester: Manchester University Press, 1995.

Hill, Joyce. "Carolingian Perspectives on the Authority of Bede." In DeGregorio, ed., 227–49.

Hoffman, Paul E. *The Spanish Crown and the Defense of the Caribbean, 1535–1585: Precedent, Patrimonialism, and Royal Parsimony.* Baton Rouge: Louisiana State University Press, 1980.

Holsinger, Bruce. "Medieval Studies, Postcolonial Studies, and the Genealogies of Critique." *Speculum* 77 (2002): 1195–227.

———. *The Premodern Condition: Medievalism and the Making of Theory.* Chicago: University of Chicago Press, 2005.

Hont, Ivstan. "The Rhapsody of Public Debt." *Political Discourse in Early Modern Britain.* Ed. Nicholas Phillipson and Quentin Skinner. Cambridge: Cambridge University Press, 1993. 321–48.

Hotman, François. *De Feudis Commentatio Tripartita.* Cologne, 1573.

———. *Antitribonian, ou, Discours d'un grand et renommé iurisconsulte de nostre temps sur l'estude des loix.* Ed. Henri Duranton. Saint-Etienne, France: Université de Saint-Etienne, 1980.

———. *Francogallia.* Trans. J. H. M. Salmon. Ed. Ralph E. Giesey. Cambridge: Cambridge University Press, 1972.

Howe, Nicholas. "Rome: Capital of Anglo-Saxon England." *Journal of Medieval and Early Modern Studies* 34:1 (2004): 147–72.

Hume, David. *The History of England, from the Invasion of Julius Caesar to the Revolution* (1688). Boston: Little, Brown, 1863.

———. *The Philosophical Works of David Hume.* Ed. T. H. Green and T. H. Grose. London, 1875.

Ingham, Patricia Clare. *Sovereign Fantasies: Arthurian Romance and the Making of Britain.* Philadelphia: University of Pennsylvania Press, 2001.

Ingham, Patricia Clare, and Michelle Warren, eds. *Postcolonial Moves.* New York: Palgrave, 2003.

Irvine, Martin. *The Making of Textual Culture: "Grammatica" and Literary Theory, 350–1100.* Cambridge: Cambridge University Press, 1994.

Isidore of Seville. *The Etymologies of Isidore of Seville.* Trans. Stephen Barney et al. Cambridge: Cambridge University Press, 2006.

Jameson, Frederic. *Postmodernism, or, The Cultural Logic of Late Capitalism.* Durham, N.C.: Duke University Press, 1991.

———. *A Singular Modernity: Essay on the Ontology of the Present.* London: Verso, 2002.

Jay, Martin. "Reconciling the Irreconcilable? Rejoinder to Kennedy." *Telos* 71 (1987): 67–80.

Jerome. "Jerome's Letter to Pammachius." Trans. Kathleen Davis. *The Translation Studies Reader,* 2nd ed. Ed. Lawrence Venuti. London: Routledge, 2004. 21–30.

Johnson, Robert C. et al., eds. *Commons Debates 1628.* New Haven, Conn.: Yale University Press, 1977.

Kabir, Ananya, and Deanne Williams, eds. *Postcolonial Approaches to the Middle Ages.* Cambridge: Cambridge University Press, 2005.

Kantorowicz, Ernst. *The King's Two Bodies: A Study in Mediaeval Political Theology.* Princeton, N.J.: Princeton University Press, 1957.

Kelley, Donald R. "*De Origine Feudorum*: The Beginnings of an Historical Problem." *Speculum* 39 (1964): 207–28.

———. *Foundations of Modern Historical Scholarship: Language, Law, and History in the French Renaissance.* New York: Columbia University Press, 1970.

———. *François Hotman: A Revolutionary's Ordeal.* Princeton, N.J.: Princeton University Press, 1973.

———. "Civil Science in the Renaissance." *The Languages of Political Theory in Early Modern Europe.* Ed. Anthony Pagden. Cambridge: Cambridge University Press, 1987. 57–78.

———. "Law." In Burns, ed., *Cambridge History of Political Thought: 1450–1700,* 66–94.

Kemp, Anthony. *The Estrangement of the Past: A Study in the Origins of Modern Historical Consciousness.* New York: Oxford University Press, 1991.

Kennedy, Ellen. "Carl Schmitt and the Frankfurt School." *Telos* 71 (1987): 37–66.

Kiernan, V. G. *Marxism and Imperialism.* London: Edward Arnold, 1974.

Klein, William. "The Ancient Constitution Revisited." *Political Discourse in Early Modern Britain*. Ed. Nicholas Phillipson and Quentin Skinner. Cambridge: Cambridge University Press, 1993. 23–44.

Knapp, Ethan. "Heidegger, Medieval Studies and the Modernity of Scholasticism." Forthcoming in Cole and Smith, ed., *The Legitimacy of the Middle Ages*.

Knolles, Richard. *The Six Bookes of a Commonweale: A Facsimile Reprint*. Ed. Kenneth D. McRae. Cambridge, Mass.: Harvard University Press, 1962.

Koselleck, Reinhart. *Futures Past: On the Semantics of Historical Time*. Trans. Keith Tribe. Cambridge, Mass.: MIT Press, 1985. 2nd ed. New York: Columbia University Press, 2004.

———. *Critique and Crisis: Enlightenment and the Pathogenesis of Modern Society*. Oxford: Berg, 1988. First published as *Kritik und Krise, Eine Studie zur Pathogenese der bügerlichen Welt* (Freiburg: Karl Alber, 1959).

Kriegel, Blandine. "The Rule of the State and Natural Law." *Natural Law and Civil Sovereignty: Moral Right and State Authority in Early Modern Political Thought*. Ed. Ian Hunter and David Saunders. New York: Palgrave, 2002. 13–26.

Laclau, Ernesto. *Emancipation(s)*. London: Verso, 1996.

Lampert, Lisa. "Race, Periodicity, and the (Neo-) Middle Ages," *Modern Language Quarterly* 65:3 (2004): 391–421.

Landes, Richard. "Lest the Millennium Be Fulfilled: Apocalyptic Expectations and the Pattern of Western Chronography, 100–800 CE." *The Use and Abuse of Eschatology in the Middle Ages*. Ed. Werner Verbeke, Daniel Verhelst, and Andries Welkenhuysen. Leuven: Leuven University Press, 1988. 137–211.

Latour, Bruno. *We Have Never Been Modern*. Trans. Catherine Porter. Cambridge, Mass.: Harvard University Press, 1993.

Lavezzo, Kathy. *Angels at the Edge of the World*. Ithaca: Cornell University Press, 2006.

Lees, Clare. "Engendering Religious Desire: Sex, Knowledge, and Christian Identity in Anglo-Saxon England." *Journal of Medieval and Early Modern Studies* 27 (1997): 17–45.

———. *Tradition and Belief: Religious Writing in Late Anglo-Saxon England*. Minneapolis: University of Minnesota Press, 1999.

Lees, Clare, and Gillian Overing. "Signifying Gender and Empire." *Journal for Medieval and Early Modern Studies* 34:1 (2004): 1–16.

———. *Double Agents: Women and Clerical Culture in Anglo-Saxon England*. Philadelphia: University of Pennsylvania Press, 2001.

Le Goff, Jacques. *Time, Work, and Culture in the Middle Ages*. Trans. Arthur Goldhammer. Chicago: University of Chicago Press, 1980.

———. "Antique (Ancient)/Modern." *History and Memory*. Trans. Steven Rendall and Elizabeth Claman. New York: Columbia University Press, 1992. 21–50.

———. "Maîtriser le temps." *Afrique et Histoire* 2 (2004): 19–29.

Lieberman, David. *The Province of Legislation Determined: Legal Theory in Eighteenth-Century Britain*. Cambridge: Cambridge University Press, 1989.

Lloyd, David. *Ireland after History*. Cork, Ireland: Cork University Press, 1999.

Lloyd, Howell A. "Constitutionalism." In Burns, ed., *Cambridge History of Political Thought: 1450–1700*, 292–97.

Lochrie, Karma. "Desiring Foucault." *Journal of Medieval and Early Modern Studies* 27 (1997): 3–16.

Lowe, Lisa, and David Lloyd, eds. *The Politics of Culture in the Shadow of Capital*. Durham, N.C.: Duke University Press, 1997.

Löwith, Karl. *Meaning in History: The Theological Implications of the Philosophy of History.* Chicago: University of Chicago Press, 1949.

———. "The Occasional Decisionism of Carl Schmitt." In Wolin, ed., *Martin Heidegger and European Nihilism*; first published as "Der Okkasionnelle Dezisionismus von Carl Schmitt" [1935], Samtliche Schrifien, VIII, 57.

Lupton, Julia Reinhard. *Afterlives of the Saints: Hagiography, Typology, and Renaissance Literature.* Stanford, Calif.: Stanford University Press, 1996.

———. *Citizen-Saints: Shakespeare and Political Theology.* Chicago: University of Chicago Press, 2005.

Luscombe, D. E., and G. R. Evans. "The Twelfth-Century Renaissance." In Burns, ed., *The Cambridge History of Medieval Political Thought, c. 350–c. 1450.* 310–16.

Mackrell, J. Q. C. *The Attack on "Feudalism" in Eighteenth-Century France.* London: Routledge, 1973.

Maclean, Ian. *Interpretation and Meaning in the Renaissance: The Case of Law.* Cambridge: Cambridge University Press, 1992.

Maitland, F. W. *English Law and the Renaissance.* Cambridge: Cambridge University Press, 1901.

Marx, Karl. *Theories of Surplus Value.* Trans. G. A. Bonner and Emile Burns. New York: International Publishers, 1952.

Mason, Peter. "The Purloined Codex." *Journal of the History of Collections* 9:1 (1997): 1–30.

Masuzawa, Tomoko. *In Search of Dreamtime: The Quest for the Origin of Religion.* Chicago: University of Chicago Press, 1993.

———. *The Invention of World Religions: Or, How European Universalism Was Preserved in the Language of Pluralism.* Chicago: University of Chicago Press, 2005.

McClure, Judith. "Bede's Old Testament Kings," *Ideal and Reality in Frankish and Anglo-Saxon Society.* Ed. Patrick Wormald with Donald Bullough and Roger Collins. Oxford: B. Blackwell, 1983. 76–98.

McCormick, John P. *Carl Schmitt's Critique of Liberalism: Against Politics as Technology.* Cambridge: Cambridge University Press, 1997.

McGinn, Bernard. *Visions of the End: Apocalyptic Traditions in the Middle Ages.* New York: Columbia University Press, 1998.

McNeil, David O. *Guillaume Budé and Humanism in the Reign of Francis I.* Geneva: Droz, 1975.

Meier, Heinrich. *Carl Schmitt and Leo Strauss: The Hidden Dialogue.* Chicago: University of Chicago Press, 1995.

Menke, Christoph. *Reflection of Equality.* Trans. Howard Rouse and Andrei Denejkine. Stanford, Calif.: Stanford University Press, 2006.

Meyvaert, Paul. "The Registrum of Gregory the Great and Bede." *Benedict, Gregory, Bede and Others.* London: Variorum Reprints, 1977. 162–66.

Mignolo, Walter. *The Darker Side of the Renaissance: Literacy, Territoriality, and Colonization.* 2nd ed. Ann Arbor: University of Michigan Press, 2003.

Molyneux, William, ed. *The Case of Ireland's Being Bound by Acts of Parliament in England, Stated.* London: Boreham, 1720.

Mommsen, Theodor. *Libri pontificalis. Monumenta Germaniae historica. Gestorum pontificum romanorum* v. 1, pars 1. Berolini: Weidmann, 1898.

Mommsen, Theodore E. "Petrarch's Conception of the 'Dark Ages.'" *Speculum* 17:2 (1942): 226–42.

Montorzi, Mario. *Diritto feudale nel Basso medioevo.* Torino, Italy: G. Giappichelli, 1991.

Mosshammer, Aldan A. *The Chronicle of Eusebius and Greek Chronographic Tradition.* Lewisburg, Pa.: Bucknell University Press, 1979.

Mouffe, Chantal. *The Return of the Political.* London: Verso, 1993.

Mudimbe, V. Y. *The Invention of Africa: Gnosis, Philosophy and the Order of Knowledge.* Bloomington: Indiana University Press, 1988.

Mufti, Aamir. "Auerbach in Istanbul: Edward Said, Secular Criticism, and the Question of Minority Culture." *Critical Inquiry* 25:1 (1998): 95–125.

———. "Critical Secularism: A Reintroduction for Perilous Times." *boundary 2* 31:2 (2004): 1–9.

Nancy, Jean-Luc. "Church, State, Resistance." In Vries and Sullivan, 102–12.

Needham, Anuradha Dingwaney, and Rejeswari Sunder Rajan, eds. *The Crisis of Secularism in India.* Durham, N.C.: Duke University Press, 2007.

Negri, Antonio. *Insurgencies: Constituent Power and the Modern State.* Trans. Maurizia Boscagli. Minneapolis: University of Minnesota Press, 1999.

Orosius. *Historiarum adversos paganos libri quinque.* Ed. C. Zangermeister. CSEL 5 (1882).

Osborne, Peter. *The Politics of Time: Modernity and Avant-Garde.* London: Verso, 1995.

Oxford Latin Dictionary. Ed. P. G. W. Glare. Oxford: Clarendon, 1996.

Pagden, Anthony. *Lords of All the World: Ideologies of Empire in Spain, Britain, and France, c. 1500–c.1800.* New Haven, Conn.: Yale University Press, 1995.

The Parliamentary History of England. Hansard. London, 1814.

Pasquier, Étienne. *Les Oeuvres d'Estienne Pasquier,* 2 vols. Amsterdam, 1723.

Patterson, Orlando. *Slavery and Social Death: A Comparative Study.* Cambridge, Mass.: Harvard University Press, 1982.

Pattullo, Henry. "Essay upon the Cultivation of the Lands, and Improvements of the Revenues, of Bengal." London: Becket and Hondt, 1771.

Pawlisch, Hans S. *Sir John Davies and the Conquest of Ireland: A Study in Legal Imperialism.* Cambridge: Cambridge University Press, 1985.

Pennington, Kenneth. "Law, Feudal" and "*Libri Feudorum.*" *The Dictionary of the Middle Ages,* Supplement I. Ed. William Chester Jordan. New York: Scribner, 2004.

Phillips, Mark Salber. *Society and Sentiment: Genres of Historical Writing in Britain, 1740–1820.* Princeton, N.J.: Princeton University Press, 2000.

Phillipson, Nicholas. "Propriety, Property and Prudence: David Hume and the Defence of the Revolution." *Political Discourse in Early Modern Britain.* Ed. Nicholas Phillipson and Quentin Skinner. Cambridge: Cambridge University Press, 1993. 302–20.

Piccone, Paul, and G. L. Ulmen. "Introduction." *Telos* 72 (1987): 3–14.

Pocock, J. G. A. *Virtue, Commerce, and History: Essays on Political Thought and History, Chiefly in the Eighteenth Century.* Cambridge: Cambridge University Press, 1985.

———. *The Ancient Constitution and the Feudal Law: A Study of English Historical Thought in the Seventeenth Century, A Reissue with a Retrospect.* Cambridge: Cambridge University Press, 1987. Original published in 1957.

———. "Political Thought in the English-Speaking Atlantic, 1760–1790: The Imperial Crisis." *The Varieties of British Political Thought.* Cambridge: Cambridge University Press, 1993. 246–82.

Pollock, Sir Frederick, and F. W. Maitland, *The History of English Law before the Time of Edward I,* 2nd ed., 2 vols. Cambridge: Cambridge University Press, 1923.

Prakash, Gyan. *Bonded Histories: Genealogies of Labor Servitude in Colonial India.* Cambridge: Cambridge University Press, 1990.

———. "Writing Post-Orientalist Histories of the Third World: Perspectives from Indian Historiography." *Comparative Studies in Society and History* 32:2 (1990): 383–408.

Preuss, Ulrich K. "The Critique of German Liberalism: Reply to Kennedy." *Telos* 71 (1987): 97–109.

Quayson, Ato. *Calibrations.* Minneapolis: University of Minnesota Press, 2003.

Quesnay, François. *Tableau Économique des Physiocrates.* London: Macmillan, 1972.

Rabasa, José. *Inventing A-M-E-R-I-C-A: Spanish Historiography and the Formation of Eurocentrism.* Norman: University of Oklahoma Press, 1993.

———. *Writing Violence on the Northern Frontier: The Historiography of Sixteenth-Century New Mexico and Florida and the Legacy of Conquest.* Durham, N.C.: Duke University Press, 2000.

———. "Franciscans and Dominicans Under the Gaze of a Tlacuilo: Plural-World Dwelling in an Indian Pictorial Codex." Morrison Library Inaugural Address Series No. 14. Berkeley, Calif.: Doe Library, 1998.

———. "*Without* History? Apostasy as a Historical Category." Unpublished paper.

———. "Decolonizing Medieval Mexico." Forthcoming in Davis and Altschul.

Rabin, Andrew. "Historical Re-Collections: Rewriting the World Chronicle in Bede's *De Temporum Ratione.*" *Viator* 36 (2005): 23–39.

Reeves, Philip. "Pakistanis Criticize Influence of Feudal Families." NPR World News, *Morning Edition,* June 18, 2007. *http://www.*npr.org/templates/story/story.php?storyId=11151854.

Renan, Ernst. "What Is a Nation?" In *Nation and Narration.* Ed. Homi Bhabha. Trans. Martin Thom. London: Routledge, 1990. Originally a lecture delivered as "Qu'es-ce qu'une nation?" at the Sorbonne, March 11, 1882.

Reynolds, Susan. *Fiefs and Vassals: The Medieval Evidence Reinterpreted.* Oxford: Clarendon, 1994.

Robbins, Bruce. "Secularism, Elitism, Progress, and Other Transgressions: On Edward Said's 'Voyage In.'" *Social Text* 40 (1994): 25–37.

Robinson, Fred C. "*Medieval,* the *Middle Ages.*" *Speculum* 59 (1984): 745–56.

Rowan, Steven. *Ulrich Zasius: A Jurist in the German Renaissance, 1461–1535.* Frankfurt am Main: Vittorio Klostermann, 1987.

Rufinus. *Eusebius Werke,* vol 2. *Die Kirchengeschichte.* Ed. Eduard Schwartz; *Die Lateinische Übersetzung des Rufinus.* Ed. Theodor Mommsen. Leipzig: J. C. Hinrichs'sche Buchhandlung, 1903.

Ryan, Magnus. "*Ius Commune Feudorum* in the Thirteenth Century." *Colendo iustitiam et iura condendo.* Ed. Andrea Romano. Rome: Edizioni De Luca, 1997. 51–65.

Saldana-Portillo, María Josefina. "Developmentalism's Irresistible Seduction." In Lowe and Lloyd, eds., 132–72.

Santner, Eric L. "Miracles Happen: Benjamin, Rosenzweig, Freud, and the Matter of the Neighbor." In Žižek, Santner, and Reinhard, 76–133.

Sarkar, Sumit. "The Fascism of the Sangha Parivar." *Economic and Political Weekly* 27:5 (1993), 163–67.

Scheil, Andrew. *The Footsteps of Israel: Understanding Jews in Anglo-Saxon England.* Ann Arbor: University of Michigan Press, 2004.

Schmitt, Carl. *The Concept of the Political.* Trans. George Schwab. New Brunswick, N.J.: Rutgers University Press, 1976. First published as *Der Begriff des Politischen* (Munich, 1932).

―――. *Political Theology: Four Chapters on the Concept of Sovereignty.* Trans. George Schwab. Cambridge, Mass.: MIT Press, 1985. First published as *Politische Theologie: Vier Kapitel zur Lehre von der Souveränität* (Berlin: Dunker and Humblot, 1922).

―――. *Roman Catholicism and Political Form.* Trans. G. L. Ulmen. Westport, Conn.: Greenwood, 1996. First published as *Römischer Katholizismus und politische Form* (Hellerau: Jakob Hegner Verlag, 1923).

―――. *The* Nomos *of the Earth in the International Law of the Jus Publicum Europaeum.* trans. G. L. Ulmen. New York: Telos, 2003.

Schmitt, Jean-Claude. "Appropriating the Future." In Burrow and Wei, 3–17.

Schwartz, Seth. *Imperialism and Jewish Society, 200 B.C.E. to 640 C.E.* Princeton, N.J.: Princeton University Press, 2001.

Selden, John. *Titles of Honor.* London: W. Stansby for J. Helme, 1614. 2nd ed. London: Tyler and Holt, 1631.

―――. *Of the Dominion or Ownership of the Sea.* Trans. Marchamont Nedham. London, 1652. Originally published as *Mare Clausum,* 1636.

Sen, Sudipta. *Empire of Free Trade: The East India Company and the Making of the Colonial Marketplace.* Philadelphia: University of Pennsylvania Press, 1998.

Simpson, James. *Reform and Cultural Revolution. The Oxford English Literary History, Vol. 2. 1350–1547.* Oxford: Oxford University Press, 2002.

Skinner, Quentin. *Foundations of Modern Political Thought.* Cambridge: Cambridge University Press, 1978. Vol. 1.

Smith, David Baird. "François Hotman." *Scottish Historical Review* 13 (1916): 328–65.

Smith, D. Vance. "Irregular Histories: Forgetting Ourselves," *New Literary History: A Journal of Theory and Interpretation* 28:2 (Spring 1997): 161–84.

―――. *Arts of Possession: The Middle English Household Imaginary.* Minneapolis: University of Minnesota Press, 2003.

Smith, R. J. *The Gothic Bequest: Medieval Institutions in British Thought, 1688–1863.* Cambridge: Cambridge University Press, 1987.

Smith, Steven B. *Reading Leo Strauss: Politics, Philosophy, Judaism.* Chicago: University of Chicago Press, 2006.

Spelman, Henry. "Feuds and Tenures." In *Reliquiae Spelmannianae: The Posthumous Works of Sir Henry Spelman Relating to the Laws and Antiquities of England.* Ed. Edmund Gibson. London, 1698.

Spiegel, Gabrielle. *The Past as Text: The Theory and Practice of Medieval Historiography.* Baltimore: Johns Hopkins University Press, 1997.

―――. "Epater les Médiévistes." *History and Theory* 39 (2000).

Spivak, Gayatri. *A Critique of Postcolonial Reason: Toward a History of the Vanishing Present.* Cambridge, Mass.: Harvard University Press, 1999.

Stein, P. G. "Roman Law." In Burns, ed., *The Cambridge History of Medieval Political Thought, c. 350–c. 1450,* 42–47.

Stokes, Eric. *The English Utilitarians and India.* Delhi: Oxford University Press, 1959.

Stoler, Ann Laura. *Race and the Education of Desire: Foucault's History of Sexuality and the Colonial Order of Things.* Durham, N.C.: Duke University Press, 1995.

Strohm, Paul. *Theory and the Premodern Text.* Minneapolis: University of Minnesota Press, 2000.

Suárez, Francisco. *De Legibus ac Deo Legislatore.* Ed. James Brown Scott. Trans. Gwladys L. Williams et al. Oxford: Clarendon, 1944.

Summit, Jennifer. *Memory's Library.* Chicago: University of Chicago Press, forthcoming.

Summit, Jennifer, and David Wallace, eds. *Medieval/Renaissance: After Periodization*. A special issue of *Journal of Medieval and Early Modern Studies* 37, no. 3 (2007).

Sutherland, Lucy. *The East India Company in Eighteenth-Century Politics*. Oxford: Clarendon, 1952.

Thomas, P. D. G., ed. "Parliamentary Diaries of Nathaniel Ryder, 1764–7." *Camden Miscellany XXIII* 4th series, vol. 7. London: Office of the Royal Historical Society, n.y. 229–351.

Travers, Robert. *Ideology and Empire in Eighteenth-Century India: The British in Bengal*. Cambridge: Cambridge University Press, 2007.

Tuck, Richard. *Natural Rights Theories: Their Origin and Development*. Cambridge: Cambridge University Press, 1979.

Tully, James. *A Discourse on Property: John Locke and His Adversaries*. Cambridge: Cambridge University Press, 1980.

Ullmann, Walter. "Arthur's Homage to King John." *English Historical Review* 94 (1979): 356–64.

Viswanathan, Gauri. *Masks of Conquest: Literary Study and British Rule in India*. Oxford: Oxford University Press, 1989.

———. *Outside the Fold: Conversion, Modernity, and Belief*. Princeton, N.J.: Princeton University Press, 1998.

Vries, Hent de, and Lawrence Sullivan, eds. *Political Theologies: Public Religions in a Post-Secular World*. New York: Fordham University Press, 2006.

Wallace, David. "Carving up Time and the World: Medieval-Renaissance Turf Wars; Historiography and Personal History." Center for Twentieth-Century Studies, University of Wisconsin, Milwaukee. Working paper no. 11 (1990–91).

———. *Premodern Places: Calais to Surinam, Chaucer to Aphra Behn*. Malden, Mass.: Blackwell, 2004.

———. "Periodizing Women: Mary Ward (1585–1645) and the Premodern Canon." *Journal for Medieval and Early Modern Studies* 36 (2006): 397–453.

Wallis, Faith. "*Si Naturam Quaeras*: Reframing Bede's 'Science.'" In DeGregorio, ed., 65–99.

———. Introduction, Notes, and Commentary to *The Reckoning of Time*, translation of Bede, *De temporum ratione*.

Warren, Michelle. *History on the Edge: Excalibur and the Borders of Britain (1100–1300)*. Minneapolis: University of Minnesota Press, 2000.

Weber, Samuel. "Taking Exception to Decision: Walter Benjamin and Carl Schmitt." *diacritics: A Review of Contemporary Criticism* 22:3–4 (1992): 5–18.

———. "'The Principle of Representation': Carl Schmitt's *Roman Catholicism and Political Form*." *Targets of Opportunity: On the Militarization of Thinking*. New York: Fordham University Press, 2005. 22–41.

Wei, Ian P. "Predicting the Future to Judge the Present: Paris Theologians and Attitudes to the Future." In Burrow and Wei, 19–36.

Weston, Corinne C. "England: Ancient Constitution and Common Law." In Burns, ed., *Cambridge History of Political Thought: 1450–1700*, 379–38.

Whelan, Frederick. *Edmund Burke and India: Political Morality and Empire*. Pittsburgh: University of Pittsburgh Press, 1996.

Wilson, Jon. "Governing Property, Making Law: Land, Local Society, and Colonial Discourse in Agrarian Bengal, c. 1785–1830." D. Phil., Oxford, 2001.

Wolin, Richard. Introduction. *Martin Heidegger and European Nihilism*. Trans. Gary Steiner. Ed. Richard Wolin. New York: Columbia University Press, 1995.

Wormald, Patrick. "Bede, the *Bretwaldas* and the Origins of the *Gens Anglorum.*" *Ideal and Reality in Frankish and Anglo-Saxon Society.* Ed. Patrick Wormald with Donald Bullough and Roger Collins. Oxford: B. Blackwell, 1983. 99–129.

Zasius, Ulrich. *Opera omnia.* Ed. Johan Ulrich Zasius and Joachim Münsinger von Frundeck, 7 vols. Aalen, Germany: Scientia Verlag, 1964–66.

Žižek, Slavoj, Eric Santner, and Kenneth Reinhard, eds. *The Neighbor: Three Inquiries in Political Theology.* Chicago: University of Chicago Press, 2005.

Index

absolutism, 8, 9, 24, 25, 35–36, 39, 41–42, 51–52, 55, 90
Accursius, 27, 36
Æthelberht, King of Kent, 128–29
Agamben, Giorgio, 57, 108, 109, 111, 121–22, 123, 138 n.50, 160 n.55
Alciato, Andrea, 30
Altdorfer, Albrecht, 91–92
"ancient constitution," 53, 55, 64, 71
Anderson, Benedict, 101
Anderson, Perry, 41
Anidjar, Gil, 77, 81
anno domini dating, 1, 3, 4, 16–17, 104, 105, 113, 114, 127, 129–30, 135 n.3, 162 n.6
anno mundi dating, 105–6, 112, 113, 126, 135 n.3
anthropology, 2, 4, 15, 90, 118, 120
Antichrist, 93, 108
Asad, Talal, 11–13, 97
Auerbach, Erich, 84, 119
Augustine, Saint, 16, 83, 84, 103–4, 105, 107, 108, 110, 112, 113
Augustine of Canterbury, 124, 125, 126

Balibar, Étienne, 79, 159 n.47
Bartolus of Sassoferrato, 30, 36
Bede, the Venerable, 1, 2, 16, 53, 103–14, 123–30
Benjamin, Walter, 7, 14, 74, 78, 79, 82–83, 85, 99, 100–101, 119
Bhabha, Homi, 72
Biddick, Kathleen, 66, 92, 119, 120
Blackstone, William, 9, 10, 26, 53, 54, 61, 62–66, 69, 71–72
Bloch, Marc, 61, 153 n.60
Blumenberg, Hans, 85–87, 88, 89
Bodin, Jean, 8, 24, 25, 31, 38, 39, 43, 44, 45, 46–50, 56
Bolt, William, 70
Bracton, Henry, 55
Brown, Elizabeth, 153 n.60

Brunner, Otto, 90, 140 n.10, 160 n. 50, n.
Buck-Morss, Susan, 45–46, 50
Budé, Guillaume, 35–36, 37
Burridge, Kenelm, 135 n.8

Caesar, Julius 105, 109–10, 125
capitalism, 2, 3, 4, 5, 71, 72, 74, 85
"Case of Tenures," 54–58, 72, 149 n.17
Certeau, Michel de, 10, 17–19, 60, 83, 97, 128, 138 n.49
Chakrabarty, Dipesh, 4, 5, 98–100
Charles I, 53, 54, 56
Charles V, 36, 51
Cheyette, Fredric, 141 n.16
Chomsky, Noam, 23
Christianson, Paul, 55
circumcision, 118, 121, 122
Clive, Lord Robert, 61
Codex Mendoza, 51, 53
Cohen, Mark, 119–20
Coke, Edward, 52, 60, 148 n.5
Cole, Andrew, 8, 45
Colebrook, Sir George, 67
colonial archive, 17, 115
colonial conquest, 9, 10, 40, 54, 56–58, 61–65, 67, 69, 71
colonial historiography, 11, 120
colonial politics of knowledge, 17, 104, 114, 116, 117, 124
colonialism, 5, 6, 7, 10, 18, 20, 119, 133; and feudal historiography, 19–20, 32–34, 40, 44–50, 53–59, 61, 63, 65, 71–74; and medievalism, 104, 117–20; and secularization, 3–4, 15, 98–100
Commission of Defective Titles, 54, 67
"common era" (c.e.), 3
computus, 105, 107, 162 n.5
Comte, Auguste, 83
consilia feudalia, 28
Constantine, Emperor, 128
Conze, Werner, 90

Acknowledgments

In its earliest stages this book seemed a solitary project, and the greatest pleasure of writing it has been the widening circle of conversations that it has brought with friends and colleagues. Derek Attridge, Andrew Cole, Rita Copeland, Simon Gikandi, Bruce Holsinger, Gyan Prakash, Vance Smith, and Paul Strohm graciously read early drafts of chapters, and gave guidance, ideas, and encouragement. With unconditional generosity and patience, Bill Jordan helped me think my way into feudal historiography, providing help and answers whenever I asked. At crucial moments and at short notice, Sally Poor, Joseph Patrouch, and especially José Rabasa and Eduardo Cadava read chapters and gave wonderful advice. I can never thank Dipesh Chakrabarty and Carolyn Dinshaw enough for reading the entire manuscript, and for the gift of unhurried intellectual exchange. Felice Lifshitz read and reread the manuscript with unflagging energy, patiently nudging the book toward its final form. The smart, meticulous work of my graduate assistants Aaron Hostetter and Wesley Yu saved me from many headaches and gave me a boost when I really needed it. The marvelous energy of the graduate students in my course on "Sovereignty," which I will always remember, sustained me as I completed revisions. From the inception of this book to its completion, Susan Crane, Derek Attridge, and Vance Smith helped to foster my resolve and keep me going, sometimes just by being there. I cannot imagine a more caring, supportive editor than Jerry Singerman at the University of Pennsylvania Press, who is one of the kindest people I've had the pleasure to know.

An earlier version of Chapter 1 appeared in *Journal of Medieval and Early Modern Studies* 36, no. 2 (2006). Leave time afforded by a Laurance S. Rockefeller Preceptorship with the Princeton University Center for Human Values greatly aided my research, and thanks go to the Princeton University Committee on Research in the Humanities and Social Sciences for generous support at several stages of this project.

My deepest thanks are for my family, who with humor, support, eventfulness, and love are the compass of life.

www.ingramcontent.com/pod-product-compliance
Ingram Content Group UK Ltd.
Pitfield, Milton Keynes, MK11 3LW, UK
UKHW032030240225
455518UK00001B/61